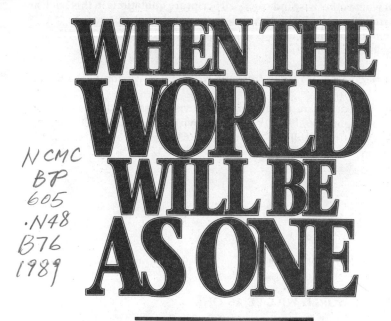

WHEN THE WORLD WILL BE AS ONE

The Coming New World Order in the New Age

TAL BROOKE

HARVEST HOUSE PUBLISHERS, INC.
Eugene, Oregon 97402

WHEN THE WORLD WILL BE AS ONE

Copyright © 1989 by Tal Brooke
Published by Harvest House Publishers, Inc.
Eugene, Oregon 97402

Library of Congress Cataloging-in-Publication Data

Brooke, Tal.
    When the world will be as one : the coming new world order / Tal Brooke.
        p. cm.
    Bibliography: p.
    ISBN 0-89081-749-9
    1. New Age movement—Controversial literature.   2. Brooke, Tal.
    I. Title.   II. Title: Coming new world order.
    BP605.N48B76   1989   133—dc19   89-1654
                                                                                CIP

In memory of my father
Edgar Duffield Brooke
(1906-1988)

Other Books By Tal Brooke

Lord of the Air
The Other Side of Death
Avatar of Night
Riders of the Cosmic Circuit
Harvest
(coauthored with Chuck Smith)

CONTENTS

ACKNOWLEDGMENTS

My special gratitude for exceptional generosity to—

Daniel Dominick Meyer. Indeed, more than being a former two-term Yale University student body president, or beating Harvard in crew, perhaps the greatest challenge for Dan was to become my next-door neighbor during our Princeton era in Brown Hall. In addition to being an outstanding friend, he topped it all by sharing his house in Burlingame for almost a year in order for me to write much of this book! Congratulations to you and your new bride, the former Amy Ballard.

Doctors Mike Esposito and Glenys Thomson of the University of California at Berkeley's Department of Molecular Biology and Genetics—for feeding me lavish meals time and again while being my sounding boards late into the night as we explored wide-ranging perspectives.

Frank Ordaz, who spent six years with George Lucas as a member of the Industrial Light and Magic team while helping to create the scenery of Star Wars and other ground-breaking films—perhaps all in preparation for the cover illustration of this book! Thanks.

INTRODUCTION
The New World Order

The Global Age is right upon us. It is on the horizon of our lifetime. This New World Order has been anticipated with hope. It has been seen as a necessity for planetary survival and heralded by a multitude from among the world's most esteemed and renowned leaders in every field. It has been a long time in the making, its pieces fitting into place from divergent realms. The arguments calling for its existence are formidable.

There is the ecological argument of Greenpeace, The Club of Rome, and other groups stating that mankind has come of age—that now we must be planetary stewards of the earth's ecology before the world's ecosystem is irreversibly damaged from industrial pollution by selfish nations who are accountable to none but whose irresponsibility directly affects the lives of other nations. The neighboring nations along the coast of the Mediterranean Sea have watched as unchecked sewage has turned a once sapphire-clear sea with endless underwater vistas into a murky grayish soup. All this in 20 years!

There is no denying the even greater global dangers as we see the ozone layer being eaten away daily, with conditions changing before our very eyes. So too with the greenhouse effect, from other atmospheric pollutants, that is changing weather patterns around the world. Meanwhile industrial pollutants flow out by the millions of tons into oceans, seas, lakes, and streams, causing in mere decades what it may take thousands of years to reverse. This ecological argument for globalism is so compelling as to be almost beyond questioning.

There is the "global village" argument of Marshall Mc-Luhan—that modern technology has altered the landscape of the earth, and that what were once great natural barriers of distance, thought, and language have been collapsed by the myriad jets and airwaves filling the sky. All the world can watch rock stars perform for a global audience in the "Live Aid Concert" singing "We Are the World" as billions of satellite-linked television sets show the same well-known stars to what were once remote cultures. Scandinavian rock groups sing in English, while Parisians are suddenly becoming addicted to "Dallas" and fascinated with JR.

Scientists use the analogy of computer interfacing and neurology to show that as parts of the earth hook up, it becomes almost an organism with an intact nervous system. Cambridge scientists like Peter Russell then come up with the term *Gaia* to give this a metaphysical aspect—that in a way the earth is a goddess coming alive as human consciousness becomes unified.

Recent media guru Joseph Campbell talks about the need for a shared mythology for the earth—that this earth which has now come of age needs a unifying nondivisive planetary religious experience and a more universal creed from this awakening. Campbell's erudite and mature syncretisms are seen as true peacemaking in a world whose disharmony comes from immature religious creeds at odds because they misunderstand each other's language. They are children throwing stones, this pundit observes. They must grasp the true underlying unity that already lies beneath them all, flowing like a universal archetypal stream of collective human experience. Thousands of television stations replay this Bill Moyers series again and again. One soon gets the idea that the media barons are pushing it from backstage.

A flood of New Age thinkers are there to pick up the ball from Joseph Campbell. Bantam starts its New Age book line. Bestsellers dealing with New Age themes fill *The New York Times* bestseller list. Compelling arguments for a common global creed based on mystical experience mount up. New Age thought goes on to penetrate almost every aspect of life, always pointing to global unity. The landmark bestseller of this trend—Marilyn Ferguson's *The Aquarian Conspiracy*—quite frankly admits that this movement is a conspiracy coming from many divergent groups who see a global creed as the final hope for man if he is to survive. On board are Buckminster Fuller, the scientist and architect, Robert Muller, former assistant secretary general of the United Nations, plus many other impressive people. The argument is compelling.

There is the economic call for globalism. Virtually every major name in banking from Rockefeller to Rothschild to Robert McNamara (president of The World Bank) has spoken of the reality of an interlocking global economy—that what happens on Wall Street one minute is felt in London or Tokyo the next, that the complex jigsaw puzzle of world economy is moving into an oscillating ball that will eventually unify nations and currencies in the global marketplace, and that the economic forces of the earth are moving relentlessly toward a unified world system.

On top of that, certain social and political voices talk about the unfair distribution of wealth and resources—that a global system of sharing and redistribution could remedy the social problems of cross-national envy, and that if this were addressed, a major component of international strife and war would be removed forever.

A pooling of resources for medical care, for feeding, and for clothing the underprivileged and the Third World is another argument. Good health is seen as a right that every citizen of the earth must be guaranteed. Toward this end there is the World Health Organization. Brock Chisolm, director of the World Health Organization, has been an outspoken voice for globalism. He and many other world leaders have agreed on the basic agenda. Brock Chisolm spelled it out:

> To achieve world government, it is necessary to remove from the minds of men their individualism, loyalty to family tradition, national patriotism and religious dogmas. . . .

>   We have swallowed all manner of poisonous cer-
> tainties fed us by our parents, our Sunday and day
> school teachers, our politicians, our priests, our
> newspapers and others with vested interests in con-
> trolling us.
>   The reinterpretation and eventual eradication of
> the concept of right and wrong which has been the
> basis of child training, the substitution of intel-
> ligent and rational thinking for faith in the cer-
> tainties of the old people, these are the belated
> objectives . . . for charting the changes of human
> behavior.[1]

One of the most compelling arguments for globalism is the
danger of global annihilation. A multitude of voices warn that
this danger alone warrants the final sacrifice required
to bring about global peace—that if nations surrender their
sovereignties and armaments in a manner consistent with
United Nations planning, this will end the threat of global
war and inaugurate an era of unprecedented peace and safety.
But this will require the supreme sacrifice of nationalism.
Only then will the world be one.

John Lennon, the rock legend and visionary, came up with
the consummate creedal statement and description of what a
New World Order would be like in his most famous song of
all, "Imagine." Lennon entreats a divided world to imagine
with him no heaven, no countries, all people living in peace
as one brotherhood of man, with the final and only option if it
is to survive, a world united as one. "Imagine" has been
compelling beyond belief as its melodic lyrics continue to fill
the airwaves of the world again and again until one day it
really happens.

Now let us look behind the scenes over the centuries at the
incredible building blocks of this enormous structure coming
together from all sides. The various rainbow filaments pulling together the disparate pieces are a thing of wonder as we
peer behind the main stage of the world.

WHEN THE WORLD WILL BE AS ONE

1
Contact

The course of modern history has been changed by contacts with the other side, contacts with nonhuman or superhuman intelligences. Since the 1960's, these events have greatly increased in frequency. It has been like the faint crackles of a Geiger counter going wild as it approaches the heart of a radiation zone. Spiritually, we have been opening one door after another, and what were once faint crackles have become thunder. There seems to be a reason for all this, but it takes layers of examination to reveal that the outward manifestations are only one level of operation.

There has been vast and elaborate background preparation for this present reality. It did not happen overnight; it has been building up. One could even say that it has been building up for centuries, as we shall later discover.

With these contacts have come messages. What is interesting is that these messages have woven together to form an interesting pattern—indeed, a belief system. The synchronicity of these messages and their divergent points of contact keep suggesting that these communications are most deliberate, and that something is being orchestrated from beyond our known world. But for what reason? And why is it happening now at an accelerating pace?

The answer: *To bring on the New Age.*

CONTACT: A Famous Medical Pioneer

James Pearre of *The Chicago Tribune* had some inside information on a celebrated medical authority and pioneer in the field of death and dying. It could have been a scene out of Steven Spielberg's film *Poltergeist.*

The incident occurred in the office of Dr. Elizabeth Kubler-Ross at the University of Chicago, where she was an associate professor of psychiatry. Pearre reported:

> Dr. Elisabeth Kubler-Ross, whose work has revolutionized attitudes about death and dying, says the spirit of a deceased former patient helped dissuade her nine years ago from abandoning her work... she since has become convinced that it was a "spontaneous materialization of somebody who had died almost a year before." Kubler-Ross discussed the mysterious incident reluctantly. She said her experience "will sound so crazy that I wouldn't be surprised if people think, 'Oh, she's now becoming an occultist, a spiritualist.' "

Here are the details. A woman appeared at her office and introduced herself as a patient who had died ten months before, Kubler-Ross says. The visitor looked identical to the former patient, but Kubler-Ross refused to believe it could be the same person. "She said she knew I was considering giving up my work with dying patients and that she came to tell me not to give it up," Kubler-Ross recalls. "She said the time was not right. I reached out to touch her. I was reality testing. I was a scientist, a psychiatrist, and I didn't believe in such things.

"I told her a white lie and said I wanted her to write a little note I could give to her minister.

"She smiled in this all-knowing way, like she knew very well what my intentions were." But the woman wrote the note and signed it, and handwriting analysis indicated that it matched the handwriting of the deceased patient.

Kubler-Ross says the incident "came at a crossroads where I would have made the wrong decision if I hadn't listened to her," and that her subsequent work has convinced her that "there is life after death." Pearre then proceeds to quote Kubler-Ross's involvement with mediumism as a source of evidence of afterlife. She has even worked out a system so that her deceased patients can get in touch with her. That short visit has resounded around the world

Since that time, Kubler-Ross has gotten to know her spirit guide, "Salem," well enough for him to materialize in her room. For those who understand spiritism, that signifies a very advanced involvement.

Yoga Journal, that same year, 1976, that Pearre reported the incident, had an article entitled "Elisabeth Kubler-Ross: Messenger of Love" describing Kubler-Ross's appearance before a large gathering. The famous doctor admitted:

> Last night I was visited by Salem, my spirit guide, and two of his companions, Willie and Anka. They were with us until three o'clock in the morning. We talked, laughed and sang together. They spoke and touched me with the most incredible love and tenderness imaginable. This was the highlight of my life.

Kubler-Ross wrote the bestselling and authoritative book on death entitled *Death and Dying*. Her peers in the medical establishment use it as the primary textbook on the subject. Nurses, doctors, psychologists, and psychiatrists use that and her other books constantly. She has been at the vanguard of the hospice movement. Kubler-Ross is an ally of another medical doctor, Dr. Raymond Moody, who wrote the most famous book of all on near-death experiences and contacts with "beings-of-light": *Life After Life*. Moody and Kubler-Ross have repeatedly addressed conferences and symposia together.

What has Kubler-Ross learned about the other side through her contacts with the dead and with spirit guides? She wrote *Death: The Final Stage of Growth* (Prentice Hall, 1975). It could be a preamble to what has since been called the New Age movement. Its message to the world in the midseventies was:

There is no need to be afraid of death . . . death is the key to the door of life. . . . The answer is within you. You can become a channel and a source of great inner strength. But you must give up everything in order to gain everything. . . . When human beings "find a place of stillness and quiet at the highest level of which they are capable, then the heavenly influences can pour through them, recreate them, and use them for the salvation of mankind" [Kubler-Ross quotes *The Quiet Mind*]. . . . There is no total death. Only the body dies. The Self or spirit, or whatever you wish to label it, is eternal. . . .

CONTACT: The Super-Channelers

Jane Roberts was perhaps the most famous and prolific of all contemporary channelers. She became the channel for an entity named Seth. It started on an early September day in 1963 in her apartment in Elmira, New York, when this aspiring novelist suddenly began to have some very strange experiences. Her encounters changed her life as well as the lives of countless thousands of people who have since read her numerous bestsellers that fill the New Age/Occult sections of countless bookstores.

In her book *The Seth Material* Roberts tells her story. She portrays herself as a liberated graduate of Skidmore University who was an honest seeker of truth. One day she and her husband decided to write a book on ESP. To prime the pump, they used a Ouija board the night of December 8. After a few sessions they were able to receive messages from someone who initially identified himself as "Frank Withers." Soon, however, it claimed to be more than this, and no longer wanted to be known as Frank Withers. "To God, all names are his name." Then it said, "You may call me whatever you choose. I call myself Seth; it fits the me of me."

Jane soon reached a threshold where she went from being able to race the pointer all over the board to being able to anticipate the whole words in her mind before the pointer spelled them out. At that moment the pointer paused, and she felt as if she were standing at the top of a high diving board. It was as if she were trying to make herself jump as spectators below egged her on. She took the leap and immediately began speaking for Seth. Jane Roberts was now a full-fledged channel. Seth initially acted like a jocular, wise, paternal old friend from some past life. Yet it made no mistake in showing that it was fully superhuman and, among other things, had a mission to get across to our world the wisdom that it was only now ready for.

Jane decided to conduct a seance for her ESP book. Her tone was that of a high school girl following a cooking recipe. She got her money's worth; Seth stunned Jane, her husband, and friends: He transmogrified her body. It was not exactly a thing of beauty, but it was, after all, a supernatural manifestation. Those at the seance table were told by the voice to concentrate on Jane's arm. One witness, Robert Butts, said that the hand began to change in appearance and resembled a paw. It gave him an eerie feeling. He said the hand became stubby and thick for a moment. Then it resumed its pawlike appearance. Then Seth told Butts to reach out and touch the hand. He touched it cautiously. It felt very cold, wet, and clammy, and seemed unusually bumpy. Then Seth made the whole forepaw glow before the stunned table.

But as if this gesture were not enough, Seth had another sign for them. They faced a mirror, and Seth told them to look at their reflections in the mirror. As they watched, Jane's image was suddenly replaced with another image. The head dropped lower and the shape of the skull and the hairstyle changed. The head in the mirror leaned down even though Jane was sitting erect, looking straight ahead. Naturally, it would take the three people a while to acclimate themselves to such bizarre antics, but they would soon triumph and transcend their visceral horror.

The Seth sessions continued. The next breakthrough in the taking over of Jane's body was the appearance of a deep masculine voice, which issued from her body. Seth told Jane's husband that he had been an extremely vain woman in a former life. Seth also started calling Jane "Ruburt," a male name. Then Seth commented philosophically that the name "Jane" would sound rather unmelodious as a man's voice.

Jane, who was by now called Ruburt, observed that they did not realize she would receive what was known as the Seth material through "the psychic structure." She acknowledged a sense of great power in Seth's voice. It made her feel very small, as if surrounded by a great energy. In time she would learn to remain in a deep trance while being able to talk, walk, and gesture. She would even learn to sip wine at times when Seth spoke through her.

But there was an incident that almost ended the sessions. Jane, who by now had had a series of out-of-the-body experiences, said she was in her bedroom when she suddenly became aware of a dark, looming figure menacing her. She had not previously believed in demons, but changed her mind when the attacker dragged her around and even bit her hand. Finally the thing tried to kill her and she screamed.

Seth explained it all away. It was merely a projection of her own mind, the energy of hidden fears. Seth assured Jane and her husband, who transcribed the sessions, that the evil that Ruburt imagined did not exist.

Later, a fairly well-known psychologist interviewed Seth to see if it was a double personality. It was his opinion that Seth had a "massive intellect" and did not seem to be a secondary personality, as in the case of multiple personality. This was further borne out by a number of telepathic and clairvoyant tests. Seth, in a ten-year period, produced over 5000 typewritten records and analogues of higher esoteric truth. Some of this material was most subtle indeed, though much of it was a redundant weaving of semantic spells, as Seth formulated the same ideas again and again. Invariably it was in abstract and often abstruse, erudite, and elusive language, with as much scientific and technical jargon as possible. In this sense Seth's material greatly resembled the earlier teachings coming through Edgar Cayce, who was the most prodigious channeler of the modern era. Seth's teachings are almost identical with those of one of the most famous "entities" of the 1980's, "Lazaris," who channels through Jach Pursel.

What are some of Seth's revelations to the world?

God is an "energy gestalt" who has passed through human stages, and in a Hegelian sense is still evolving. This energy forms all universes. Seth names God "All That Is." God is not personal but is the sum of all consciousness. Humans are cocreators who contain this God within them; they evolve through reincarnation. Apparently Seth evolves too.

Something came along named "Seth II," an ancient friend of Seth I who gave Seth I a punt out of Jane, as though he were a soccer ball.

Ruburt, or Jane, tells what happened one night in April 1968 during the fifth year of the Seth sessions. By then Jane had been forbidden by Seth to read "religious books."

With massive power the voice started to break through, and Jane was hurled off into a void. The voice sounded clear though distant. Jane felt as if a cone had come down over her head. The voice claimed to come from an alien dimension— so alien that the contact was almost a miracle.

Two months later, the pyramid effect started again. Now the voice was plural, speaking of itself using the royal "We." They described themselves as an entity which existed before our own time frame, and which was instrumental in building the physical cosmos—this entity helped form pure energy into physical matter.

Jane said that under this new Seth's influence, her body became like a puppet and her face expressionless.

After the visitation, Jane encountered difficulty getting back into normal consciousness, and Seth had to help her.

When Jane went back into a trance, she had a trauma. She had been not only the recipient of words, but of direct spiritual revelations and experiences as well. She says that the entity referred to individuals returning in the future to peer into physical reality like giants upon the floor. At that point she saw a giant's face peer into her living room, its face filling up the entire window. Then her body, the room, and its contents all grew to enormous size. She screamed and began to tremble violently.

Jane had one more bout with the higher Seth, Seth II, but she became so shaken that the regular Seth did not allow it to continue for a long time. Again she felt the cone above her head and saw the giant looking in at her. At this point she struggled to get in touch with her vocal cords. She was beginning to feel violated by this being, a problem she had never felt with the lower Seth. Yet the unpleasantness of the experience, she conjectured, could have been due to her lack of evolution of consciousness.

The last statement from Seth II was a godlike declaration; it claimed to have given man the mental images from which man formed the known world and his own physical self. By 1984 the pluralistic Seths had written a compendium of revelations for the human race. Today these teachings are readily available to anyone who walks into just about any bookstore.

"Ruburt" has gone on to be with Seth, and newer channels have come on the scene to replace Jane Roberts (Ruburt). New entities have in turn replaced Seth—such as "Ramtha" and "Lazaris"—who feature among the bright new stars of Shirley MacLaine's autobiographies such as *Out on a Limb* and *Dancing in the Light*.

Yet these newer entities have arrived with exquisite timing to a world in waiting. The advance work has been done. Unlike Seth, who only muttered in dark rooms before a handful of observers, Ramtha and Lazaris have spoken on live television before hundreds of millions of viewers. Both Ramtha and Lazaris have appeared on the Merv Griffin Show, the Phil Donahue Show, and the Oprah Winfrey Show, among others. And news teams such as ABC's 20/20 have done specials on these entities and their human channels. Compared to Seth, they have achieved superstar celebrity status.

Time magazine's December 1987 cover story on the New Age movement mentioned that the enormous gate fees of these entities and their channels comprised only one indicator of the surging popular interest. That month's *New Age Journal* featured channeling on its cover story and stated that J.Z. Knight, who channels Ramtha, "on an average weekend draws up to 700 participants at $400 apiece (280,000 dollars); she admits to earning millions of dollars from 'Ramtha.' "[2]

If you wander through Marin County's Corte Madera Mall, up Highway 101 from the Golden Gate Bridge, there is an elaborate art store there that stands out from everything else.

The expensive lettering says *ILLUMINARIUM*. In the spacious plate-glass window displays are expensive carved gems, ancient Chinese curios, lifelike porcelain statues of Diana the goddess of Wicca, gnomes, and paintings of Atlantis. Then there is this brilliant formless being who keeps appearing in different paintings. He is what Ray Moody in his bestseller of the 1970's, *Life After Life*, called a "being-of-light." It is *Lazaris*. And his channeler, Jach Pursel, happens to own the Illuminarium. In the doorway stands a large, impressive fountain with the goddess Diana cast in bronze, kneeling over the flowing water. At the front desk are videocassettes of Jach Pursel channeling Lazaris.

The New Age Journal cover story reported:

> "Lazaris's" themes should by now seem quite familiar to us, since they closely echo what we have already found in "Seth," *Course in Miracles*, "Ramtha," and Ryerson material. It is basically a spiritual, united universe, "Lazaris" says, and we are essentially evolving, spiritual, immortal beings within and at one with it. Self-empowerment includes the causal, creative, intuitive ability to access what we need from our higher selves and from the universe as "God/Goddess/All That Is." And to realize these two truths, we must work to overcome our negative programming, our debilitating self-image, and our limited world view.[3]

We will later examine exactly what these entities consider to be negative programming.

When Jach Pursel, owner of the Illuminarium, tuned in on Lazaris, he had been a regional insurance supervisor in Florida and had started to dabble in meditation. On one of these occasions his wife addressed him and a different voice came through Jach. It was "Lazaris." The voice had a Chaucerian Middle English quality that has over the past 14 years "stayed impeccably consistent throughout thousands of hours of channeled talking, as has the personality supposedly doing the talking."[4]

CONTACT: A Bestselling Author

Whereas Jane Roberts was out there eagerly fishing for entities with a Ouija board, offering herself as a willing vessel, this was not the case with several others who have gained notoriety recently. And some of the things they have hooked into have been a little more strange and a little less friendly than some of the more famous entities. This would be a little hard to take for Harvey Cox, a noted Harvard theology professor, whom *The New Age Journal* quotes as saying of such entities as Lazaris, "They're so cuddly and friendly. They seem to be yuppified versions of the demons and spirits of another time."[5] Some contactees seem less fortunate.

In the case of one of these "victims," a well-known author by the name of Whitley Strieber, he has parlayed his chilling encounters into the number-one spot on *The New York Times* bestseller list twice—first as a hardback and then, in January 1988, as a paperback, earning more than he ever did writing horror novels like *Wolfen*. In fact it makes you wonder if his present bestseller, *Communion*, is not somehow his ultimate horror novel. He is certainly the right man for the job as "a chosen one," according to the aliens that abducted him. Who else is better suited to report on the sheer terror of such an encounter than a horror novelist?

Strieber has changed his mind a number of times about who these aliens are. In early 1988 Strieber was on the Larry King Show and was formative in his speculations about the origin and purpose of these beings. But he remained vehemently defensive about the authenticity of his encounters. One could say he looked almost paranoid about them, and with good reason; according to what he learned under hypnotic regression, these beings have been spying on him from the time he was a small child.

But the big trauma happened one night recently.

Whitley Strieber, on the night of December 26, 1985, was in his secluded log cabin in upstate New York with his family. In the early hours of the morning he had a visitation. Small, terrifying humanoids crept up to his bedside. They mentally controlled him by paralyzing him. Then they quietly carried him out of his house naked. They seemed to levitate him to an examination theater in the sky from some spot in the snowy woods.

Once in the small, round theater, he felt like an animal in a medical experiment, one of those monkeys whose skullcap has been sawn off and replaced by diodes. He sat nude and helpless. This was by no means a positive experience:

> The fear was so powerful that it seemed to make my personality completely evaporate.... "Whitley" ceased to exist. What was left was a body in a state of raw fear so great that it swept about me like a thick, suffocating curtain, turning paralysis into a condition that seemed close to death. I do not think that my ordinary humanity survived the transition to this little room.[6]

The gray-and-brown-skinned creatures closely resembled the two types of aliens that emerged from the saucer in Spielberg's film *Close Encounters*, except that these were fierce. There were the three-foot variety and the elongated, delicate, and spindly five-foot variety. But unlike the creatures in the film, there were two other types as well. The massive eyes of these creatures seemed like infinite shafts, black abysses. They had an insectlike quality, almost an exoskeleton. The smallest ones moved with rapid, ugly mechanical movements as they sped around Whitley Strieber.

As he was examined, one creature in particular—the spindly leather-skinned, five-foot variety—observed him: "She had those amazing, electrifying eyes ... the huge, staring eyes of the old gods.... They were featureless, in the sense that I could see neither pupil nor iris."[7] In her presence he "had no personal freedom at all." When he looked into her eyes, "It was as if every vulnerable detail of my self were known to this being.... I could actually feel the presence of that other person within me—which was as disturbing as it was curiously sensual. Their eyes are often described as 'limitless,' 'haunting,' and 'baring the soul.' "

Later on, Strieber would think of this creature as being like Ishtar, the ancient Mesopotamian "Eye-Goddess" with the huge staring eyes. He would observe that the closest he could come to an unadorned image of these beings was "the age-old, glaring face of Ishtar. Paint her eyes entirely black, remove her hair, and there is my image as it hangs before me now in my mind's eye, the ancient and terrible one, the bringer of wisdom, the ruthless questioner."[8] And like the ancients with their goddess Ishtar (or Ashtoreth), Whitley Strieber cited a sexual side to the encounter.

The examination room was untidy, even dirty. The creatures had a bad smell. A probe was jammed into his head. Then the hideously sexual aspect of this examination unfolded: "I was being shown an enormous and extremely ugly object, gray and scaly, with a sort of network of wires on the end. It was at least a foot long, narrow, and triangular in structure. They inserted this thing into my rectum . . . at the time I had the impression that I was being raped, and for the first time I felt anger."[9]

During this period the "Ishtar" creature asked him why "it" was not fully hard. Under deep hypnosis Strieber was questioned in detail about this event. He was horrified, later likening the event to a human copulating with an incubus or succubus.

The creatures couldn't have cared less about his rights; all they told him was that he was chosen for something—perhaps to be a messenger to the world. But were these creatures space aliens? Not necessarily so. At times they have seemed to be more like the ancient pagan gods and goddesses, or spirits, or incubi and succubi. Strieber has been confused. Maybe the ancient spirits were dressing up for our contemporary culture as space aliens. Their outward form only seemed like shells anyway.

Whitley Strieber conjectures about them:

> As the ages roll along, it could be that what changes is not our visitors but our way of installing them in the culture. Maybe they did not come here in 1946, 1897, 1235, or even A.D. 300. I have reported

that the being I have become familiar with looks like Ishtar. Maybe she is: she said she was old. . . . It would seem that our civilization is not paying attention to what may be the central archetypal mythological experience of the age. If so, then this is the first time that man has simply refused to respond to the ghosts and gods. Is that why they have become so physical, so real, dragging people out of bed like rapists in the night—because they must have our notice in order to somehow be confirmed in their truth? . . . Something is out there and it wants to get in.[10]

Before we can let them in, they claim, we must be prepared. Some people claim that they are in fact being prepared. Indeed, they claim that the whole human race is being prepared for the New Age, but that only the worthy will make it all the way. And this depends on the ability of individuals to absorb the new teachings and the new models of reality, and to abandon the old negative programming.

2

The Rainbow Bridge

In his movie *2001*, Stanley Kubrick had the edge 15 years before Marilyn Ferguson ever portrayed where things were going in her bestseller, *The Aquarian Conspiracy*. By the midsixties, Kubrick was both a change agent and a prophet who spoke through the medium of the 70-mm film. He created whole new realities before audiences of millions. Long before New Age terms were popularized by the masses, Kubrick showed the world what a "paradigm shift" was really like in his portrayal of Arthur C. Clarke's mystical science fiction epic *2001*. It was quite an experience sitting in a huge cinerama theater, in a packed audience, while the vast screen engulfed us with this new vision of reality.

QUANTUM LEAPS

Kubrick had us sitting in his Darwinian time machine, as the vast solar orb rose slowly to illumine the dawn of human intelligence in reddish-golden light. Simian packs roamed the scarred primitive face of a prehistoric world. Some of the ape-man faces were less monkeylike and more human. The camera angle seemed to show intelligence in the eyes. Grunts were on the verge of becoming words. Then one type of simian tribe began to move in on another. They moved in place for battle. Mounting shrieks became physical attacks. It was a war between the species. Suddenly one of the more intelligent ape-men picked up what was to be the first weapon in history, a large thigh bone. That gave him the critical edge. He beat the opposing simian to death. Others of the same species, with their greater intelligence, imitated what their leader had just done. Suddenly, they all held large bones and started smashing their enemies, the more apelike creatures.

In the silence after the battle, the winning species yelled in exuberant triumph. Apelike screams filled the air. One superior species suddenly replaced another. But something far more significant was going on than one species replacing another. What was really happening was the indwelling faculty of consciousness suddenly leaping to a greater magnitude on the earth, from one type of simian to another. In reality it was a moment of pure Hegelian consciousness evolution. It was a glimpse at the real subject behind the shifting actors. Consciousness was the true timeless protagonist of the vast epic—"the eternal charioteer," to use an expression from the *Bhagavad Gita*, and apparently it "was up to something."

Then came Kubrick's supreme moment of genius. The humanoid ape leader then hurled his large thigh bone into the air in triumph. The bone filled the screen as it spun in slow motion. It kept ascending, and then suddenly its same basic shape became enormous, filling the whole sky. It had suddenly become a vast machine as it drifted in outer space. Below it shone the huge, bright, bluish-green planet earth. It was no longer a bone. The leap of intelligence had dwarfed time and turned the simian bone into an interplanetary vessel whose inhabitants—evolved human simians—were a quantum leap beyond the ape creatures. Soon the third quantum leap would begin when this vessel reached Jupiter and its human inhabitant crossed the next catalytic threshold into some kind of supermind, represented by the star baby.

This epic is not about creatures but about evolving consciousness reaching what New Agers call *critical thresholds* for the next *transformation of consciousness*. Kubrick's vision is indeed the stuff out of which pantheism, monism, and cosmic humanism are built. As old as the Vedas of India, consciousness is portrayed as ascending up the evolutionary ladder in the act of becoming godlike. The leap in conceptual understanding is called a *paradigm shift* by the New Age movement.

Stanley Kubrick's paradigm shift represented the new myth. The biblical/monotheistic view of existence had become eclipsed by the pantheistic-mystical New Age view. It was dazzling, electric, and seemed hauntingly insightful. A generation was wooed. Opinions and lifetimes of thought were shifted in a few brief hours on the screen. It was almost like magic. To many in the audience, this film was a seed which would work away in their minds on a subconscious level. In time it would emerge as a worldview. Those on the mystical fringe of the 1960's had already caught the vision.

In the sixties there were many apostles of the new consciousness. One avenue for the new consciousness to manifest itself was through mind-altering drugs. Personal experience was key. Beliefs could easily be attached to experience, especially with mysticism. As it happened, Doctor Albert Hoffman, a pharmacologist, discovered one of the most potent mind-altering drugs ever known: LSD-25. It was in Switzerland in the late forties when by accident a few millionths of a gram lodged under Dr. Hoffman's fingernail. The resulting mystical experience was soon reported to other elite scientists. Not long after that Aldous Huxley, famed British novelist and intellectual, tried his fortune with mescaline and psilocybin, eliciting mystical experiences from these natural hallucinogens. Various shamans had been doing this for thousands of years.

If ancient Hindu rishis could ingest a plant called soma, thousands of years ago, and write the *Upanishads* in their altered states of consciousness, the same scenario could work again. But it would require finding the right mind-expanding drug, as well as respected members of society to sanction the drug. Well, the drug was in place. LSD had entered the world.

CONTACT THROUGH ALTERED STATES

The idea of chemically altered states would have to receive further sanction from the intellectual elite to reach the critical threshold of public experimentation—and it did. Harvard Professor Timothy Leary began to administer hundreds of doses of LSD-25 to his graduate students. His assistant was

Harvard psychologist Dr. Richard Alpert. They were a team, and their psychedelic road tours across the United States were famous. Meanwhile, another Harvard professor, Dr. Alan Watts of the Oriental Religions Department, had previously taken LSD and written *The Joyous Cosmology*, discussing his own mystical encounters while "tripping" on a New England farm.

By the time Leary and Alpert left Harvard, they were packing university auditoriums, conference centers, and civic centers with their exciting alternative to the straight society. This new secret, which defied the present system, carried the potent sense of mission that the early church had as it met in the catacombs beneath Rome to receive the startling message of the Christian faith. Now again there were harbingers of a new reality. And the West was like Rome, ready to crumble under its old system represented by the futility of Vietnam, the banality of Lyndon Johnson's "Great Society," traditional moral do's and don'ts, Pentagon marches, and protest rallies which all seemed to culminate in the Kent State Massacre.

Leary had become the academic celebrity-turned-guru. His cause was in high fashion among the vanguard of the counterculture. *Playboy* interviews popularized his views, and countless cover stories featured Leary's broken smile. He was a bodhisattva in tennis shoes and white chinos who merged psychedelic mystical experiences and modern psychological theories with timeless Eastern holy writ.

In the mid-1960's I encountered Timothy Leary for the first time in Washington, D.C., in a large church sanctuary overflowing with my contemporaries. In the dim light of center stage, leaning against the podium, was Tim Leary, his face creased with a strange wisdom. His soothing voice soon drew us in. It was evident that he had found a key to terrible power and knew that when it was used the world would not remain the same. Whether through flower power or mass ecstasy the world would be transformed, and nothing that the "straight society" did could stop the momentum of the truth they had found. Leary began talking under the spotlight, opening a major doorway into the New Age:

"LSD does not produce the transcendent experience; it merely acts as a chemical key. It opens the mind, frees the nervous system of its ordinary patterns and structures, and releases an enormous amount of awareness-energy. Understanding, describing and using these released energies intelligently has puzzled scholars for thousands of years. Yet here is a key to the mystery which has been passed down for over 2500 years; the consciousness expansion experience, premortem death and rebirth. The Vedic sages, the Eleusinian initiates and the Tantrics all knew the secret; in their esoteric writings they whisper the message. They figure out the pathways and landmarks. It is possible to get beyond ego consciousness, to tune in to the neurological processes which flash by at the speed of light, and become aware of the treasury of ancient racial knowledge welded into the nucleus of every cell in the body. Psychedelics can open this door."

We were dazzled. Leary then asked the audience, "Are you aware of the complexity of the human nervous system? For us, the voyagers, the following neurological numbers take on the significance of *mantras* (sacred Hindu words). The human brain receives one thousand million signals a second. We possess between ten and thirteen billion brain cells. Each neuron is connected to, on average, twenty-five thousand neighboring neurons."

Leary paused, an amazed look on his face. His tone became confidential, almost a whisper, as he went on to share profound secrets.

"During an ecstatic experience these billions of signals, which are normally registered and decoded, are no longer hindered by the conscious-logical-censor. Without the censor, we become unable to describe our experience because the mechanisms of language cannot contain the experience. It all happens too fast." Leary's tone of amazement was that of the explorer finding the secret Egyptian vault. It came from his personal experience.

What was our twentieth-century reference point in relation to this huge new discovery? Leary gave us a means of comparison as he flew through psychological and neurological models. He had walked us from Carl Jung's archetype theory to modern neurology. Now he was about to show us how language—a descriptive and conceptual medium—had limits similar to attempting to drive a Chevy, which performs reliably on land, through the Pacific Ocean depths where only a submarine can go. It was hard to argue with the full clout of Leary's credentials as an Ivy League—indeed, a Harvard— psychologist. Our academically competitive generation held intellectual accomplishments in awe. ("Getting into the Ivy League is hard enough. Try being a professor in that league!")

Leary resorted to anthropological and linguistic comparisons: "Picture in some barren, primitive region of Australia an aboriginal tribe that has been completely screened off from present-day civilization. They have not seen the world beyond a 20-mile radius of their cave dwelling; they have never seen a two-dimensional picture, and when they are shown a photograph, they are unable to decipher it, even if it is of something from their surroundings. They have never seen the wheel or woven cloth. Their only implements are stones; their only garments are animal skins and leaves. They have not even seen a truly straight line, a metallic or glassy surface. Their language possesses fewer than a thousand words, and none of them has abstract meaning. Their food is not cooked; it is wild and so depends upon the moods of the forests and the generosity of the seasons.

"Now picture the savage standing alone in the woods, then suddenly hurled into the very center of Manhattan, in front of the United Nations building or Park Avenue. Unless the savage has a stable grounding in some form of religious truth, he will experience utter terror.

"If he is later teleported back to his own culture, hopefully sane, he still has to cross the gulf of semantics to tell his tribesmen of his amazing experience. To do this, he must invent a completely new language. Yet even this is not enough. For even if he has catalogued memories of sensations into new words, he has still failed to understand the new sensations in their own context. The chances are his memory will be scrambled since his nervous censor is used to only a fraction of all that input, unlike those used to a modern city.

He will be in a chaos of car horns, sirens, construction jack-hammers, jukeboxes, underground subways, jets and heli-copters, rumbling cars and whining engines. And while hearing this cacophony, he will be seeing millions of tons of glinting glass and steel, shining metallic objects traveling at frightening speeds, colored lights and glowing neon as evening sets in. He will smell anything from Aqua Velva and Chanel No. 5 to ozone, propylene, phenylhydrazine, chewing gum, super detergents, germicides, gasoline, synthetic flavors and all manner of esters and ketones, methane and assorted sewage gases, exhaust and restaurant smells.

"After an LSD experience we emerge just as overwhelmed, intrigued, frightened and ecstatic as the savage transported to New York City. But our task of finding a language and creating a road map may well be even more difficult than his." A stroboscope flickering in the auditorium seemed to punc-tuate Leary's statement. The blinding flashes turned every-one's movements into an insect dance.

Leary closed the session with the parting admonition: "Remember that throughout human history, millions have made this voyage. A few whom we call mystics, saints, and Buddhas have made this experience endure and communi-cated it to their fellowmen. The experience is safe. At worst, all you will do is return as the same person you were be-fore."

Only months after Leary's talk, I had the mystical experi-ence of my life after taking ten times the normal dosage of LSD-25 (pure Swiss Sandoz LSD). I experienced a transforma-tion of consciousness that would take me years to understand in its true context. For the moment, everything seemed to be going my way.

Leary and Alpert (who himself was yet to go to India and become Ram Dass, a New Age celebrity guru in his own right) soon transliterated *The Tibetan Book of the Dead*, a Mahayana Buddhist text on the rite of death. They turned this ancient rite into a manual for taking LSD and entitled it *The Psychedelic Experience*. It further popularized the Eastern mystical teach-ings of reincarnation, karma, and the self being a spark of the divine.

STRAWBERRY FIELDS FOREVER

Meanwhile, LSD had come a long way from that modest molecular sample under Dr. Hoffman's fingernail. In Kool-Aid "acid tests" in Golden Gate Park during the "Summer of Love" in 1968, gallons of spiked Kool-Aid were handed out to thousands during "Be-Ins" and rock concerts. Youth chemists such as Stan Owsley in Berkeley became famous for taking an esoteric molecule like LSD and synthesizing it for the masses. Now there were new batches coming off the production line like colored candy: mellow yellow, blue cheer, and blotter acid. Leary's dream of nirvana from a pill for the youth culture was becoming a reality overnight. Indeed, much of the labor force for building the Rainbow Bridge came from the counterculture, which exuberantly explored new modes of living.

Hippie communes suddenly appeared on America's historical horizon. They creatively explored new alternatives for abandoning civilization and going back to nature. Men and women, boys and girls cohabited communally in the countryside. Colored Indian tepees, tents, geodesic domes, and other innovative structures suddenly filled the landscape as old farms and ranches were bought. Other groups invaded the woods. Bright scarves and headbands, bell-bottoms, and beads appeared in all patterns and shades. It was Thoreau's *Walden Pond* set to psychedelic communalism from Vermont to Marin County.

The ideals of marriage, college, and striving for a successful career in order to fit into traditional society were replaced by semi-Gandhian values: aesthetics, pacifism, nonviolence, and antimaterialism. But the move for more freedom became obsessive—for sexual freedom, for freedom from all restraints on personal choice. "Be bound by nothing." Freedom from responsibilities and commitments meant the freedom to explore, to fly like a bird. When the hero in Neil Simon's *The Graduate* was advised to go into "plastics," the sixties generation saw that as a cue to sneer collectively at such dull and myopic advice. Their collective response was, "What a compromise of the human spirit . . . what a sellout . . . what a way to spend your life."

Underground journals such as *The Berkeley Barb, The East Village Other, The Village Voice,* and *The Rolling Stone* proliferated the radical new viewpoint from coast to coast. A terrific sense of solidarity and mission resulted. It was almost a conspiracy, the generation gap became so vast. The counterculture had what seemed almost unlimited energy, and their mystical ideals would remain as the sixties generation replaced their peers by the 1980's and became corporate leaders and college professors.

Meanwhile, it is doubtful that Dr. Hoffman in the late 1940's, apart from his wildest acid visions, could have pictured *Woodstock Nation*, where a half a million youths invaded upstate New York for a Super Rock concert, ending the decade of the sixties stoned on his discovery of LSD and similar psychedelics. Their rock bands reflected drug synesthesia with names like: Jefferson Airplane, Big Brother and The Holding Company, The Strawberry Alarm Clock, The Grateful Dead, Iron Butterfly, Blue Cheer (a name for acid), Quicksilver Messenger Service, The Doors, Pink Floyd, Led Zeppelin, The Cream, Riders of The Purple Sage, The Moody Blues, Tangerine Dream, Buffalo Springfield, Credence Clearwater Revival, and so on—all names that are metaphors of psychedelicized perceptions of reality or a return to ethnic innocence.

Acid had even touched music. Every chord seemed to be played for the first time ever, with no repeats. Fresh and original lyrics and images filtered through millions of minds. The tunes were incredibly diverse, whether mystically blissful, erotic, haunting, celebrational, or defiant.

Psychedelic rock became the collective theme song for an explosively radical era that entered the world stage like a musical extravaganza. It made the era of the fifties, with its straight society, its decency, and its gray churches look flat, like a Lucky Strike wrapper lying on the ground. Who wanted to turn back the clock? No one from the youth culture, that's for sure. America had never had an era like this. Unlimited horizons seemed to flash into view now that this incredible bridge of consciousness was being built. New materials had suddenly appeared on the world scene to help build the Rainbow Bridge from our present world to a New World Order. This growing structure, like the tower of Babel, would likely span from one type of civilization to another. It was a paradigm shift indeed, and it promised to bring us to the shores of a new age. Delicious expectations filled the air.

3

Opening the Third Eye

, Willow extends his index finger to meet the finger of the dwarf magician. He fails the test because he went against his intuition at the last moment. The old village magician tells him that he has the whole universe inside of him. But like Luke Skywalker of *Star Wars*, he has to "believe" and trust the Force. George Lucas' *Willow* is a film that is itself supposed to be a microcosm of what is inside each individual viewing the film. The characters in *Willow* are living "myths" existing within all of us, according to Lucas. The mythic epics of Lucas are to inspire the unleashing of these inner realities. Lucas calls these creatures and characters in all of his epics his "best friends."

Joseph Campbell, the guru of George Lucas, has said that myths are representations of inner realities and truths. Joseph Campbell spelled this out in his book *Hero of a Thousand Faces*. When I read it 20 years ago, it hit me the same way it hit George Lucas. It was outrageously seductive. It was compelling and ingenious. It stated that we carried the sum total experience and knowledge of the race. We were walking microcosms; we had the universe inside, and carried the inner secrets to our own unfoldment. The name of the game was consciousness expansion through confronting inner and outer worlds, escalating to higher levels of energy and consciousness.

Fifteen years before Shirley MacLaine ever discovered New Age thought, many of us on the pioneering edge of the sixties were pursuing the identical path. We were persuaded that total awareness was possible: about nature, the cosmos, and man—from the spiritual to the mundane. We wanted simultaneous access to supramundane planes and dimensions, and command of occult realities that only a fraction of our world even knew about. In short, I and my contemporaries believed in the reality of cosmic consciousness, or superconsciousness, or enlightenment. I felt that life's greatest jewel was to attain it, and that finding this great secret was the real reason we were here. Was there outward evidence for superconsciousness? It seemed so. Leary had spoken about it—but so had Joseph Campbell, Carlos Castenada, and many others. Analogies already existed.

It was already plain to see that the elevator shaft of consciousness went from the lower floors of the animal world to the incredible levels of man's greatest achievements. If this shaft continued to the vast levels of angels, higher beings, and beyond, then by speculative extension the mystics were right and human potential did not stop until it arrived right at the seat of godhood. We were in a continuum that implied we could ride the elevator to the top floor. Lower rungs of consciousness could be used as an argument for extension.

Even among people there was a huge range of consciousness. In the same way a savvy internationalist can adeptly work through London from Belgravia to Kensington to Soho or Mile End or Hammersmith on one day, Paris the next, from the Left Bank of the Seine to Saint-Cloud, then midtown Manhattan the next, and 50 other cities with equal adroitness—flashing through a million nuances of language and culture, mastering customs and cuisine—as compared to an unschooled and unsophisticated villager living in an adobe hut or a backcountry hillbilly farmer, who would be helpless at any of these supercosmopolitan points. The same analogy points to the full range of human differences in consciousness—from a fully empowered yogi and master to someone with the depth awareness of a formica countertop, living in a world of Wheaties and McDonald's hamburgers. The span from idiot to genius had upper and lower floors to which we were only beginning to wake up; indeed, the elevator shaft broke through new levels all the time.

There were other analogies. If insight could increase a little, it could increase massively. There were a number of ways I pictured superconsciousness. One was by taking the process of insight and extending it with no upper limits. I recalled the time that I wrote a university paper on Plato's cave allegory, and had sudden breakthroughs of insight into the meaning of the concept "abstract." My awareness changed in a moment of time and would never go back. Then when I studied Jean Piaget, I realized that the mental development from childhood to adulthood had tangible barriers that were approached and transcended as growth continued. A child at the "concrete operational level" was incapable of the gear shift of more mature abstract thinking, and so on. It was like the evolutionist's maxim, "ontogeny recapitulates phylogeny." In the microcosm of the womb, the human organism, they claimed, seemed to mimic prior stages in animal evolution. Consciousness had stages as well.

"Heaven and Hell and all the gods are within us," Joseph Campbell suddenly told Bill Moyers. Yet if Joseph Campbell became the guru of George Lucas of *Star Wars* fame, Carl Jung was the source of inspiration and the teacher of Joseph Campbell. Jung's depth psychology was the source of almost every major insight that Campbell ever had. And during the six-part series by Bill Moyers on Joseph Campbell, Campbell payed homage to Jung repeatedly.

Jung talked about consciousness. The famed Swiss thinker was an important key for many of us in the sixties.

Jung had revolutionary ideas about the mysteries of the self. To Jung, man contained the universe within: The entirety of racial knowledge was welded within every cell. Within the mind lay the vast collective unconscious containing every type of character in every Shakespearean play, every mythological figure, and more. These were the inner archetypes. Jung stated that the supreme voyage—and Jung was a mystic, having written the introduction to the Evans-Wentz Oxford translation of *The Tibetan Book of the Dead*—was to boldly encounter and absorb every archetype within, to come to terms with the forbidden, the inner shadow, and ultimately to discover the higher self. To Jung, when this huge collective unconscious, this microcosm within, was fully searched out and no longer a mystery, then one was "individuated." This was a form of enlightenment.

Jung's theories did not merely go beyond Freud's psychoanalysis, but Jungian depth psychology anticipated the eventual merger of the new psychologies of the midseventies with Eastern thought. Jung was 50 years ahead of Esalen and the transpersonal psychologists of the New Age movement. Indeed, Jung was the true grandfather of transpersonal psychology. In the sixties another fan of Jung, Alan Watts of Harvard, an orientalist, wrote *The Supreme Identity*. The supreme identity, of course, was the divine inner nature that Watts had learned from studying Zen Buddhism which he then melded with modern psychological theories. For opposites to be resolved and to merge, they had to be encountered: good and evil, male and female.

The male, Jung said, had to come to terms with his opposite valence, the feminine within—an archetype known as the "anima." Where did Jung see this archetype manifesting itself? In Renaissance paintings, novels, and a thousand other places. But there was one novel in particular, H. Rider Haggard's *She*, that Jung felt most fully portrayed the anima. "She" was the embodiment of the shrouded feminine nature that had to be encountered by males, especially those who had all the defense mechanisms of modern culture. The anima also enabled men to appreciate the truly feminine in women. It was a deeper tug than the purely physical sexual drive, which was only one manifestation of the interplay between the forces of masculine and feminine. They were universal forces, and Jung turned to Taoism to explain the interplay of opposites. The masculine and feminine polarities were but one aspect of the cosmic dance.

Jung's pathway through the mysteries of the self to us in the sixties was tailor-made for the taboo-ridden Westerner with all his hang-ups, who had such an ordeal in looking within, especially when it came time to face "the shadow" and the "inner demons." Evil was now relegated to areas within the individual that were projected out; it was the other half of good. To Jung, there was no really absolute evil. It was merely one more opposite out of which the cosmos was composed—light and dark, male and female, good and evil, and so on. As Taoism stated, all life is an interplay between these opposites until they are merged into one. This was an attractive universe indeed. In a way, it made that irritant of a continually gnawing guilty conscience now obsolete and irrelevant. That carryover from Old Testament morality, the Pentateuch within, could now be "outgrown." There were times when my conscience weighed me down greatly. I welcomed a way to be rid of it, if it could be transcended as taboos and fears, the dragons at our inner gates, were defeated. Thus, as the myth of the ego dissolved, our inner potential would increase exponentially as we worked toward superconsciousness.

Superconsciousness, I believed, could more than encompass the range of intellectual knowledge. The superconscious individual could look into people and read them like a book. He was equally able to adeptly frolic through any fields of knowledge like Horowitz at the keyboard. Such a mind could picture DNA or glycolysis at a glimpse; inhale Wittgenstein or Kant's *Critique of Pure Reason* (appreciating why he evolved the solipsism he did, in T.U.A., in answer to Hume); or see all nuances of literary brilliance in James Joyce, William Blake, or Tolstoy. But beyond all this, the superconscious one was able to know all these things with an infinite depth after having attained full awareness of "the Self." It was this latter achievement that gave full scope to his awareness. It is this mystique that Westerners see in a Rajneesh or a Krishnamurti. They represent the mystical masters of superconsciousness.

It was easy to romanticize the potentials of human consciousness and its evolutionary expansion into superstates of being. Hegel had talked about it. And so had the ancient writers of the *Upanishads* of India as well as myriads of more recent voices. This challenge made the church on the corner seem dead, irrelevant, and boring. On the other hand, I felt a thrill of enthusiasm each time I thought of the possibilities of consciousness expansion just waiting around the corner.

Then one day, I experienced it all—in a glimpse, a split second in eternity. This experience radically changed the course of my life, ultimately sending me to India.

ENCOUNTERING THE GROUND OF BEING

It was a balmy evening in the late spring of 1966 when I rode my motorcycle deep into the countryside of Virginia away from civilization. The meadows seemed like a vast armchair. I sat atop a smooth, warm, grassy knoll, slightly higher than hundreds of acres of surrounding meadows and woods. My knapsack and sleeping bag were propped against a lone tree that arched into the night sky like a giant neuron or antenna reaching into the cosmos.

I took ten times the normal dosage of LSD-25—3000 micrograms—and watched my own consciousness explode open as the celestial powers seemed to speak to the deepest core of my being. The LSD I took was the purest you could find in the world—Sandoz LSD made in Basel, Switzerland, right out of the labs of the inventor, Albert Hoffman. The result of the experience is that I was sure that I was a mystic and had seen things only privy to a few. I was a master in the making, an adept. In order for me to show the lure and power of this type of experience, I shall record what happened to me. It is written up in my book *Avatar of Night* [published in India in 1982 by Vikas Publishing]:

> At a fraction past midnight, I swallowed the capsule. I accepted the fact that I was, in effect, sitting on top of an atom bomb. And I would either come out on the level of Gautama Buddha or the coyote in the Roadrunner cartoon.
>
> An hour later, what looked dead was conscious, as all of creation crackled in dialogue with itself. Meanwhile, my thoughts and perceptions began to fuse. Stars joined like drops of mercury across the night sky forming multi-colored webbs—breathing and arching across the heavens, across galaxies and onto the very ground where

I perched. Grains of sand, pebbles and trees, ebbed and flowed with this impersonal consciousness.

If my own consciousness was layered and branched in a million places like a banyan tree, it was now as though the rest of my being had squeezed what was most essentially me into the top stem of the uppermost branch. Down to the deepest root, there were a thousand astral levels at war within me, as my uppermost self was fighting to stay aloft through the aid of a million subordinate parts that were straining and tugging. Even below these, there were endless rumbles and shifts, like a subterranean city, while every archetype that I had ever encountered was presently being held at bay.

Soon I was above even the dazzling beings and demigods that were so special before. The celestial cities and realms were like the lower strata of a pyramid whose fascination I had sacrificed—things great enough to inspire the master poets and painters, I later reflected, in order to approach the level of the truly abstract, pure thought, pure knowing, pure being. If I did reach the purest state, I could diffuse like a drop of mercurochrome throughout the ocean of thought.

Every second that passed, one of my million parts was answering something comparable to the riddle of the sphinx to propel me on to the level of super-consciousness.

A new truth came. That I, like every man, was a hierarchy of men, a living society, a kingdom and a nation, and before I became enlightened I would have to bear the weight of all truths, to encompass the total history of my nation within a fraction of time. After a thousand other thoughts, I passed on to the next level of realization.

Momentarily, I shrank and became so small that "humbling" does not describe it—I became insignificant. Far less than a blade of grass that has just been given the brief consciousness to realize what it is. It might hear the voice that shakes the mountains of the worlds and announces, "You thought you were a god and you stir only to find that you are but a blade of grass lying helplessly on the forest floor. Even the ants walk over you. How tiny you are. Your delusions end. Can you bear this, and yet live?"

Then the sheer jet-like force of what was happening to my mind became too great. I became a twig riding a tidal wave. I clutched that Virginia meadow as though clutching the rigging of a hurricane-swept deck of a Galleon. It seemed that something other than the drug had taken over, something supernatural perhaps.

As a force drove my mind at a speed greater than thought, I could feel something far older than I suddenly start navigating my course. I passed ten thousand cross-roads per second, and took the proper turn on each one of them. I feared that if I tried to grind down the gears at this point, I might wake up on the outer edges of the galaxy not much higher up on the phylogenic scale than a cucumber. And after all the billions of years it took me to work my way up to to becoming a human being, I did not want to blow it now, and enter a form of loneliness that was unthinkable.

My speed increased even more, as I became a diamond wedge cutting the finest possible arcs, from one juncture to another. Then it occurred to me that on some level I was being asked questions in which a correct turn could only be made by means of a totally spontaneous truthful answer. Anything else would veer me off course. Like the Day of Judgment, a lie would be impossible damnation, because there was not an atom of time to deliberate. And anything but the truth, it seemed, would have fragmented me all over the cosmos.

Then something happened: I lost all grasp of language and thought. I saw a doorway into a new universe. It was a pinpoint of light. To fight the acceleration required to approach it was to fight the mass of the entire universe. I could not tell whether the distance within the pinpoint of light was as minuscule as the angstrom units between atoms, or almost infinitely huge, as the distance from one side of the universe to the other.

At the barrier of the pinpoint of light—*I enter the eternal present. All thirteen billion brain cells within me seem to turn inside out, as though jumping to a higher gestalt and forming into a higher structure that was previously latent. Each cell recites one of my former names, and I as a nation hear the thirteen billion names of my subjects and former earthly identities on the wheel of reincarnation. Once I enter the pinpoint of light, all ties with the world vanish. I enter the Unborn.*

A caterpillar cannot experience the butterfly transition and remain a caterpillar. One structure cannot be smuggled across into the other, that is impossible. You are either one or the other. That also applied to me. At most, my experience could be paralleled from one universe to another, but nothing could cross the barrier.

I have never been able to summon what happened to me during that stretch of time after entering the pinpoint of light. Months later, I assumed that I had entered into the ocean of being . . . "the void, also known as the clear light or the Ocean of Brahman." That I had been allowed to experience the highest mystical state, what the Hindus call *Nirvikalpa Samadhi*.[1]

By the time I went to India in 1969, I had pored through thousands and thousands of pages of mystical revelations. I understood these things as though I had written them: from the writings of Sri Aurobindo to the writings about Sri Ramakrishna; from the *Upanishads* to the *Bhagavad Gita*. They made complete sense of my mystical experience, putting flesh on it with new language. Meanwhile my life took on a thrust of manic joy that was so positive I felt unstoppable. I was in the currents of a vast wave directing my life. I felt like some Boddhidharma in the making. Inevitably, I could do no other than sell all that I owned and head East. There I spent several years as a close disciple of Sai Baba, India's greatest miracle-working super guru. This experience was beyond anything Leary had described the day I heard him.

I was a consummate New Ager before the term had been invented. My beliefs were a composite of the best I could find from the East blended together with the most radical break-throughs in the West—the new physics, new forms of psychology, psychic research, channeled information from such psychics as Edgar Cayce, Theosophy, and creative ideas coming from the psychedelic subculture. The drama of life was to ride the wave and "trust the Force" as I saw my third eye open.

4

The Coming Changes

After my powerful mystical experience under LSD, I was walking to the beat of a different drummer. I began to tune into things that I had never noticed before. I felt part of a great pattern. Suddenly I sensed that history was unfolding according to plan. A hidden army of advanced adepts were pioneering the coming of the New Age and I was among them. Overnight, my conceptual universe had altered radically. Perhaps similar changes could happen to the whole world—a global alteration of consciousness.

Before I took that leap to India, I felt new experiences beckoning me on, preparing me for new leaps in consciousness. I had to leap off the diving board of uncharted experience. I had to explore new thresholds beyond the mindset of our materialistic culture which had demystified the universe. America had become a society of people whose intellectual curiosity rarely ranged beyond the mundane and the prosaic. It was intimidated by the unknown and seemed to easily settle for a McDonald's spiritual diet and a K-Mart lifestyle. The grand summits of ancient wisdom towered above our distracted and busy culture which had lost its roots with eternity. We were ants absorbed in disposing of some small speck of waste food at the base of a grand edifice. The vast and splendid columns of the Parthenon dwarfed us into insignificance. We never looked up.

The challenge for me was to plug back into the ancient secrets of existence that our modern world had cast away. Yet in this alien and uncharted universe, I also needed some sort of compass. Like most of us in the army of mystics, I felt that my ultimate navigational instrument was my deepest intuitive promptings. Now a new door appeared and I had to open it.

THE ASTRAL TRAVELER

On many a freezing winter's night in 1968, I motorcycled down the rustic wooded lanes weaving from Charlottesville, Virginia, to the spectral ranch house of Robert Monroe, author of *Journeys Out of the Body*, poised on its many acres and beaming multicolored lights like an airport control tower. We often met several times a week. Monroe was gaining increasing fame across America among connoisseurs of the underground new-consciousness movement as a legitimate astral projector—one who was able to leave his physical body. Twenty years later, Monroe's writings were to become among the most recognized of New Age advocates, and Monroe would be a key conference speaker at New Age conventions.

At the time, Dr. Charles Tart and an array of notable parapsychologists had run a whole gamut of double-blind tests on Monroe. Skeptics were invariably baffled each time by Monroe's unaccounted-for powers. Robert Monroe would whoosh out of his body at midnight and travel to an anechoic chamber beneath Stanford University, the University of California at Berkeley, or the University of California at Davis, where Tart and others awaited. On the west coast it was only nine in the evening. Monroe would look around the room, noting people, conversations, and furniture arrangement. Then he would whoosh back to his body in Charlottesville and give them a long-distance phone call describing what he saw. He was right on target repeatedly, astounding these scientists with the fact that there are other forces operating behind the machinery of the physical universe. But what was really important to Monroe were not these trips around the country, but trips somewhere else.

Monroe and I met regularly to make sense out of the whole phenomenon of astral travel, catalyzing one another in the process. He was approaching the subject in terms of the "higher teachings" he had received while out of the body in his encounters with "higher beings," astral masters, and other entities. Monroe combined this with his diversified readings in yoga, Eastern thought, and scientific theory. I approached his bizarre exploits and spirit encounters from the viewpoint of Indian monistic philosophy syncretized with a new emerging "mystical Christianity" that came through channeled teachings of Edgar Cayce, Levi Dowling, and others combined with Jung, Tillich, and Teilhard de Chardin.

From Monroe's lonely perspective, perhaps my most important credential was that apparently I, too, had been able to leave my physical body sporadically. It had started when I was a ten-year-old battling the mumps in London, at around the same time I had started toying with a Ouija board. Half asleep in bed in our old Victorian house in Knightsbridge, I would become paralyzed, hear the sound of jets, and apparently go ripping through the roof to hover above our house. Occasionally the same thing happened during my teens, and it was starting again in college. Monroe's out-of-the-body symptoms matched mine point for point.

Monroe and I were also working on the technology to elicit astral experiences in ordinary people. Monroe was getting his ideas from his "contacts." This became the M-5000 program, a complex, multichannel recorded tape which the subject listened to on going to sleep. Cables and sound equipment trailed through the house from central command, an isolated geodesic chamber of pyramidal glass which rippled with colored lights, while pulse generators whirred and hummed to the syncopated beat of a synthesizer/organ. Monroe had been the child prodigy of a medical doctor father and college professor mother, spending much of his life dabbling with inventions. Much of what we were doing now with sound equipment came from his experience as a vice president of Mutual Broadcasting in New York City.

What was most momentous about this was that we were on the pioneering edge of occult technology. We were not closing the gap to enter the spiritual dimensions by blindly putting together the machinery. Rather, the powers on the other side had bridged the gap, with Monroe as medium, and were the ones telling him what to do. Monroe cited a long list of technological breakthroughs that came from the other side to various inventors, including the benzene ring and the Xerox copier.

We pictured the transformation of America into a spiritual technology. The story of Atlantis came to mind. Channelers such as Edgar Cayce stated that Atlantis had risen to great heights until it destroyed itself. This time, hopefully, we were wise enough not to let the power get out-of-hand. But there was something even more profound than getting millions to have occult experiences by a new technology. There was, on a deeper level, a number of revolutionary spiritual implications behind astral travel; namely, these experiences implied a whole metaphysical reality that was completely new to America.

Implicit in soul travel among the living—those who have bodies to leave—is soul travel among the dead, whose souls can freely range through other planes without need of bodies. Implied in this is soul travel from life to life, incarnation to incarnation, hence *reincarnation*. Further implicit in all of this is the concept of "old souls" who have an almost endless history of reincarnations. And what is the reason for reincarnation? The answer is central to Eastern thought itself: We reincarnate up the evolutionary ladder for the purpose of ultimate perfection and self-realization into pure consciousness. When consciousness realizes its identity with ultimate consciousness, and the mystery of being is over, then the separate ego-self ceases to exist. Then the "true self" unites with the ocean of being, the godhead. In short, as the Hindu masters have stated all along, the self or *Jivan Atma*, merges with God or the *Paramatma*, thus attaining eternal liberation or *Moksha, Nirvikalpa Samadhi, Sat-Chit-Ananda*. As our past records of karma are worked away, we evolve spiritually and climb the ladder of being. We are a composite of millions of former characters in the cosmic play. And some of us have very long dossiers of former lives.

This brings up the question of past-life speculation. For instance, if Monroe and I had been in Atlantis at the same

time, playing around with dangerous cosmic devices, perhaps we helped blow up the whole works then. Our karma,
therefore, was to correct now what we had blown up then
when the ancient civilization of Atlantis went up in a vast
explosion so great that there is no longer any record of it (this
eliminates the archeological question). I remember, after all,
at 12 years of age going to the great pyramids of Egypt with
my parents and later doing drawings of how they were built
using antigravity "Atlantian" technology; colossal blocks
hovered in the air above the Sphinx en route to Cheops.

I also remember an epiphany I had in the Egyptian city of
Alexandria at the age of 14—I suddenly felt this blissful sense
of connectedness—that I was experiencing a *déjà vu* from a
past life. As we took a horse-drawn carriage through the royal
gardens of Alexandria, I had this overwhelming nameless
emotion, a timeless yearning. Later in India I was told such
signs in my early childhood indicated I was an advanced
adept. Now I could see these bits to the puzzle fitting together.

I speculated about my own past lives just as people do in
today's New Age circles. These days you can go to a Hollywood cocktail party where all kinds of incredible past lives are
spoken of with this sense of profound knowing, heroic lives
from King David to Abraham Lincoln, to Atlantian priests.
Five people present all claim to have once been Abraham
Lincoln. A means of sifting was needed. How do you discern
the real Abe Lincoln? Then you might encounter someone
trying out for a bit part with Metro Goldwyn Mayer. He
announces he was once Lao Tse or a top disciple of Gautama
Buddha. You quietly wonder about his Hollywood incarnation as he is now playing a werewolf in some horror movie. It
seems a bit disconcerting for a former pupil of the Buddha to
be playing a werewolf. The answer: He is working off some
last traces of karma.

There was an aspect to some of Monroe's and my encounters with the other side that threatened our notions of a peril-
free universe void of absolute evil. Some of these spirit
encounters had a brutal, almost demonic concreteness. This
cut away at the stereotype I was forming of an almost sym-
phonically gentle and peace-pervading cosmos whose evil

was so wispy and illusory that apparent evil was little more than good English humor turned up to a cosmic scale.

One morning, Monroe looked quite shaken as he rubbed his bleary eyes over a cup of coffee at our usual meeting place, the kitchen table. I had spent a fitful night alone in a far-wing bedroom, with earphones on while lying flat on my back in an attempt to enter what I called "the buzz region." I had been trying to discorporate, kick out of my body and control its sojourn. Monroe, meanwhile, had been assaulted by alien beings at about 3 A.M. That and other encounters had lasted till dawn. I was absolutely fascinated by his report at the breakfast table.

"I felt about as significant as an ant compared to these two beings," Monroe confessed. He said he had perceived clair-voyantly two massive beings of light, brighter than stars and of vast power, drifting deep in the heavens like two meteors. Then they stopped their drift and honed in on him, begin-ning a terrible drilling down upon him like huge, sparking hornets. They descended with great speed while Monroe remained in the paralyzed "buzz region." These beings soon reached his room and went through the hidden records of his mind like speed-readers flipping through a card file. After about ten minutes they evidently had gotten what they wanted—or as he suggested later, implanted what they wanted—and then pulled away, much like a huge hypoder-mic being pulled out of a patient. This experience brought up the question of victimization and cosmic bullying, and indi-vidual worth and privacy, but we preferred to theorize more in the direction that the incident was an act of charity, that the two beings had probably left a subtle implant which would germinate when Bob Monroe was ready, perhaps years in the future.

In a guarded manner, Monroe said that these two beings might have had some connection with UFOs which he be-lieved were not necessarily machines, but celestial beings, almost angels of a sort.

Since that time in 1968, Robert Monroe has written several sequels to his bestseller, *Journeys Out of the Body*. They follow up on his experiences and contacts with the beyond. He has also entered the New Age movement as a sort of guru—as have several other friends of mine from that era, such as Raymond Moody, who wrote the bestseller *Life After Life*. By the time I left for India after graduating from the University of Virginia, fellow student Raymond Moody was getting a Ph.D. in philosophy. Later Moody returned to the University of Virginia as a medical intern while he was a local celebrity with his Bantam paperback bestseller filling shelves all over the country. By then I was back from India, having lived through something that felt like a motion picture.

INDIA

I had been absolutely compelled to go to India. After my psychic dabbling, I realized that my first love remained the sheer genius of India's spiritual philosophy. Its depth and range were light-years ahead of what I considered to be our psychic hobbies in the West. We were just discovering spiritual realities that Indian sages had exhausted millennia ago. We were exulting over novel toys that the ancients had abandoned as tokens of spiritual infancy. Astral travel to a rishi is like the neon lights of Broadway to a native New Yorker who looks on in disdain as some visitor from the Third World stands with his mouth hanging open over the blips and flashes of neon at Times Square. Or it's like a New Yorker watching some foreigner who can't get over discovering and reveling in, time and again, some techno-trinket at Toys-R-Us—say a dayglow robot that follows you around the store speaking in metal-voiced banalities. To a jaded New Yorker, such foreigners are mental midgets. So are we when we go into silent awe before some Indian yogi who makes deep penetrating insights into our character or family history. These are party trinkets to an *advaitin*, the cream of the crop of India's spiritual elite, who admit of no subject-object distinctions in the universe including between self and God.

In truth, Monroe's contact teachings did not reach what I considered to be the highest truth of all: the ultimate oneness of all things, which is at the kernel of India's perennial philosophy. To me, his contact teachings from astral classes seemed little more than the low-level pyrotechnics that the Indian masters had been warning against all along. His teachings were fragmented interpretations of reality taught by demigods and entities which, though higher up the evolutionary scale than your generic citizen, still fell vastly short of the absolute. These entities were way down the scale of consciousness compared to an enlightened master who had reached unity with the godhead. Such entities ultimately had to take up human form anyway in order to make that final leap into enlightenment in the first place.

The teaching of the enlightened masters is simply this: The very highest state of being in the cosmos exists in the one who has become enlightened, when the overmind, the void, suddenly becomes incarnate or manifest in a human body. Even the hierarchies of celestial beings are subject to such a one.

Bingo: Seth or Ramtha are to sit at the feet of Krishna, not the other way around. The last leap-off point was when a superevolved being joined once again with God; this was the stage of enlightened master. Therefore, why ask a disincarnate Tibetan priest a question that only a full master can answer? The entity or being would not be an entity or being in the first place unless it still had things to go through, lessons that awaited it before it could merge with the absolute. It was in the karmic classroom and could never be any more than a pupil of a fully enlightened master as long as it remained "an entity." That was the very uppermost peak of the evolutionary ladder in the entire cosmos. So why, I asked, bother hooking up with space visitors or drifting entities who are still learners themselves and have only incomplete answers at best?

Inevitably, the next major door to open in my life was India. But as always, there were dragons at the gate.

En route to India, I met the head swami of the Ramakrishna Mission in London. He walked with me through Holland Park to quiz me on my understanding of India's nondual philosophy known as *advaita*. I was considering joining the Ramakrishna Mission in Bengal. Yet I knew only a handful of Westerners ever made it. Then, the day after our initial encounter, the swami amazed me. He gave me a letter of recommendation. I had apparently passed his tests. I knew in my heart of hearts that my awareness came only partially from reading the great mystical books. The main source of my understanding came from that massive mystical experience induced by LSD. The swami's parting words were encouraging: "Your understanding of advaita philosophy is as advanced as the best young Brahmin men I have seen in India. I will write a letter of recommendation to the Ramakrishna Mission in Calcutta recommending you for *sanyas* (initiation as a renunciant and monk wearing the ochre robe). I believe you are sincere and have real understanding." Those who read Christopher Isherwood, a well-known author, orientalist, and follower of Ramakrishna, will learn from his own testimonial that I was given a very rare appraisal and invitation for a Westerner. But other things awaited me in India than ordination into the Ramakrishna Vedanta Society.

Within six months of my arrival in Delhi, I was rewarded by the powers that be for my costly leap of faith. I became, after some months of wandering across India, the top Western disciple of Sai Baba, India's most powerful miracle-working godman. His following numbered over 20 million in India alone. I lived with him in South India for two years, gaining a rare residence permit in the process. I meditated and practiced a range of yogas under Baba. I also became a privileged spokesman under Baba. A number of times I joined Sai Baba onstage at his massive ashram, *Prasanthi Nilayam*, to speak before vast crowds.

Before I had left for India, I still saw some value to contemporary channeled information, such as Edgar Cayce's contacts with the Akashic Records. I was intrigued by their ultimate endorsement of Eastern mystical revelation. They brought me to the shores of India, to the heartland of Vedanta, but no further. Their truth value seemed to stop there.

But perhaps psychic/channeled information had another purpose: Since the world was being prepared for a leap in evolution, new paradigms of the ancient wisdom were needed to reach that critical threshold of people sent to catalyze "the time of changes." Therefore, hidden in these channelings were personal directives to us, the agents of change. We were among the predicted higher souls to incarnate in our time to help bring in the New Age. Cayce described our "descent into the earth plane." The cosmic teletype had some updated information on today's events that the rishis of ancient India did not need to write about in their time.

Later, many of the sixties pioneers would abandon their mystic attire, join the establishment, and become yuppies. But their understanding of reality would infiltrate the world. They would remake the corporation. They would fill the ranks of influential occupations and, from their prestigious vantage points, they would then parlay this new belief system into acceptability as it descended down the slopes of the pyramid into the average living room of middle America.

These embryo mystics of the sixties were destined to grow up and take over the gears of society: publishing, movies, news magazines, television shows, schoolrooms, government agencies, science labs, academia, banking, even Wall Street. It was a *coup* of quiet succession, of one generation replacing another. A whole new world was waiting in the wings. It just needed time. It also needed a line of credit from some quiet insiders behind the scenes. There were many players in this drama of shaping global history. Some were actors in the parade, some were movers and shakers. The plan for a New World Order was not a new one. But certain things needed to be aligned before it could even be discussed. The spiritual structure of this was absolutely crucial.

The New Age movement is the spiritual structure for globalism; it is a critically important adhesive to hold all of the other elements in place. As a spiritual system, naturally it must have its human agents—its mouthpieces in contact with powers beyond this world. They themselves look to higher guidance and then transmit this guidance to others. The guidance itself is not without purpose. Clearly a plan is unfolding. It has everything in the world to do with the New World Order.

5
Higher Guidance

"Higher guidance" is crucial for the process of spiritual transformation from normal consciousness to cosmic consciousness. This axiom is universal among New Age luminaries. Ken Wilber, David Spangler, Fritjof Capra, Elisabeth Kubler-Ross, Marilyn Ferguson, Shirley MacLaine, and other well-known figures emphasize the need to be guided by higher powers. They have been foremost among the new wave in letting go and letting the process of guidance from beyond take hold in their own lives. There are many forms of guidance. It is an open field. Any technique that works is fair game in this new renaissance, whether it has come out of the ancient mystery religions, India, or the very newest experiments in producing altered states.

To the zealous mystic, the smallest perception or event can be loaded with significance. Intuition alone can go a long way. Then there are higher octane methods such as the tarot, visualization, meditation, shamanistic techniques, drugs, the Ouija board, astrology, and the I Ching. The higher powers can use these things as mediums through which to guide inquiring minds. Things did not start to happen to channeler Jane Roberts until she started using a Ouija board—that opened the door. After that, her life was never the same.

Certainly in my own life, once I crossed the threshold I quietly watched for signs from the cosmic gatekeeper to direct my course. I knew the higher sources could break through

59

into our material domain to direct spiritual adepts such as myself—of that I was positive.

Once I gained the ability to see things "from the plane of the gods," I was able to look back and suddenly see meanings behind events in my early life. I could detect patterns of "guidance," such as when I got a Ouija board at age ten and subscribed to a spiritualist newsletter when my father was a diplomat in London; or when I left my body for astral travel at the same age; or when I became obsessed with the wider field of psychic phenomena at 12. Invisible hands were directing my course.

It was therefore no accident that I met a classmate when I was 13 who was psychic. He would receive mental pictures of distant events like a cosmic television station. He blanked out his mind and in they would come. He also received images from people's minds that we called "pictures." We engaged in a kind of psychic voyeurism. We sat at the back of the class, eyes closed, waiting for impressions to come from the prettiest girls in the class. What usually came through was fragmented and odd. But we were compelled by the sheer fascination of the unknown.

By high school there was a lull as new interests filled the gap, yet cosmic tidbits did come through. I was in an advanced English class under a teacher who had just come back from Oxford. J.D. Salinger was required reading. There it was, another tidbit—the short story entitled "Teddy." It was about an "embryo mystic," a precocious ten-year-old boy crossing the Atlantic on an ocean liner (at age ten I too crossed the Atlantic on an ocean liner). I walked home rehearsing Salinger's story in my mind. It brought back my fascination. One passage in particular between ten-year-old Teddy and an adult had great impact:

> "From what I gather, you've acquired certain information, through meditation, that's given you some conviction that in your last incarnation you were a holy man in India, but more or less fell from grace—"

"I wasn't a holy man," Teddy said. "I was just a person making a very nice spiritual advancement."

"All right—whatever it was," Nicholson said. "But the point is you feel that in your last incarnation you more or less fell from grace before final Illumination. Is that right, or am I—"

"That's right," Teddy said. "I met a lady, and I sort of stopped meditating."

. . . Nicholson was looking at him, studying him. "I believe you said on that last tape that you were six when you first had a mystical experience. Is that right?"

"I was six when I saw that everything was God, and my hair stood up, and all that," Teddy said. "It was on a Sunday, I remember. My sister was only a very tiny child then, and she was drinking her milk, and all of a sudden I saw that *she* was God and that the *milk* was God. I mean, all she was doing was pouring God into God, if you know what I mean."[1]

It kept echoing in my head on the way home from high school: ". . . all she was doing was pouring God into God, if you know what I mean."

THE BIG PICTURE

When I was a bit younger than Teddy, we lived in George-town, Washington D.C., not far from Dumbarton Oaks. One day I wandered down to the Georgetown theater after school. I used to go to movies alone so I could concentrate without interruption. On the marquee it read: THE DAY THE EARTH STOOD STILL. I was haunted, invaded by the film. It touched a primal nerve in me. There it was, the earth in chaos, a hostile planet whose nations were at war. Suspicion and weaponry were everywhere. The earth was like a big ship out-of-control, with no one at the helm to steer it. People battled and tugged on the wheel—frightened, warlike people with hair-trigger responses to threats, real or imagined. At any moment the ship might collide with any number of things and that would be it—down it would go. So too with an earth run by unenlightened people who were always on the brink of war.

In *The Day the Earth Stood Still*, a saucer fills the sky and glides down into the park behind the White House. The alien visitor, played by Michael Rennie, is an infinitely noble-looking man whose handsome, refined, and intelligent face is grieved by people who cannot handle their own affairs. The earth is given an ultimatum. If it wants to survive and join the planetary confederation, it must abandon national rights, surrender to global government, and immediately disarm, otherwise the earth will be reduced to cinders. An elite of the world's top intellectuals, of course, understood this like the ABCs. Presumably they would be among the elite of the global government. But military men and politicians needed a show of power, which they got. Gort, the robot with the one eye, a supertitanium cyclops, could melt anything in sight if he so chose, from Sherman tanks to the entire planet. Idiots with guns finally got the point and backed off after he vaporized numbers of them.

The alien visitor was what all earthlings needed to become: an infinitely noble and wise being with a cosmic outlook and who detested violence, valued all things—including the sacredness of life, was impartial, peace-loving, and who held an air of unshakable superiority. He was among the enlightened. He was the ultimate role model. The producer, Mr. Blaustein, made a deep point to my tender young mind in a post-World-War-II world. After the afternoon matinee, I walked through Dumbarton Oaks—an ironic act, though I did not know it at the time.

Indeed, I used to love exploring Dumbarton Oaks, the beautiful estate where a handful of intellectuals, some who were acquaintances of my father, had held strategy meetings preceding the formation of the United Nations. It was also the meeting place of another group of intellectuals, physicists such as Robert Oppenheimer, Enrico Fermi, and Edward Teller, who had met eight years before the first group. Their purpose was to explore the feasibility of building the world's first atomic bomb—what was known as the Manhattan Project. All this was just around the corner from where I lived—a peaceful and innocent-looking place with stunning fountains, flower gardens, woods, and red-brick buildings, and where global war and global unity had been discussed and planned. It implied a planet in chaos, without peace and order, where perhaps an elite group of men might intervene to keep a great tragedy from happening. All someone needed was to go along with the plan. It was democracy in action. In those days, all I could see glinting within the walls of Dumbarton Oaks were the bright coins shining at the bottom of the fountain.

The truth seemed simple then and many years later: All the world needed was a change of consciousness, of mind-set. That was it. Then people could put down their arms and live in peace, sharing selflessly the resources of the world. Indeed, a new viewpoint was needed—a sense of the cosmic and, of course, a change of self-orientation so that universal love could take root. This didn't seem to be asking too much.

By the time I went to India I was convinced that there was a fundamental and supreme basis for unity that few people saw or understood. It was a unity that we already had in our very deepest natures—that if we were all sparks of the divine, then to be anything but united in global peace and love was a miscarriage of highest truth. "I am you as you are me" sang Lennon and Harrison of the Beatles in "I Am the Walrus." If I am shooting a fellow human being, then I am shooting myself—that is what the mystic finally realizes. Once you can see the divine within, then you can see the divine without— because it is within others. Then boundaries of the ego dissolve and only love can exist. This was cosmic love "for all people" about which the yogis of India and the mystic masters spoke.

This was also an essential tenet of New Age thought. Peace is a by-product of our realizing our mutual divinity through planetary evolution of consciousness. This was the true cement for global unity—a change of consciousness. New Agers use the term "planetization." Until we did that, the threat of a planet in chaos capable of destroying itself almost any time in nuclear fire loomed on the horizon. This is the platform of Greenpeace and a thousand other New Age groups.

But there is a hidden work: networking groups have to reach a critical threshold of people, a minimum number required to catalyze the New Age planetary *transformation*. This is viewed as a necessary evolutionary event without which the planet might not survive. The catalytic threshold occurs when that minimum number of people experience "consciousness-raising."

Events like Hands-across-America and the Harmonic Convergence are events that the public can role-play which have far deeper significance than they realize in acclimating them for globalism and the new consciousness. It is like getting millions of people to recite a mantra on a TV program; the act itself is an unconscious invocation. Hands-across-America was the seeding among the people of a mind-set. It was a dress rehearsal for universal brotherhood, gearing the public for world cooperation. It is the fishnet approach. First you identify and then catalyze those among the masses who will be future beacons to help steer this process of public influence.

The film, *Close Encounters of the Third Kind*, carried this message—the gathering together of those from out of society who were receptive to higher guidance. They were ready for change and ready to take the leap to leave the old world behind.

Again, it involved alien intervention. It included a seeding process and a gathering process. By the late seventies, people were ready for aliens who did not need to look like the ultimate role model. We could now accept things that were more dehumanized and alien. This time Spielberg replaced Blaustein as the director of a landmark film about aliens arriving.

In *Close Encounters of the Third Kind*, a giant mental pulse goes out worldwide in the form of a primal melody, almost a nursery rhyme. The experts are baffled. Those that are being called learn to surrender to a deeper impulse behind the tune.

They zone out, trance out. The chosen few around the world chant the melody as the experts look on. Ochre-robed Brahmins chant the cosmic melody in Rajasthan while little Johnny plays it on his xylophone. It is a global Rice Krispies commercial.

Guidance continues. The meeting point is Devil's Tower, Wyoming. Many have telepathic images of it. Only the chosen will get there, and that includes little Johnny. Awed faces drift along. The same faces that were once awed at Christ in *Ben Hur* and *The Robe* now shine with reverent awe at the strange-looking aliens. But this new awe has taken a left-hand turn; it is zoned out. The players in the game look like a long line of Rajneesh disciples staring at their guru.

The aliens coming out of the saucer greatly resemble what Whitley Streiber reported in his contact. It is a cosmic omelette of mixed emotions—"love the alien"—not the powerful romantic love of Zeffirelli's *Romeo and Juliet*, where your guts are on fire. No, this is different. This is the zoned-out grin of the Zen master or a member of a transpersonal encounter group—not always a thing of beauty, but cosmic.

Spielberg and Lucas were able to hammer this message home again—love the alien—when they made *ET*. People wept over a creature with messianic powers that looked like a reptilian foot upside down. Its poignant moments of helplessness made the hideous creature endearing—the koala-bear effect. The message was Love that which is strange, breaks convention, is unacceptable, monstrous, even grotesque; and Only those who are ready can experience such cosmic love. In the words of the Indian yogis, "Learn to love all—including things which are ugly or may even appear evil—by seeing the unity in all, the divine in all." Again, as Luke Skywalker was told, "Let go. Trust the Force."

6

Voices from Out
of the Rainbow

It is the late 1980's and things are exploding in all directions. Esoteric spiritual paths that I had explored for years, placing me in a distinct minority, have become by now almost the consensus view of America. The plan is unfolding with the force of a charging freight train. Perhaps the few are becoming the many.

1987 starts out with a bang. As 1986 passes by on New Year's Eve, millions have gathered in convention halls and stadiums and even churches to invoke the New Age. It is International Meditation Day for World Peace. Hundreds of organizations in 60 nations have sponsored this event. New Age leader John Randolph Price calls the event:

> A planetary affirmation of love, forgiveness and understanding involving millions of people in a simultaneous global mind-link. The purpose: *to reverse the polarity of the negative force field in the race mind, achieve a critical mass of spiritual consciousness, usher in a new era of Peace on earth, return mankind to Godkind.*[1]

By mid-January of 1987, the big TV miniseries that everyone has been waiting for is on the air. Famed actress Shirley MacLaine has finally found it, and she is telling the world in her autobiographical miniseries "Out on a Limb." The ABC television network has sunk a fortune into this one, while media previews and feature articles have netted everyone's attention months ahead of time.

By early February 1987, downtown Pasadena has thousands of people with badges flowing through the streets. A line stretches for blocks, leading into the main auditorium of the Pasadena Convention Center. It is Jach Pursel who is channeling "Lazaris" that night. Kevin Ryerson is on the bill as well. Hundreds of booths inside the convention center offer endless New Age techniques and technologies. Scores of seminars are going on. "We are taking over," someone announces in line, smiling knowingly.

The summer of 1987 has brought in the Harmonic Convergence, with scores of people worldwide invoking the higher powers from the spiritual realms as they flock to the Great Pyramid in Egypt, Stonehenge in England, Machu Picchu in Peru, and Mount Tamalpais in California's Marin County, plus thousands of other "sacred" places.

The year of 1987 closes out with Shirley MacLaine on the front cover of *Time* magazine. The cover story is about the New Age movement, and Shirley is smiling with crystals in her hand.

The TV miniseries "Out on a Limb" is key. Fifty-million-plus American homes are treated to the following scenes:

Shirley MacLaine walks Malibu beach with her artist companion David who has wiggled his way into her confidence with fortune-cookie observations dropped with impeccable timing. He is ready to give her another dare. A slightly crooked, all-knowing smile passes across his face. "Now open out your arms, face the ocean, and repeat after me. 'I am God.' Go ahead, say it."

Shirley looks awkward, embarrassed. Tentatively she mouths the words, "I am God." Inhibitions keep her from a full-hearted acclamation.

Dave is like a surfing instructor dealing with a novice who keeps wiping out. "Come on, yell it out, don't be chicken, say it convincingly. I am God."

Shirley's chant mounts in volume. She forces herself to act out the conviction. "I am God, I am God, I am God." David has chimed in, helping her to build up steam.

She is breaking through the resistance, the cold barrier. "Hey, it isn't so hard. Just say it." By the end of her repetitions, Shirley is celebratory, liberated. That wasn't so painful. Wow! What a lesson.

Fifty million Americans get the message: "Hey, we are God." That is the cornerstone of the New Age movement: *Man is God*.

So how does Shirley go from just chanting it to experiencing it? She needs a little consciousness-raising. It will soon be time for her to go to Peru, to the Andes. She must follow the paths of the mystics. Meanwhile, she is to go to the Boddhi Tree bookstore on Melrose Avenue, Los Angeles—the biggest occult bookstore in America—and buy stacks of books, from Edgar Cayce, Gurdjieff, and Ouspinsky, to Muktananda and Sai Baba. Then she meets some channelers—first the one in Sweden. Then she is ready for Kevin Ryerson. Later it will be J.Z. Knight and Jach Pursel. The entities speaking through the channelers have the same message: Man is God. But Shirley still has an area of resistance. It's that old puritanical conscience. The old paradigms from the West's biblical foundation are still hanging on.

Shirley needs some signs and wonders and so does America. The miniseries takes us with Shirley and David to Peru. David is doing the Harrison Ford routine—time for the old Panama hat and Banana Republic gear. He's still sporting the all-knowing look.

It is bitingly cold outside that night, high up in the Andes, even in the summer. Shirley and David have discreetly disrobed and are experiencing one of nature's wonders. They are in a bubbling pool carved out of the rock and fed by a warm natural spring. They have talked about Atlantis, about soulmates. Shirley is still hung up over her English lover, a married laborite member of Parliament who is a this-world-only materialist. She is unable to share her deepest and most sacred passion with him—her new emerging spiritual awakening. He will have nothing to do with it. He mocks her. There is a strong sense that they were married before, in Atlantis. One of the channelers has already said this. But they had the same sort of spiritual disagreement they had had in

Atlantis. Shirley has moved on and the Englishman is back into changing the world through politics: a kind of updated Fabian socialism. Shirley goes in and out of a trusting vulnerability with David, her present spiritual mentor.

"Have you ever left your body?" David asks bluntly. He is preparing the famed actress for astral projection. "I have, scores of times. It's really no big deal. Just relax, trust the process, let go. Go on, let go."

Shirley MacLaine is surrounded by bubbling water. Then her voice narrates what is happening to her in a stream-of-consciousness musing. She becomes stunned, overwhelmed. This incredible feeling comes over her. It's really happening. She feels this incredible oneness with all things, that she is experiencing universal reality. Then her body becomes paralyzed, and this blissful charge of energy runs through her like electricity. The next thing is that she fires up into the mountain sky looking down at her body lying in the pool. She sees a long silver cord attached to her body. When it is over, David is nonchalant. He now begins teaching again. He is the nonchalant guru, full of deep mystical truth.

The message to watching America is: You are not your body. You are a timeless soul evolving through many lifetimes to a definite goal. Each life is a classroom experience, a chance to learn. Every time you learn, you move on to the next lesson. In doing this, you are working off karma. Sin is really ignorance. There is no personal, transcendent God to sin against. God is impersonal consciousness, an ocean of being. It, God, is in all things. Now that you know this, then you know that our world is only an illusion. It can keep us from knowing the deeper realities going on. These foundational truths of the New Age movement are absolutely central.

Shirley MacLaine gains credibility with her massive TV audience by well-timed moments of skepticism of the you-can't-really-mean-that variety. Now and then, when things really get unconventional—alien, if you will—Shirley gets shrill. One such moment occurs after she has just plain had it and has asked David to let her out of the Land Rover on the mountain road. The reason is that David is now beginning to prepare her for the next phase of training. She, Oscar-winning actress Shirley MacLaine, has been chosen by the higher powers to be a New Age teacher, a guide who is to affect millions. Not just that, but one extraterrestrial with whom David has been in touch for a long time, named "the Mayan," is strangely present. She is a being, an entity, who is non-physical and is from Pleiades, a distant star system. "She" is to become Shirley MacLaine's guide.

To prove it, "the Mayan" tells David in his mind to utter the following words to Shirley MacLaine: "In order to get the fruit of the tree you have to go out on a limb." These are the identical words that "John," an entity channeling through Kevin Ryerson in Los Angeles months before, told Shirley. David could not have known this.

Now things have gotten too far-out. Shirley's laugh becomes the kind of laugh that people have when it is time for the men in the white coats. It is fractured, shrill, loony—time for her to get away from David immediately. She insists on leaving him. We can read her thoughts. He is nothing more than a spiritual opportunist, a con artist, a flunky without a track record bragging his way into her graces.

She gets the Land Rover and goes off to be alone for several days. She is lost. It breaks down. Now she is hungry and afraid. Being alone on the Peruvian mountainside was just too weird.

In the next scene, through "the Mayan's" psychic guidance David locates the lost Shirley. She has been sending out mental signals for help. His arrival is another sign for her. As he is driving her he now has a captive audience. They are blasting along the narrow mountain road. There are some lethal drop-offs on the side. There is also a presence in the truck. Now it is time for another sign. David lets go of the steering wheel and lets "the Mayan" drive the truck. Shirley's mouth is wide open and she is hysterical. She is back to the barrier of natural revulsion. She is again told that she has been chosen as a world server, a luminary to bring in New Age realities to a world in waiting.

Shirley now becomes especially aware that a nonphysical hierarchy exists and is waiting to intervene in the affairs of the world. It is New Age lesson number three. Famed author Ruth Montgomery spoke of these celestial beings as "Walk Ins" and that they are waiting to walk into prepared bodies of surrendered subjects who have obeyed the *impulse*. America now knows that they are out there as well. We just need to get ready to surrender to the intuitive impulse.

THE NEXUS OF NEW AGE BELIEFS

Shirley MacLaine's TV miniseries, "Out on a Limb" has pulled together the central nexus of New Age beliefs. Virtually all New Age thinkers are in basic agreement. For the sake of clarity, these central beliefs will be reiterated below. The core can be found in the basic tenets of Eastern mysticism with some modern ideas added from the West.

Eastern Influences

1. *THE IMPERSONAL GODHEAD.* God is the *Brahmin* of Hinduism. It is impersonal, like the Force in *Star Wars*, or the ocean of supreme consciousness. It is the Ground of Being and non-being, the static eternal, the overmind, the consciousness within all things and sustaining all things. Hence, New Agers talk about the *sacredness of all things*. It is beyond all attributes and all polarities.

The yin/yang symbol of Taoism expresses the One as being beyond all polarities. It is indeed composed of them: light and dark, masculine and feminine, good and evil, etc., for all polarities are composed of the godhead. White light going into a prism comes out as differentiated colored rays on the other side. The phenomenal universe is like the differentiated colored rays. They are no longer unified. But if you examine the unified white light, the source of all color, the colors can no longer be differentiated. Blue, red, yellow cannot be seen in the white light. There is not even a hint of their existence without the prism. This is how consciousness emerges from the godhead and forms the phenomenal universe.

On the other side, within the ocean of pure consciousness, all seemingly separate forms are perceived as being the One. It is their appearance of differentiation that is the illusion. An impersonal god has no forgiving grace, no personal love, no higher morality, and is not the transcendent personal creator of the universe. To an impersonal consciousness, the lives of struggling individuals rate no higher on the scale than ants being swept off a tree trunk in a summer thunderstorm. Older cultures, such as the Hindus of India who have lived under this perennial philosophy for many centuries, understand the downside of an impersonal godhead, and it can be a source of great despair as they struggle to escape the great wheel of karma.

2. *THE DIVINE WITHIN.* The mystery of man's ultimate identity is finally revealed as his divinity within. It is the basic tenet of pantheism, the core belief of Hinduism: All things are One, since all energy is divine consciousness "frozen" into matter. Since all things are made of God, man in his deepest self is none other than God. But without "enlightenment," he does not know this and, in effect, lives as an amnesiac. The purpose of man is to realize that he is God, thus ending the "illusion" of separation.

3. *THERE IS NO DEATH.* As parts of God we are immortal, and death is only an illusion as we evolve throughout eternity. Death is only a veil between one lifetime and another. Reincarnation is one element of this scheme. Others speak of continuation on other planes; the Tibetans use the term *bardos* in Mahayana Buddhism.

4. *GOOD AND EVIL ARE ILLUSIONS.* Evil is just the reverse side of the coin of good. It is the back side. Each is incomplete without the other. In effect, both good and evil are part of the illusion of existence. Good and evil merge at an upper threshold, and both are necessary in the phenomenal universe. Indeed, both are parts of the godhead, as polarities that unify in the One. An aspect of the godhead is evil, as we see represented in Kali and Siva who wreak death and destruction as the dark underbelly of reality. Because of this, sin is ignorance. Both polarities are to be transcended; they are not absolutes in the biblical sense.

5. *ALL PATHS LEAD TO GOD*. Through a higher under-standing, it can be seen that all world faiths point to the same spiritual reality and are all paths up the mountain to the godhead. The goal is to show that all religions are saying the same thing. Syncretism is a central goal of the New Age movement.

New Western Hybrids

6. *SPIRITUAL EVOLUTION*. The New Age view of history is one of spiritual evolution, almost in Hegelian terms. History is seen as a kind of cosmic genetic code that unfurls the divine dimensions of man as consciousness evolves. Consciousness, in the act of self-discovery, must answer the riddle of its true nature. The cosmos is purposeful as it moves inexorably toward its final goal: global enlightenment and the deification of man. New Age theoretician Ken Wilber says, "... if men and women have ultimately come up from amoebas, then they are ultimately on their way towards God."[2]

7. *SHIFTING PARADIGMS*. This is the shift in the way reality is perceived due to the inevitable momentum of the evolution of consciousness. Virginia Hine, the respected sociologist, has mentioned this shift as our leaving the Faustian myth of scientism. And Ferguson spoke of the need to shatter the confines of the present "crust of custom." In short, New Agers anticipate the collapse of the Old Age and the birth of the New Age by means, in part, of the paradigm shift in the way reality is perceived. Rationalism and Christian mono-theism will be supplanted by mystical monism, as the intu-itive right hemisphere of the race is brought into equal footing with the long-reigning logical left hemisphere of Western consciousness, as Peter Russell observes.[3]

8. *OPTIMISM*. Though New Agers are deeply aware of the precariousness of human existence due to such things as the nuclear threat and the ecological and population crises—from which they cite dire statistics such as the Global 2000 Report (to show how the old paradigms have failed)—they

nevertheless brandish a positive spirit, rising above contemporary despair. With Marilyn Ferguson this mood of optimism is almost a manic expectancy. Secretary General of the United Nations Robert Muller exults, "The next stage will be our entry into a moral global age—the global age of love—and a global spiritual age—the cosmic age. We are now moving fast towards the fulfillment of the visions of the great prophets who through cosmic enlightenment saw the world as one unit, the human race as one family, sentiment as the cement of that family, and the soul as our link with the universe, eternity, and God."[4]

9. *CRISIS AS TRANSFORMATION.* The dark and foreboding horizon of impending global holocaust is an important catalyst that will help thrust the planet into a new awakening, breaking down walls of resistance like a tidal wave crashing through a seacoast village. Man stands at the crossroads about to make a quantum leap forward. Such things as atomic threat raise the global temperature to the boiling point where human ego structures are forced to break down in the manner that hostages trapped in a hijacked airplane suddenly feel the futility of worrying about their belongings. Outward necessity forces the dire realization and the transformation.

10. *HOLISM.* We must relate to our world from the viewpoint of the solidarity of all reality, the "all is one" of Eastern thought. When we do, things that are presently out-of-balance will be restored—whether ecological, political, or geophysical. Human health will be restored and earth itself will reach a kind of planetary consciousness that Cambridge-educated New Age apologist Peter Russell calls "Gaia Consciousness."[5] In short, for those who are ready it will be a new heaven on earth, a New Age millennium.[6]

TRIGGERING THE GREAT EVENT

Alice Bailey spoke of "The Externalization of the Hierarchy" (also the title of her major work) to help bring on the New Age. It would be a broad-range release of forces on every level of the continuum of consciousness, from ascended masters to impulses coming from deep within "the godhead." These were all seen as manifestations of the One in a grand concert. In a talk in Geneva, Switzerland, before the Arcane School, which she founded, Bailey thrilled her audience with descriptions of this release of forces:

> The decision to release the Shamballa force during this century into direct contact with the human kingdom is one of the final and most compelling acts of preparation for the New Age.
> The Shamballa force is destructive and ejective... inspiring new understanding of The Plan. ...
> It is this force ... which will bring about that tremendous crisis, the initiation of the race into the mysteries of the ages.[7]

These mysteries of the ages are now being revealed before the world. We glimpse them in Shirley MacLaine's televised account of her own birth into the New Age. In this lies the central creed of New Age beliefs. Most central of all is the discovery of the divinizing of man. Not just the discovery of the divine within—the heart of pantheism—but a global process of objective and conscious divinizing of the race that will change the entire earth.

If true, it is a titanic event. And it cannot help but affect all and everyone. Those that go along with it are told that they will apparently experience heaven on earth as they become gods. Those that resist it because of outmoded beliefs will apparently have some rough lessons in store for them. And why should it be any other way? The brutal facts of evolution, they point out, have told us this. Life is a spectacular passing show of variant creatures, from bright-green frogs to behemoths. But invariably some species are discarded as they are replaced by more evolved species. It is just one more a cappella note coming from the voices from out of the rainbow.

Wheels of Influence:
The Therapist's Office

The current wave of New Age beliefs may endure or it may change, but it is this: Given that the self is God, then once it is unleashed, it can control reality. Indeed, this God-self can remake the world by its own power. The more minds that awaken and tap this reality, the faster the great changes can occur. At a certain critical mass, the process will become a millennial explosion. A critical threshold of collective human minds that have been "awakened" and are working in synchronicity would have the power to transform the world in the twinkling of an eye. If this is done right, a utopian world will emerge. Man can literally wish away the problems that have plagued the earth for millennia, from disease to poverty. Consciousness is the hidden messiah.

Those who stop and question this emerging conventional wisdom, wondering if it doesn't sound like *The Emperor's New Clothes*, are perceived to be among those in the resistance whose force fields of doubt are keeping the global event from happening. They must either be converted or rendered ineffectual so that their "negativity" does not interfere with the great plan.

The plan is this: Enlighten through various wheels of influence as many people as possible. A critical threshold of people must be reached. It is like electing someone into office. Campaign rhetoric can only become a reality once that person is elected into office and then empowered by the office.

But enough votes must be gathered to get that person into office first of all. Germany soon changed once Hitler became chancellor. Novels like Frederick Forsythe's *The Fourth Protocol* illustrate the historical reality of someone with a hidden agenda trying to acquire the power of political office. Forsythe pictures a top KGB mole using the English labor party platform to gain the office of prime minister. While the film version merely emphasized the drama around the KGB effort to create a nuclear explosion at a U.S. air base, the more sinister underlying theme of the novel involved the progress of the KGB candidate into the most powerful office in Britain.

If we pictured that critical threshold of people spoken of by New Age advocates as representative of Forsythe's KGB mole, then it would mirror the type of conspiracy described by Marilyn Ferguson in her 1980 bestseller, *The Aquarian Conspiracy*. It is a conspiracy of gradualist penetration and takeover. It is a numbers game that involves such key arenas as the marketplace, the schoolroom, and the therapist's office, for these are all places with captive audiences where the power to influence is considerable.

THE THERAPIST'S OFFICE

One highly captive audience is the hurting, vulnerable, and receptive client sitting in the therapist's office. The mind and heart of such a client are wide open for direction, for answers, for the truth about the meaning to life.

The power to influence that lies in the hands of the psychotherapist is considerable. His guidance, insights, and beliefs can affect the patient for life. The therapist's view about the nature of reality becomes the foundation stone upon which his therapy is based. It can be no other way. His understanding of reality cannot help but influence the patient directly or indirectly. The therapist is a guru about reality and the self. He is both an authority as well as a confidant—perhaps more intimate than a best friend or spouse. If he is among the many humanistic or transpersonal psychologists or psychiatrists, the winds of New Age thought will inevitably blow into the soul of the willing client.

The field of psychotherapy has gone a long way since it first started. During the course of this century, from Freud to Ken Wilber, it has covered the entire map of beliefs, from atheism to mysticism, from nihilism to existentialism. Over this same period, it has gathered under its umbrella over a hundred different schools of thought about the nature of man and the universe and the appropriate therapy required. It has tried to call itself a science, but how can it be! It is so complex as to defy verifiability. How can the unseen workings of the psyche—the very consciousness of an individual—ever be exposed and examined by any device for scientific verification? And how can any individual psyche ever be subjected to scientifically valid lab experiments? We're still struggling to pinpoint the electron—is it a particle or does it sometimes lapse into waves?

What scientist could ever create the identical individual and then grow him up in a thousand different environments, to test the effects of those different environments—each time perfectly monitoring them and controlling them? And if you say that each one is the same test-tube clone, can you prove you gave him the same soul? (Are you so sure there is not a soul?) And if there were, could you ever discover the soul through science?

And here is an added problem: Which mortal scientist could ever live long enough to do this experiment? Likewise, how can the scientist even come to terms with all the environmental influences of a single day within a single environment? The problems of verifying the psyche through pure science are titanic, insurmountable—indeed, beyond the range of science.

In the end, the gurus of human nature, the psychotherapists, are forced to generalize. They must play the role of wise pundits, and so they claim to be. But when they disagree, as when Carl Jung parted ways with Sigmund Freud, what court of wisdom is able to prove which one is right? Again, psychotherapy is no science at all; it is a battleground of different schools of belief. Inevitably, it comes down to a faith issue about the nature of human identity and ultimate reality. Is

Freud's psychoanalysis right or is Jung's depth psychology right? What if they are both way off base?

Sigmund Freud's psychoanalysis reflected his beliefs and opinions. Freud's sample cases were mostly affluent and neurotic Viennese women. His subjects by no means encompassed all peoples and cultures. Freud synthesized the reigning beliefs of his day—the popular conceptions of humanists on the vanguard of liberated thought—into a pseudoscience. Above all, Freud was an atheist. For him, quite simply, neither the universe nor psychoanalysis had a place for God. That was a closed issue.

In Freud's day, philosophers believed in a contingent and closed universe. At the head of the pack were the Logical Positivists of Cambridge. Scientific determinism was the order of the day. Popular wisdom claimed that we were all products of long, complex causal gateways confining the course of our existence to a choiceless determinism. Man was merely a by-product of genetics and environment.

Freud propounded the above and also borrowed from Darwin and assorted anthropologists. The biblical God was now seen as an internalized surrogate father figure originally projected out into the world by a tribal people. Freud used Greek mythology to press this theme into respectability. As in the story of Oedipus Rex, Jehovah was seen as the jealous and feared father figure holding back the threat of incest. Morals and religion were built on these strange ancestral psychodynamics of tribal rule. The conscience was a learned response to taboos created by the tyrannical father type who became a tribal god. The Judaism of Freud became the random saga of a tribal horde that imagined its God from its ancestral memories of wandering. It was the cosmic "no" to lust and assorted hedonisms in order for the tribe to survive and not dissipate into chaos and anarchy.

There was no ultimate hope in the universe for Freud. And the fruit of despair that came with this was inevitable. What psychoanalysis did offer to sophisticated society, in the same era that D.H. Lawrence was breaking ground, was freedom from the dictates of the conscience and moral restriction. It offered sexual liberation to a world still under the dictates of moral propriety and biblical moral law. Moral customs still created pangs of conscience; they still inhibited free expression. And liberated intellectuals were trying desperately to break down the doors of sexual "repression" and find a haven of free expression. Freud helped provide the door, but behind that door, as was noted, was the deeper despair of determinism, of man's lack of significance in a godless universe. Some people got their orgasm, but it took place in a huge cosmic vacuum. Others, seeing through the implications of the psychoanalytic system, became dysfunctional and despairing in other ways. Woody Allen is a living example of the psychoanalytic mind-set. Sex and death are his obsessions. He looks into the mirror to remind himself what will be erased from the universe when he dies—himself. His angst keeps him frustrated, forever kept apart from the illusory sensual moment. It is like watching a dog slobbering at a ham sitting in a plate-glass window. The void becomes too close to escape into the sensual dreamland.

By the sixties, people had had it "up to here" with Freud and the impasse of scientific determinism. Now that they had finally acquired their freedom from moral restraint, they were tired of the downside of Freudian deterministic gloom. Freudian psychology was referred to as First Force psychology. Then came behaviorism which utterly rejected the theories of Freud as scientifically unfounded speculations and opinion. The behaviorists resolved to camp out in the lab with animals and not venture beyond this. They were the Second Force psychologists. Anything that could not be scientifically verified they considered to be myth. They were hard-core materialists. Beginning with Fechner and Wilhelm Wundt and going through Pavlov's stimulus-response experiments, the behaviorists have logged thousands of lab hours testing simple things that can be tested. Their most famous recent pioneer has been B.F. Skinner of Harvard, inventor of the Skinner box.

Skinner took determinism to its limits in his book *Beyond Freedom and Dignity*. Skinner announced that basically man was a soulless animal who had no free will, no guarantee of meaning or happiness. Therefore man had no basis to object when social engineers came on the scene to behavior shape him to fit into a world that the intellectual elite planned to create. War could be driven out of the human race in the lab. With the right probes and enough current, the job could be done. Skinner's daughter grew up under the Skinner box (Skinnerian behavioral conditioning) and ended up in a mental institution not far from Harvard. She knew no love (for love does not exist), merely positive and negative reinforcement. The scientist who had assumed the task of changing the world through operant conditioning had failed on his own daughter. His behavior modification had starved her soul and dehumanized her. Yet Skinner proclaimed his school of psychology as bearing the solution to human ills.

To the generation of the sixties, the above mind-set summed up the grotesqueness of the humanistic experiment. They could not wait to enter Freud, Skinner, and others into the museum of obsolete thought. So when the Eysenck study was released at the University of London, there was a furor. Eysenck's study simply showed that among neurotics divided 50/50, those that underwent psychoanalysis had no better recovery rate than those who just lived life and saved the massive therapy fees. The recovery was the same, plus or minus a .02 percent statistical error factor. In other words, psychoanalysis did nothing. Eysenck drove home the fact that psychoanalysis was anything but scientifically proven. All it could do was hide behind its terminology and verify itself by its own closed definitions of reality. Freudian psychoanalysis became discredited among all but the most loyal followers and/or those who had spent 20,000 dollars in training to become highly-paid psychoanalysts.

When the sixties hit, there was a rediscovery of the spiritual and the intuitive, realms that such intellectual Model-T Fords as Freud and Skinner had not sanctioned. The birth of Third Force humanistic psychology took place in the sixties, arriving on the scene in time to restore dignity and value to men after Freud and the behaviorists had confiscated them. Though they could not prove the foundation upon which they stood, humanistic psychologists like Abraham Maslow and Carl Rogers assured the world that there was meaning to life after all and that there was a good deal of room for optimism in the universe. Humanistic psychology declared that people had free choice and were not the random collocations of molecules deterministically gathered into human biocomputers, but rather were part of a larger spiritual dimension. "Feel-good" psychology made its entrance. At the forefront of this was Carl Rogers, at one time president of the American Psychological Association and winner of numerous awards for his nondirective therapy. At one point, I tried it and liked it. I too had felt the despair of atheism in the sixties and hated the small space into which I was boxed.

Under Rogerian therapy and transactional analysis (I'm okay, you're okay) I felt good because I could write my own ticket to reality. That gnawing conscience that burdened me with guilt was being selectively cut away by a scalpel of permissiveness. This new psychology brought a sweet-sounding creed—that conscience and guilt were like vestigial organs, such as the appendix, that no longer served a useful function. The conscience was part of my primitive brain holding me back from full self-expression, from freedom, creativity, and joy. In Rogerian client-centered therapy, I the patient had all the answers within. All I needed was a good psychic plumber to help me find them. In time my angst began to lift away. My mood became an almost reckless abandon—the Zorba the Greek approach. Respectability and conformity were limitations to radical human freedom that were carryovers from the old order. I was assured that human nature was basically good, so why be afraid to change? Experience and change became prized ideals in this psychic gold rush.

Humanistic psychology pointed to the idea that self-actualization could be speeded up by exploring within and overcoming all inner fears and areas of darkness by a total nonjudgmental self-acceptance. Then the unfathomable depth of human potential could be tapped. It was upbeat and optimistic. Change was never bad; it was always good. Rogers spoke of the next evolutionary leap into the new man. But society would have to be radically changed first. A revolutionary agenda was needed for this to happen, a kind of psychological Marxism that repudiated institutions and traditions. By the midsixties, Esalen at Big Sur had become a think tank for many of these famed psychologists: Fritz Perls, Rollo May, Carl Rogers, and the rest. Their message was that it was a no-lose universe.

Yet there was an underside to such positive acclamation. As Barbara Ehrenreich observed in her article entitled "The Psychology of Growth," which appeared in *Mother Jones*, April 1983: "If the human potential was intrinsically good, then there was no firm ground left from which to attack the deviant or nonconformist. All trajectories were possible as each unique and groping 'self' reached toward fulfillment." Thus there were no standards left to judge undesirable deviance, nor could you find standards to judge what desirable growth was. As long as the self was doing its own authentic thing, it was okay. Growth and fulfillment were life's new ideals. It was a perfect creed for a culture of narcissism.

Indeed, humanistic psychology undermined the traditional structures of society while using the most gentle and accepting language. Such stabilizing institutions as marriage were questioned. After all, they confined the new freedoms. Ehrenreich observed in her above article: "Psychologists had always seen marriage as 'work'; the doctrine of growth transformed it into a navigation feat which would have challenged a ballistics expert." Self-interest could now be selfish and morally blind. Hedonism was okay, and feeling good was okay. Anything could be questioned, especially sacrosanct institutions. Freedom meant you could do almost anything.

The creed of Third Force psychology indeed sounds like the slogans of the sixties. Maybe we could say that the slogans and peoples movements of the sixties got much of their impetus from humanistic psychology, which became the special ally of the sixties revolution. What were the new directives of the sixties youth culture? Christopher Lasch's *The Culture of Narcissism* spells them out: nonbinding commitments, freedom from guilt or failure, personal fulfillment, the neurotic need for affection, reassurance, and gratification, as well as an inability to internalize clearly defined criteria of right and wrong. Under these new rules what you end up with are manipulators who are on the take. They can quickly assess how to use others to get what they want from them, then dump them as soon as they have used them. Loyalty is not their strong point. Communal experiments become a free-for-all without reference points—from egalitarian tribes to cultish dictatorships. Communal anarchy brought out the full fruits of character traits which pointed to a new barbarism further down the road.

The founders of humanistic psychology anticipated and then built the bridge to transpersonal psychology. Again, Esalen Institute rates high as a power point in this bridge. Abraham Maslow traced a hierarchy of seven levels of need. When basic needs like food and shelter were taken care of, the higher needs—which were the spiritual ones—could then be addressed, leading to self-actualization. This was the key part of the bridge that led from the humanistic psychology of the sixties to the transpersonal psychology of the seventies.

Posturing as "experts," these psychologists had clearly left all pretense of science and entered the domain of faith. It was indeed a creed of humanism, and it was most definitely in opposition to the creed of the cross. However, the other mystery creed—the creed of the pyramid—had an open door through which to pass. Not surprisingly, a number of the founders of humanistic psychology had their own experiences which took them into the cosmic humanism of transpersonal psychology.

Maslow inaugurated transpersonal psychology by making popular the idea that human consciousness could be the link between man and the fundamental realities of the universe. He was deeply into oriental metaphysics, even coauthoring a book with Zen adept D.Z. Suzuki. Maslow pointed toward Buddha constantly. Carl Rogers crossed a different barrier. Prior to his wife's death, he tried spiritism. Today we would call it channeling. The spirit that addressed Carl Rogers spoke to him in the language of a nondirective therapist. It seemed the guru of unhooking the debilitating effect of the conscience was feeling a few pangs himself. He had had an affair on the side and needed positive reinforcement (for-giveness, if you like) from his wife. The spirit, claiming to be Ruth, told Carl: "Enjoy, Carl, enjoy! Be free! Be free!" These words certainly anticipated the permissive creed of Indian guru Acharya Rajneesh. Here was a form of spirituality with-out the inhibiting moral influences of biblical faith. Indeed, it had arrived just in the nick of time. When Carl Rogers wrote *A Way of Being*, he could say: "I now consider it possible that each of us is a continuing spiritual essence lasting over time, and occasionally incarnated in a human body" (p. 177). Psy-chology had just fused with the faith of its choice, Eastern mysticism. It would now be hard for this growing branch of psychology to be neutral to other faiths and traditions.

By the late seventies large gatherings of transpersonal psy-chologists, representing the wave of the future, met in major cities across the United States. Harvard-trained psychologist Dr. William Kirk Kilpatrick attended the Fifth International Conference of Transpersonal Psychology in 1979. He came, he saw, and he was concerned. In a brilliant essay in his book *The Emperor's New Clothes* entitled "The Brahmin in the Ba-hamas," Dr. Kilpatrick described a group who used the re-spectability of science to wear the ochre robes of the priest-hood of a new mystery religion.

Swami Muktananda, whom I had met nine years earlier in India, graced the convention as the guest of honor. He was one of India's preeminent "Shakti-pat" and *kriya* power yogis who claimed to be fully self-actualized into God-conscious-ness. He had attained what Maslow anticipated was at the top of his scale of consciousness. Muktananda was the living example, the proof of cosmic consciousness. Psychologists could touch him and hear him. He was also the former guru of Werner Erhard and Da Free John, among many others.

Psychology's most recent progeny had fully entered the New Age. At the conference, as Kilpatrick describes, were cowbells from India, pamphlets from a Tibetan monastery, polarity charts on the wall, mantra meditation beads for sale, and so on. The theme of the annual conference was "The

Nature of Reality." Reincarnation was taken for granted. Past-life recall through regressive hypnosis was a hot topic. Now one's problems could be explained by a radical new viewpoint: Problems today stemmed from events in former lives. The Hindu concept for this is past *karma*. And now twentieth-century psychologists were learning how to unearth this esoteric information from past lives by regressive hypnosis. Everything could be viewed as a learning experience of the self—from life to life—on up the scale of consciousness to godhood.

The transpersonal psychologists were a legitimate branch of the American Psychological Association and by far their fastest-growing branch. They had the following seminars at their fifth annual conference: "Shamanic and Spiritist Modes of Healing," "The Tibetan Image of Reality," "Ancient Indian Concepts of Sex and Love," "Siddha Meditation," "Living Tao," "Archetypal Stages of the Great Round," "Evolution of a Yogi Trip to Awareness," "Kundalini Awakening and Spiritual Emergency," and "Aikido as a Spiritual Discipline."

William Kilpatrick relates an encounter of the transpersonal variety among psychologist professionals at the conference. At the time he was reading a book entitled *Profound Simplicity*. The psychologist who wrote the book relates the following theories that are consonant with Eastern thinking:

- There are no accidents.
- Events occur because we choose them to occur.
- Every death is a suicide.
- A rape "victim" is choosing to be raped.
- Social minorities are oppressed only if they allow themselves to be put in a position they call oppression.

One of the psychologists at the conference commented that it was a great book. He too was in the business of past-life therapy. Kilpatrick was not so sure. He relates:

I asked if he thought there was anything of value in the Western tradition or in Christianity. Christianity, he explained with an amused smile, makes people feel guilty; guilt is a crippling emotion. The others at the table nodded assent, and the psychologist settled comfortably back in his chair. It was an open and shut case.[1]

To this enlightened crowd, reincarnation settled the problem of evil, the problem of suffering, and the problem of life's victims, such as the girl born crippled. By this new view, everyone gets what he deserves, what he wishes for. It's just that some people are not very good at wishing. The crippled girl's present sufferings stem from her past life. She is now getting what she deserves for failing to make the right choices in former lives. It is her own fault.[2]

One psychologist observed: "You choose everything that happens to you, and you pretty much get what you deserve." He had learned this at an est seminar. At this point, his wife, a social worker, added that the same ideas were corroborated by the *Seth Journals*.

Kilpatrick responded that this is the most guilt-provoking scheme he had ever heard. "You're telling this crippled girl, in effect, that she has no one to blame for her handicap but herself."[3] He might have also noted that she cannot even remember what she did in the first place to deserve such a condition (a statistical microfraction even claim to have past-life recall, which itself is far from being beyond the realm of dream material). If you cannot remember what you did to deserve punishment, it is a wasted and cruel lesson. It is like punishing a dog a month after it did something. It howls and cringes in ignorance. The dog's suffering is futile since it cannot connect what it did to deserve punishment, nor will it learn its intended lesson. So too with us and the hypothetical mistake we made 20 million years ago. To make it fair, all of us should remember millions of past lives for these lessons to make ___ ___ hether we are mongoloids or millionaires.

___ critic of the East told Kilpatrick later, "Being ___ never having to say you're sorry." She noted it ___ that left India's caste system unchanged for ___ nd groaning under travail. Now India's phi- ___ ome the darling of Third and Fourth Force psychology. To quote "The Brahmin in the Bahamas" about the crippled girl, "She's only getting what she deserves."[4]

Freud, who had declared God irrelevant, was now as dead as a fossil to the psychologists of the late 1970's. And Jung, Freud's rival, was now the favored figurehead of psychology. The search for the self had led the way to the overself, the *Atma/Paramatma* of Hinduism. Alan Watt's book *The Supreme Identity* had anticipated this fusion. And now we had living examples of psychologists who had turned into holy men. One of them was Ram Dass, the former Doctor Richard Alpert, Harvard psychologist. He had gone to India and found his guru and a new name. Today he speaks at many transpersonal and New Age gatherings. Alpert had watched Skinner and other behaviorists; he had also done his psychoanalytic stint, and found them all wanting—indeed, bankrupt. In the end he looked east to the watering hole of India. Perhaps Ram Dass (Sanskrit for "the Servant of Ram") would be the first Westerner to become the new man of Carl Rogers. Time would tell.

But what cannot be denied is the current growing army of transpersonal therapists, moving across the land from seminars to conventions, spreading the good news. They are a growing storm. They call themselves the Fourth Force psychologists, after the Third Force of humanistic psychology. Maybe they should just call themselves *The Force* as their wheels of influence spread through society.

Transpersonal psychology has embraced the New Age views that were stated at the beginning of this chapter. Now this core of beliefs will be repeated. If the self is God, then once it is unleashed, it can control reality. Indeed, this God-self can remake the world by its own power. The more minds that awaken and tap this reality, the faster the planetary change will occur. At a certain critical mass, the process will become a millennial explosion. A critical threshold of collective human minds that have been "awakened" and are working in synchronicity will have the power to transform the world in the twinkling of an eye. If this is done right, a utopian world will emerge. Consciousness is the hidden messiah. But minds must be awakened!

Wheels of Influence: The Marketplace

The millions of members of the corporate and business work force comprise a significant captive audience. Why? Because they live in a competitive environment that is full of peer pressure, the need for corporate approval and advancement, as well as one of the deepest human needs: the need for financial security. The latter is a survival need. Upon it rests the family. For these reasons there is considerable stress in the workplace. There are fears of failure, fears of missing a promotion, insecurities about job stability, and so on. This stress is a gauge of the power the workplace has over lives.

When employees are told to attend a seminar or undergo further training, they are indeed a captive and vulnerable audience. Their careers and their very livelihoods are at stake. They have conformed to get where they are, and they will continue to conform to get ahead. If the seminars they attend employ the very psychotechnologies that have emerged from breakthroughs in behavior shaping over the last decade or two, this audience becomes very malleable indeed. They are willing and eager to believe, and they do believe, for it is in their best interests to believe. But what is it that they are to believe?

Those who shape beliefs in the marketplace have formidable power. In the last few years *The Wall Street Journal* and *The New York Times* have begun to write about an emerging trend in corporate America.

In the July 24, 1987, issue of *The Wall Street Journal*, Peter Waldman described the trend in a headline article:

> Abuzz with buzzwords, corporate America has launched one of the most concerted efforts ever to change the attitudes and values of workers. Dozens of major U.S. companies—including Ford Motor Co., Proctor & Gamble Co., TRW Inc., Polaroid Corp., and Pacific Telesis Group Inc.—are spending millions of dollars on so-called *New Age workshops*.

Waldman cites numerous examples, among them the Krone seminars put on by Pacific Bell that would ultimately cost 30 million dollars and either come out of the ratepayers' or stockholders' pocketbooks. Publicity brought the program under scrutiny:

> . . . Pacific Telesis (Pac Bell) began a series of quarterly two-day training seminars for its 67,000 workers to give them a common purpose and common approach to their work.
>
> To foster greater creativity, for example, trainers discussed different "levels" of thought, energy, and behavior. (In ascending order, the six levels of energy were described as automatic, sensitive, conscious, creative, unitive, and transcendent.) That session, loosely based on the teachings of G.I. Gurdjieff, an early 20th century Russian mystic, was supposed to inspire more analytical thinking among employees. In it, workers broke into groups to discuss issues like the difference between "knowledge" and "understanding." . . . Shortly after the program began, workers were quoted in articles about the training in local newspapers as saying that the workshops smacked of mind control, Eastern mysticism, and coercion.
>
> "Dissenters are referred to as 'roadblocks' or having 'Bell-Shaped Heads' " by supporters of the training, wrote one company employee, in response

to a California Public Utilities Commission survey on the sessions.[1]

Fortune magazine on November 23, 1987, had a feature article on New Age corporate seminars and workshops. One is called MSIA and pronounced "Messiah" and is led by Mystic Traveler Consciousness in the person of John-Roger. It is an offshoot of John Hanley's Lifespring, another potent New Age consciousness-raising group that has also invaded the business world as well as the military establishment.

One observer notes in the *Fortune* article: "It's one thing if an individual walks in off the street and signs up for a course, but quite another if your boss sends you. Then there's a level of coercion. Does my boss have the right to put me through training that conflicts with my religion and world view?"[2] Some protest at what seems forced vulnerability.

One of the more potent New Age seminars/workshops was once called est, then out of it came The Forum. From out of that has come a franchise called Trans Tech or Transformational Technologies. The Forum is one of hundreds of seminars, but we will look at it as a case in point. The man behind it is not new to New Age seminars. He is Werner Erhard, who invented est (Erhard Seminars Training) which in the 1970's had 500,000 people who passed through the course. Erhard has commented that it is interesting that most of these half million graduates are today holding positions in corporate America. They are also loyal converts willing to open the doors of their companies to Trans Tech and its affiliates.

How did est philosophy come about? Through mystical peak experiences that Werner Erhard underwent. When I was in India under Sai Baba, Werner Erhard made several trips to India to sit under Swami Muktananda, the power yogi whose headquarters were in Ganeshpur, near Bombay. Muktananda came to America on one occasion by invitation from Werner Erhard, who gave large contributions to the guru. Erhard used to boast that Muktananda hit him with a power touch on the third eye, *Shakti-Pat*, giving him an enlightenment experience. But as his success with est grew, Erhard went more and more on his own and became a self-styled guru. Like Bubba

Free John, another American ex-Muktananda disciple, Erhard left the guru's fold claiming equality of consciousness with the Indian power yogi, but some of Muktananda's techniques—such as psychically disemboweling the *chelas* or pupils—have appeared in the est seminars.

In the est seminars, people were undone and shocked as barriers were broken. Few of them had anything in their field of experience to prepare them for the barrier-breaking ruthlessness, albeit watered down and with a Western slant, that came out of the tradition of Indian Kriya *Shakti-Pat* yoga. Muktananda had been on the receiving end of this from his own guru, Avadhut Nityananda, the famous *Siddha Guru* or power yogi. Some of these same techniques can also be found in the Rajneesh camp. The explanation is simple: To find the overself, the false identity that keeps us from divine realization—known as the ego or self with a small "s"—must be destroyed. The "proof" that the method works is seen in the many crisis and transformational experiences that accompany these techniques. This is straight Vedanta, nothing else.

The leaders in est seminars were dictatorial. Picture a lady whispering to a leader for permission to go to the bathroom. She is publicly railed at with shocking obscenities and told to hold her bladder. She is then made to take part in a psychodrama before 500 people. You bet she will have a transformational experience. She will be broken down. There will be real tears, real horror, and real peak experiences.

John Bode of *The Chicago Tribune* writes about The Forum and est and interviews former est graduates to see if The Forum is any different. First of all est: Steve Brown claimed that est training gave him new insights, but thinks est robs people of their identity. Brown is quoted as saying, "The control Werner exercises over his followers is really frightening." Suzanne Perkins, a former est worker, said that during her est training she was deprived of food and sleep by confrontational, abusive trainers. "They broke down my moral and emotional standards," said Perkins. "They said it was all right to sleep with your friend's husband because you can create the feeling of being guilty or feeling fine. You are your own God."[3] Such was est.

The est teaching was that people had "total responsibility" for creating reality and had to claim that they had created everything in their lives, positive and negative. Now The Forum uses the word "choice." People choose things to happen. They formulate life scripts. The Forum does not have est's guided fantasies preceded by body-relaxation techniques, and the old "rules" are now "suggestions." But people are still encouraged to reveal themselves on the most intimate levels in order to free themselves from the need of protecting their images and the fear of being stigmatized. With this "sharing" comes a breakdown of personal autonomy. Participants are still abused by leaders, and the est exercises known as "Truth Process," "Fear Process," and "Danger Process," are carried over into The Forum.

In essence, The Forum has been repackaged for business and is sleeker, more professional, and milder, but its philosophy and central techniques are the same as est—and little wonder if you learn how the founder has repackaged his own identity while remaining the same. What is hard to imagine is that the Fortune 500 companies that have spent millions to be trained by The Forum would outlay that sort of capital with so little scrutiny—or worse, they don't care for other reasons. What companies has The Forum and Trans Tech trained? *Fortune* magazine in its November 23, 1987 issue in an article entitled "Trying to Bend Managers' Minds," mentions Allstate and Sears, General Dynamics, the Federal Aviation Administration, IBM, Boeing Aerospace, and Lockheed, among others. *Image* magazine, October 12, 1986 (p. 25), quotes Werner Erhard's partner, Jim Selman, as saying that Trans Tech franchises have made inroads in 100 of the Fortune 500 companies including Ford, TRW, General Electric, McDonald's, Manville, and RCA, plus eight federal agencies, the Justice Department, NASA, and The White House. Again, who is Werner Erhard and what kind of experience could launch him into having this wide-ranging effect?

Mark Dowie in his article "The Transformation Game" in *Image* magazine (Oct. 12, 1986, p. 24), reveals the moment of change for Werner Erhard:

His first major metamorphosis occurred somewhere between Corte Madera and the Golden Gate Bridge one morning in 1971 while commuting to work at an encyclopedia company, when the wisdom of Est was suddenly revealed to him. "I realized that I knew nothing," he later recalled of that magic moment. "In the next instant, I realized that I knew everything. . . . Suddenly I held all the information, the content of my life, in a new way, from a new mode, a new context."

Earlier in life, Erhard had made less lucrative leaps, transforming himself from Philadelphia used car salesman Jack Rosenberg to San Francisco encyclopedia peddler Jack Frost. . . . The second big transformation in his life began about the time his wife of 24 years filed for divorce.

John Bode in his *Chicago Tribune* article mentioned that Jack Rosenberg "married at 18, but abandoned his wife and four children in the early '60s and ran away to California with another woman. To conceal his identity, he changed his name to Werner Erhard, and for the next 13 years worked selling used cars, correspondence courses, and encyclopedias. (His own biographer, referring to this period, calls Erhard 'a liar, an imposter, a rogue.') In the meantime, he began to explore the then emerging human potential movement, studying Zen Buddhism and hypnosis, taking courses from Dale Carnegie, Scientology, and California's Esalen Institute." It is interesting that he has become one of the gurus of New Age business workshops and commands millions of dollars—an interesting foundation stone on which to build the New Age. Again, Erhard's seminar is one among hundreds.

The deeper issue is that hundreds of similar seminars are going on all across the country, and they are having an effect. Is this new to business? No. The oldest mystically inclined group to penetrate the international business world are the Masons. The Grand Orient Lodges of Europe have wielded vast political power, including fomenting the French Revolution and spreading enlightenment philosophy. The Masons have been supremely closed and silent about their upper-level initiations. Only recently have books like *The Brotherhood* come out in England showing the extent of Masonic influence within the banking and political elite. For centuries the Masons have affected commerce and politics but they have done it virtually undetected, hidden by a glove of invisibility. What is different about the explosion of New Age thought into business is that this explosion is so widespread and blatant as to represent the new norm—and this is greatly different from those past eras when occult groups had to lie hidden from public view. The hidden mysteries have come out of the closet; they are being revealed. Indeed, it looks like the All-Seeing-Eye of the pyramid is floating down Wall Street and Fleet Street these days in the full light of day.

Wheels of Influence: The Schoolroom

One very captive audience is the vulnerable young child sitting in the schoolroom who is just opening his eyes for the first time to a world that is totally strange and new. Such a child is looking for meaning about life and the world to satisfy a cardinal need: the need to find a secure context for his own life. Trustworthy figures become automatic sources in this quest for the meaning to life. Teachers are primary among a child's trustworthy figures. They carry natural authority because they are adults, but also because the adult world has appointed them to be teachers. Children may still misbehave and act inattentive, but statements of "fact" from these adults sink deep into their minds.

New Age leader John Dunphy made a telling observation in *The Humanist* magazine in its Jan./Feb. 1983 issue, in his award-winning essay entitled "A Religion for the New Age." Dunphy remarked:

> I am convinced that the battle for humankind's future must be waged and won in the public school classrooms by teachers who correctly perceive their role as proselytizers of a new faith: a religion of humanity that recognizes and respects the spark of what theologians call the Divinity in every human being. These teachers must embody the same self-less dedication as the most rabid fundamentalist preachers.

> The classroom must and will become an arena of
> conflict between the old and the new—the rotting
> corpse of Christianity, together with all its adjacent
> evils and misery, and the new faith. . . .

John Dunphy and Marilyn Ferguson are very aware that
the schoolroom is a critical arena and that teachers are
powerful opinion-shapers of the young captive minds under
their care. Ferguson, in the New Age bestseller, *The Aquarian
Conspiracy*, observed, "Even doctors, in their heyday as godlike paragons, have never wielded the authority of a single
classroom teacher, who can purvey prizes, failure, love, hu-
miliation and information to great numbers of relatively
powerless, vulnerable young people."[1]

As well as the role of the teacher, there is also the equally
influential role of the peer group. If other children go along
with an idea, its acceptance is that much more likely with a
child. The reality of influence in the schoolroom spurred John
Dewey, the father of American progressive public education,
to write *My Pedagogic Creed*. In it, Dewey discusses public
education as being a massive behavior-shaping tool and
enterprise. Dewey knew that you could sway the beliefs of a
generation in the classroom and thereby alter the course of
society. He saw the public school system as an ideal platform
to proselytize his radical socialistic views. Regardless of what
the parents believed, it was only a matter of time before the
successive generation took over. What a way to remake the
world!

But John Dewey's ideas did not just come out of a vacuum.
He was influenced by an insider group of intellectuals in
England known as the Fabian Socialists. Dewey was an American ally of this clique. It is important to glimpse the Fabian
agenda of gradualist global penetration and their views of
using education as a tool of influence in this process.

THE FABIANS OF ENGLAND
AND THEIR AGENDA

The Bloomsbury Fabians of London were an elite intelligentsia of world socialists who envisioned an end to war and

poverty by a united world order dedicated to the ideals of socialistic humanism.

The Fabian Socialists formed within a year of the death of Karl Marx, who died in London. They were captivated by Marx and Darwin. Dewey was one of the first of the liberal elite in America to embrace their beliefs. He later signed *The Humanist Manifesto*. His meetings with key leaders of the British Fabian society allowed Dewey to incorporate their ideas of socialist penetration in their mutual educational agenda. The League for Industrial Democracy (which before 1921 was the Intercollegiate Socialist Society) of which Dewey was president in 1938-39 as well as honorary president for the next 13 years, was one of America's cousins to the British Fabian Society.

Unlike Marxists, who advocated bloody revolution for world socialism, the Fabian Socialists of Britain advocated a more gradualist path to socialistic globalism. The plan of these early one-worlders was to use intellectual penetration, from the top of the pyramid down, into key areas of influence on society. Elite minds were to influence and change the social order. Their symbol was the slow-moving turtle which would pass the sleeping rabbit. Bertrand Russell referred to the Bloomsbury group as a mutual admiration society. But they penetrated one major field after another—literature, politics, education, science, and the media—and had some of the most renowned figures in the world.

English Fabians such as H.G. Wells, Rupert Brooke, Aldous Huxley, George Bernard Shaw, G.M. Trevelyan, Lord Haldane, Arnold Toynbee, Sir Julian Huxley, Virginia Woolf, Arnold Bennett, Rebecca West, E.M. Forster, J.B. Priestly, and other similar luminaries greatly influenced the public mind and the academy through literature, letters, and the laboratory. Oxford and Cambridge became central recruiting grounds. One recalls the Fabians at Cambridge University in the film *Chariots of Fire*, with their large banner next to the Gilbert and Sullivan Club.

One of the most effective Fabians was famed Cambridge University economist John Maynard Keynes who turned Harvard on its ears when he came and charmed the students and faculty with his socialist economics. Keynes said that the state should guarantee welfare for all, that it should provide guaranteed employment through government programs, and that all of this could be financed by his revolutionary scheme.

How? By supreme Keynesian alchemy—that of turning paper into gold! The gold standard could be dropped for paper currency, then deficit spending through government loans would open up a money vault of endless supply. Indeed, it was a "New Deal," to use the Roosevelt expression—maybe too good a deal to be true.

Another Fabian to hit Harvard was Harold Laski, who with avowed socialist Lord Haldane eventually started the London School of Economics. He later obtained an instructorship at Harvard in 1915 through invitation of Felix Frankfurter, Byrnes Professor of Law at the Harvard Law School. Frankfurter became Laski's closest friend. During the four years Harold Laski taught at Harvard, he edited the Harvard *Law Review*, inoculating the prestigious publication with socialist ideas. The Harvard Law School eventually adopted a socialist leaning through its Fabian liaison. Justice Frankfurter of the U.S. Supreme Court, a member of the Harvard faculty, as well as his former pupil, Justice Louis Brandeis, also a Supreme Court judge, kept a line of communication going with their Fabian friends in England. This was important for the agenda of penetration.

Laski, for 25 years, remained an honored houseguest of Supreme Court Justice Frankfurter, especially when the latter was a member of Roosevelt's New Deal brain trust. By that era, Harold Laski was chairman of the Fabian Society of Britain (from 1946 to 1948). Employing Fabian gradualism, one of the most long-range and penetrating legal statements that Frankfurter ever made was that *"through the use of due process the justices could read their own economic and social views into the neutral language of the Constitution."*[2] This statement has spelled out the very agenda adopted by lawyers in dismantling the U.S. Constitution. This Trojan horse rolled through the Fabian doorway right into the U.S. Supreme Court and has affected legal decisions across America.

Meanwhile, the far-ranging effects of the Bloomsbury group is seen in England today after its decades of socialist penetration. The Fabians started England's influential labor party and never looked back. Edwardian England and the era of the aristocracy is no more. A more plebian England has replaced it, though it has used those from the intellectual aristocracy to bring this about. The glamor of the left remains a compelling mystery as it seduces bright and ambitious university youth, artists, and assorted aspiring intellectuals.

THE TROJAN HORSE OF PROGRESSIVE EDUCATION

John Dewey, who remained close with Fabian leaders, had his own circle of academic disciples at Columbia University, especially Kilpatrick and Counts, who influenced textbooks and school curricula for decades. Through Dewey's influence, Harold Laski, right before becoming chairman of the British Fabian Society, lectured at Columbia Teacher's College for a semester in 1939 amidst John Dewey's best and brightest disciples.

What did all this mean for American public education? Columbia Teacher's College influenced other graduate schools and colleges of education. Before too long, progressive education—Dewey's tool for reshaping America—was a public school reality all across America.

Dewey knew that to penetrate the existing social order a united front of educators, who embodied the new viewpoint, needed to emerge from graduate schools. These teachers of teachers would then influence future teachers. Among the new views was a national self-criticism that spurned narrow patriotism for a broader globalism. At the same time all traditional values were to be questioned, from parental authority to the validity of established religion.

Rather than equipping the child to handle the demanding academic and moral standards of the old order, with its McGuffey Reader and its implicit moral virtues, Dewey's progressive education considered behavior-shaping as its highest educational priority. "Socialization" was now defined as a type of learning at least equal to traditional learning. Now the old morals and ethics could be replaced by situational ethics or "values clarification." Reading, writing, and arithmetic took a backseat to an array of experimental programs such as "sensitivity training." The virtues of hard work were replaced by new permissive standards that would pass a failing child rather than "harm" him by labeling him a failure. Total equality was the new ideal: It would jealously guard against too much excellence in any child that might show others to be less endowed, thus implying that abilities were unevenly distributed.

FROM PROGRESSIVE TO
NEW AGE EDUCATION

Since Dewey's time, public school programs have been behavior-shaping children without even pretending to impart useful skills or academic knowledge. "Confluent education" is a recent example. One contributor to this was the late Dr. Beverly Galyean. Galyean's beliefs are part of her program. In 1981 she said:

> Once we begin to see that we are all God, that we all have the attributes of God, then I think the whole purpose of human life is to reown the Godlikeness within us; the perfect love, the perfect wisdom, the perfect understanding, the perfect intelligence, and when we do that, we create back to that old, that essential oneness which is consciousness.[3]

Scores of children, starting from Los Angeles and moving across the country, have been affected by Dr. Galyean's approach. Picture first graders being made to lie down on the floor of their classrooms while being told to relax and then visualize such "positive" things as the sun radiating within them. They picture the light of the sun filling their entire being. Then the teacher tells them: "You are inwardly perfect and contain all the wisdom of the universe within yourselves." First graders are introduced to spirit guides in the

Galyean approach, although as she remarked at a plenary session at the conference entitled *Education in the 80's*, "Of course we don't call them that in the public schools. We call them imaginary guides."[4]

The Supreme Court, although banning prayer, has no laws against simple classroom exercises in visualization which are seen as merely creative exercises expanding the pupil's imaginative and creative potential. Besides, positive affirmations such as, "You contain the wisdom of the universe," might elevate the pupil's self-esteem. Knowing educators argue that first graders certainly won't take this too seriously. The legal system has agreed, winked, and looked the other way. Lawyers and not professors of philosophy are being asked whether there are issues of ontology and metaphysics beneath such exercises and "affirmations." An Ivy League philosophy professor like Allan Bloom, who wrote *The Closing of the American Mind*, or my old mentor at Princeton, Dr. Diogenes Allen, could see through this issue in a fraction of a second. But then again, they do not write the laws of the land or govern public school curricula, which is very convenient for educators with a particular agenda.

In 1984, the U.S. Department of Education conducted hearings to gauge public opinion and propose regulations regarding the implementation of "The Protection of Pupil Rights Amendment" otherwise known as the Hatch Amendment. Testimonials that went on record across the country consistently wove a pattern of classroom activities that revealed the new agenda was well under way. "Values clarification" had been included and surpassed. Earlier door openers like MACOS, for fifth graders in the 1970's, introduced open discussion of what were once taboo topics in the schoolroom such as genocide, homosexuality, and euthanasia. Teachers could talk about alternate sexualities with liberal candor, while dissenting voices with old-fashioned views could be easily quashed by majority consensus. This door opened so widely that by 1988 parents of kindergartners in Marin County learned that the latest sex education programs required their young children to learn slang terms for body parts, including genitals. According to *The San Francisco Chronicle* (April 5, 1988, p. A2), kids in lower primary grades were also to explore the meaning of sexual fantasy and discuss alternate lifestyles.

In the 1984 hearings, one witness displayed a future studies publication, produced with support from the National Institute of Education. It was entitled *Future Studies in the Kindergarten Through Twelve Curriculum* by John D. Haas, and it recommended how teachers might subtly introduce certain key topics into the classroom such as: fertility control, contraceptives, abortion, family planning, women's liberation, euthanasia, New Age consciousness, mysticism, ESP, new religions, changing older religions, guaranteed income, and so on. These issues had become hot stuff in many classrooms anyway. But how might the system reach down into the lower elementary school grades to expedite the process of preparing children for the new order?

There was a time when Johnny was happy to be a boy and Susan was happy to be a girl. Now the kids of the eighties, with the help of the experts, believe in the new myth of androgyny. A case in point is the Title IX-funded Sex Equity Program, or the Women's Educational Equity Act Program tested in five counties across the United States as test sites. The plan is to change the thinking patterns of America's children, starting with the kids in these five counties who have acted as guinea pigs for the greater national experiment. What happens in classrooms under this program?

On March 13, 1984, in Seattle, Washington, at the official proceedings before the U.S. Department of Education, one observer described this program—the Sex Equity field experiment—in Lincoln County, Oregon:

> One of the demonstrations was in a 1st grade room. The students each had two naked paper dolls, one male, the other female. They were asked to dress the dolls in work clothing to show that both genders could work at any job.
>
> The thing I found interesting was there were no dresses. All clothing was male oriented. Then the teacher had the students sit in a circle while she pulled out objects from a

sack, like a pancake turner or a tape measure. She asked, "Who uses this, mom or dad?"

If the student did not answer the way she had wanted, she would say, "Well, who else uses this?" Finally, one little boy raised his hand and said, "I don't care. Men ought to be doctors, and ladies nurses."

The teacher then asked how many students agreed with the little boy. By the tone of her voice, they knew no one should raise a hand, so no one did. The little boy was so humiliated by the peer pressure and class manipulation by the teacher that he started to cry. This is classic of the type of discrimination, bias, stereotyping, and harassment that this program has included.

As I reviewed different manuals that teachers were using in the schools . . . questions on family values, self-analysis, opposite role-playing, unisex ideas, discussion of family roles in students' homes, and sex-role values were discussed. One book said, "Students are no longer to be called helpers, or boys and girls, or students, but WORKERS" (a part of the Socialist lexicon).

Another book showed *only* pictures of opposites to traditional roles, such as the father feeding baby, or mother holding a firehose in her "fireperson" job. The children didn't realize they were being fed only one side of the picture.

. . . Our school district received federal funds to teach "Sex Equity." . . . The teaching is firmly intact in the system after five years of funding. Teachers are required to attend sex equity workshops sponsored by Northwest Regional Laboratory in Portland, which received federal funds. They provide resource material and teachers.

I discovered there was no set curriculum. Teachers chose what to teach from several manuals. They were to integrate the teaching into the entire day's classes. Women were really exalted in all the material I viewed, while male minorities were almost ignored. The goal of the Sex Equity program was to eliminate traditional roles of male and female.

Clearly the above is a behavior-shaping program that uses the classroom as a laboratory under the cloak of education. More and more, the classroom has become a test site for human guinea pigs. Dr. Benjamin Bloom, the father of mastery learning, in his recent book, *All Our Children Learning*, states, "The purpose of education is to change the thoughts, feelings, and actions of students." Again and again two names keep appearing in this effort of changing thoughts and feelings: Sidney Simon, the "expert" who introduced values clarification, and Lawrence Kohlberg, who introduced moral reasoning. Both programs annihilate traditional values. Again, the Fabian theme emerges: A handful of "experts," in this case psychologists, presume their views upon millions with impunity. They arrogantly become founts of wisdom about the family, about sexuality, and about ultimate reality. In a sweep they can destroy the student's faith, beliefs, and moral system. Occasionally we learn of their handiwork. On October 9, 1987, *The Los Angles Times* headlined a story with the words: "Alcohol Used by 45% of 7th Graders." That is merely the tip of the iceberg.

England might even be ahead of us in this arena of shattering boundaries of morality. In the news recently was a book introduced by English liberal educators for children. *The San Francisco Chronicle* on March 16, 1988 in an article by Adrian Peracchio described outrage in Britain: "It began last year with parents' howls of outrage at the publication by local municipal councils of *Jenny Lives with Eric and Martin*, a graphically illustrated pamphlet showing a cherubic little girl smiling at her father, naked in bed with his live-in gay lover."

The *Chronicle* then reported: "The pamphlet, printed with British government funds, attempted to prove that young children brought up by homosexual couples could adjust and thrive just as well as those reared in more traditional households.

"It appeared in local school libraries alongside, *How to Be a Happy Homosexual*, and *The Children's Playbook of Sex*, two other publicly financed pamphlets in which homosexual themes were explicitly treated." But the values barrier is only one barrier. In breaking the New Age barrier, the United States might be ahead of England.

In other testimonials before the U.S. Department of Education, which were compiled from across the country in 1984, there were numerous examples of New Age thought flooding classrooms. Common activities involved learning how to do horoscopes, conduct seances, cast the witch's circle, use a Ouija board, meditate, and role-play such characters as warlocks and spiritists which appeared in required readings. Wiccans (witches) and neopagans were invited on public school premises to speak about their alternate views (they do not use the word "religions"). Witches could now enter where ministers were forbidden to tread, a new milestone in America's "liberation." Children also partook in the visualization of invisible guides not just through the Galyean approach but through Silva Mind Control. They would lie on the floor and empty their minds, invoking the invisible presences within them. In Buffalo, New York, students were required to learn Silva Mind Control and reportedly contacted the spirits of various long-deceased historical figures—a new way to study about George Washington and Lincoln! Why read about historical figures when you can invoke them from the dead?

The State of Connecticut presents a case in point of how New Age curricula is creeping through the doors of the public school system. First of all, there comes the federal grant. In the case of Connecticut, several million dollars were granted to develop the Connecticut Teachers' Center for Humanistic Education. The loophole was the Department of Health, Education and Welfare's allocation of 75 million dollars for the teaching of humanistic education nationwide via the 1978 amendments to the Higher Education Act, Title 5. Stratford's Board of Education initiated the first grant for one million dollars to have humanistic education taught in the Connecticut public school system, thus becoming the *legal* education agency and employer. This was the machinery of how the door opened up.

For input, the Connecticut center had a number of resources including the Aspen Institute for Humanistic Studies in Aspen, Colorado, which has a worldwide reputation. A closer source of input was the Institute for Wholistic Education in Amherst, Massachusetts, codirected by Jack Canfield and Paula Klimek, who came and led workshops at various Connecticut Teacher's Center sponsored programs. They were featured in a brochure entitled "Education in the New Age," a training program that took place in Madison, Connecticut, November 17-18, 1979, and sponsored by the then fully operational Connecticut Teacher's Center for Humanistic Education. One workshop was entitled "Meditation and Centering in the Classroom," the other was "Guided Imagery."

The conference "facilitators," Canfield and Klimek, had written an article for *The New Age Journal*, February 1978, entitled "Education in the New Age," which essentially spelled out the New Age agenda for penetrating and using the public school system across the United States. Their biography in *The New Age Journal* stated, "They consult with schools, train teachers, and have co-authored numerous books such as, *The Inner Classroom: Teaching with Guided Fantasy*, and *Wholistic Education*." Not surprisingly, some Connecticut parents began to take note when their children returned home from school with new ideas. They were quietly moving into the new paradigms, beyond the obsolete mind-sets of their parents' generation. It was all happening with the quiet sense of *Invasion of the Body Snatchers*. A consortium of parents described what was happening in the classroom with the words, "In the name of discovering their 'life purpose,' children are encouraged into trance-like states of mind where they communicate with 'guardian spirits.' The use of Yoga exercises and mind control techniques are other examples of the format of this program."[5]

The media followed the footsteps of Jack Canfield and the high-powered groups of educators and lawyers he was addressing. A Canadian journal, *The Editonion Journal*, on October 11, 1979, had an article by Marilyn Moysa entitled "Improving Images Seen as a Key to Help." It reported:

> Imagine more than 800 of North America's top judges, lawyers, education professors, social workers and just plain parents chanting an Indian mantra.

Even Meyer Horowitz, University of Alberta president, sang along in the guitar-accompanied chant. "What ever happened to the keynote address? I kept asking myself. Wasn't this supposed to be the big opening number of a national conference on children with learning disabilities?"

What happened, quite simply, was Jack Canfield. Director of the Institute for Wholistic Education in Amherst, Mass. . . . Images, claims Dr. Canfield, can have power beyond the will of an individual when it comes to change.

The article then showed how Canfield took a learning-disabled sixth-grade girl and had her go through guided imagery with a "wise old woman" up a stairway of light. Through this the girl discovered the meaning of life. The 800 lawyers and educators applauded this profound experiment and its insight.

Canfield's extremely long feature article in *The New Age Journal* is packed with material, techniques, and insights. Canfield and Klimek state that New Age education has arrived and that "more and more teachers are exposing children to ways of contacting their inner wisdom and higher selves."[6]

The coauthors diagnosed breakthroughs in the sixties when the educational system began to break down, saying:

At the same time, an influx of spiritual teachings from the East, combined with a new psychological perspective in the West, has resulted in a fresh look at the learning process. . . . People everywhere are looking for a new vision, a new approach, a new paradigm of life. . . . A new vision is beginning to manifest.[7]

Much of guided imagery begins with Roberto Assagioli's *psychosynthesis*. This is the creative root to reaching the all-knowing higher self within.

Canfield and Klimek's article states:

Within the past five years we have also witnessed the birth of "transpersonal education," the acknowledgment of one's inner and spiritual dimensions, through working with such forms as dreams, meditation, guided imagery, biofeedback, centering, mandalas, and so forth. Now is the time to combine both of these focuses, for the New Age means integrating the soul and personality. . . . Holistic education . . . views the student as being engaged in an integral process of unfoldment under the direction of his/her higher self. This process is perceived as taking place in a universe that is also constantly evolving: each of us is seen as an important part of the larger planetary and universal evolution of consciousness.[8]

There were endless pointers: "Children of all ages love physical exercise and seem to be particularly fascinated with yoga: they move easily into all sorts of contortions. . . . There are numerous books on yoga for children. One of our favorites is *Be a Frog, a Bird or a Tree*, by Rachel Carr (New York: Doubleday)."[9] Intimacy games are described, as are sensory awareness games, in which children get over inhibitions against touching one another. "Centering" becomes the more acceptable word for meditation. "Relaxation and centering exercises are a fundamental process for New Age education, because they provide a space for listening to the voice within."[10] Sufi dances are mentioned.

Chanting is recommended to reach the transcendent within. The best place to learn chanting is at workshops and yoga retreats. Resources listed are: *Jewels from the East* and *Spiritual Nation* by the Khalsa String Band as well as Baba Ram Dass' *Love, Serve, and Remember*. One chanting method is called "seed planting" (in India we used to call them *Bija mantras*) in order to plant the chants deep into the consciousness. It is a group event with one child sitting in the middle of the room. They take turns sitting in the middle.[11]

Then there are meditation techniques that use media ideas. Canfield observes:

A wonderful way to do this, we have found, is to use the tools the media are providing. An example might be to ask, "What's this thing called The Force in *Star Wars*? How does Luke communicate with it? How does it help him?" The next question is, "Well, would you like to have this kind of experience?" (The answer is always an overwhelming "Yes!") "Well, we can try this and see what happens. There are some ground rules you will need to follow." At this point the kids are more than ready. The media has done a lot of the work for us.[12]

Canfield and Klimek conclude their extensive article with some telling insights regarding children of the New Age. They no doubt share these same insights in their coast-to-coast teacher training seminars. They conclude:

We believe that guided imagery is a key to finding out what is in the consciousness of New Age children.... Children are so close to spirit if we only allow room for their process to emerge. We celebrate to fantasize what is in store for all of us.... Additional emphases in the transpersonal dimension are using nature as teacher, and aligning and communicating with the other kingdoms such as the elemental and *devic** realms...working with children's psychic capacities (such as seeing auras); working with astrological charts.... The souls that are presently incarnating seem to be very special.[13]

The coauthors end their article on education in the New Age with the words: "We must not get caught in the trap of putting them into developmental models which will soon be irrelevant.... The only requirement is to provide a space and an environment where these beautiful young spirits can open up and allow their wisdom to be seen."[14]

---

* The term *Devic* is a Vedantic Sanskrit word for the realm of the gods. The complete Sanskrit term is *Deva Loka*.

The present generation of latchkey kids, whose parents are busy with dual careers, operates almost unsupervised in a permissive world. They are indeed a lonely and captive audience, ready to sponge up the new agenda. As former Yale professor Allan Bloom observes in his bestseller, each succeeding group entering college from public school comes less equipped to deal with the university world—an index of a tragic and costly experiment. Bloom says they are coming out of the educational experiment "impoverished."

High school "grads" of the 1980's come out semiliterate, passive, hedonistic, as they live for the moment, have no goals, no concept of history, no discipline, no real mental furniture, no sense of what is noble or good. Instead they specialize in taboo-breaking decadence and grin cynically at moral correctives. They have earned self-esteem cheaply by being told that they are gods. Now they don't have a thing to prove, nor are they capable of the sort of commitment and virtue required to run a society, whether in the workplace or in human relationships. They are ready to fall into the hands of almost anyone who comes along. The new youth resemble the effete Eloi in H.G. Well's futuristic *The Time Machine*. They have become *The Less than Zero Generation*, dropping by the wayside on cocaine and perversion. Yet they have been assured by educators of their own self-worth and freedom to self-actualize as long as it feels good. They have tried that and they have emerged impoverished both intellectually and morally. They have empty heads and hard hearts and the self that they have spent so much time pursuing vanishes like a ghost every time they think they have found it.

A whole generation of teachers today went through the humanistic programs of the 1970's. What will be the story when the New Age children in elementary school reach high school? They are the next generation, and are vastly more behavior-modified than any group to precede them. Will they be part of the collective global messiah, or will they turn out to be part of something far more sinister? Truly they are modeling clay in the hands of the educators and experts, and are wards of the state, whether anyone realizes this or not. The Trojan horse has entered the gates.

10

Dress Rehearsal for a New Age Christ

We have seen one front after another penetrated by the wheels of influence of the new world mentality: books, movies, television, psychology, education, the corporate world, political platforms, and so on. The rapid changing of the guard from the old world to the new has been remarkable. The march ahead has almost been unimpeded . . . almost. But there are a few obstacles left and they represent considerable barriers, in some cases fortresses. As we will see, the traditional family is one of them, traditional gender roles another. But the greatest barrier of all is the unyielding stand of genuine Christianity that cannot and will not accommodate itself just to have a kind of spiritual *détente*. It cannot be syncretized into the new temple that is being built by new world visionaries who want to show, as John Lennon stated in his last interview, that "Christ, Mohammad, Krishna, the Imam Mahdi, Maitreya are all equal and represent God equally in different ways. We don't say one is more important than the other." Lennon perfectly captured this emerging viewpoint when he said this—so has Joseph Campbell on his much-televised "Bill Moyers Special" on mythology. But the unadulterated Christian faith will not yield to this multifaith juggernaut. It stands exclusive and alone, and as such it is a supreme obstacle for the simple reason that the reigning view of the old order of Western civilization is Christian-based.

As an obstacle it must be remade into a new form or utterly

115

destroyed. Either there must be created a New Age Christ, lifted out of the confines of history, or the memory of this faith must somehow be expunged from the record books of history. It is a double-flanked approach, and it is going on: 1) Create a New Age Christ and 2) In a propaganda campaign, caricature the historical faith and Christians, making them supremely unpopular, irrelevant, and out-of-touch.

Something has to be done with Christ and Christianity. It's that simple. No matter what, this reality cannot be ignored. Christ is seen as either an impediment or a doorway. It is surprising how many groups have an obsessive preoccupation with Christ and with hammering him into place. It seems they feel a need to have his sanction, as though their consciences cannot rest until they have somehow included him into their beliefs.

But these same groups insist on taking Christ to the make-up artists and tampering with his attire. What they need is a broad-minded, nonjudgmental, cosmic Christ. Somehow he must be unearthed from history or rediscovered; a Christ who sanctions all paths as leading to God, who is not exclusive or judgmental, who in fact teaches the ancient mystery religions of the divine within, that spark of divinity within all men waiting to be awakened.

This cosmic Christ is to be one facet of the capstone atop the massive pyramid now being built. It must be a Christ who will syncretize with Buddha, Krishna, the Imam Mahdi, and perhaps some future Jewish Messiah. This Christ will be seen as a type of the new man, a perfect master among other perfect masters, who is leading the way for the whole human race to enter into the secrets of enlightenment. He is an exemplar, at the head of the pack.

But certain things need to be done to bring about this cosmic Christ. Hidden writings must be discovered after having been buried for 2000 years, revealing a different Christ from the powerful figure in the New Testament. Channelers and psychics must communicate with this cosmic Christ to the world-at-large and divulge his new teachings because the world is "now evolved enough to handle the deeper teachings." A few must encounter a being-of-light in near-death experiences who claims to be Christ and who bears this universal creed of spiritual evolution.

There must also be new systems of interpretation for going into the New Testament and ferreting out this mystery Christ. New meanings must be given to ancient phrases and words. For instance, when Christ told Nicodemus, "You must be born again," the new hidden understanding is that he was speaking of reincarnation, and so on. But only certain "advanced" teachers will know these hidden meanings—a closed union of mystics who will appear before the world, as they did during the ancient era of the Gnostics and mystery religions.

The new teachers will announce, as some already have, that these higher teachings have been hidden and suppressed by the church—that they were quashed at the ancient councils, such as Nicea and Constantinople. The new teachers will claim that the church was engaged in a cover-up operation of obscuring the very mystery-Christianity which would have so perfectly fit like a piece to a puzzle to the other world religions, especially Buddhism and Hinduism—that this suppressed mystery-Christianity would have helped to provide the groundwork for a universal faith based on the universal nature of God, the brotherhood of man, and the divine basis for all life. These teachers will show that, instead, the historic church has become a divisive obstacle that is not tolerant of all paths. It obstructs the smooth flow of this effort at world unity.

But now it is time for a universal creed. Planetary needs demand it. A universal, nonoffensive creed will be a major element in providing so that the world might be one. It *must* be brought about and *anything* divisive must be permanently quashed. Christ is to be rediscovered as the avatar, gnostic redeemer, incarnation of the godhead, and mystery figure who fits the pages of the world creeds. For historical accuracy, it must be observed that this mystery Christ is far from the Jesus who hurled accusations at the Sanhedrin, overturned the tables of the money changers, and bodily rose from the dead. The mystery Christos is light-years removed from Jesus Christ who was born in Bethlehem, healed lepers, spoke pointedly about sin and moral condemnation, fed thousands miraculously, and claimed to be the unique son of God, without peer, who existed before time began, and who foretold his return to judge the world. The mystery Christ is a different Christ altogether from the New Testament Christ, and he emerges from countless peripheral sources—except from the canon of the New Testament. From this sealed canon he cannot emerge, for the early manuscripts and autographs don't breathe a word about this other cosmic Christ.

This presents a problem which must be addressed. It must be dealt with from all sides in a pincer movement, logistically and strategically. It is a little like the problem of the Marxist who wishes to change the common understanding of the United States Constitution so that a gradualist skewing of word meaning can enable a socialistic interpretation of words whose intended meanings in the original were clearly different. He must deal with language manipulatively.

On one level, it is a problem of hermeneutics and exegesis. In the case of the Bible, if you can editorially cancel out certain words and phrases, or invent new contexts surrounding statements, you can skew the entire meaning of a major passage. Literal realities can be conveniently thrust into a symbolical context. Paul Tillich did this all the time. Then you can look for "Jungian" meanings behind ordinary events as these moments in history are doubted and now ascribed to being symbolic. Academic criticism provides this mode of attack. You begin by absolute doubt. You doubt the books and parchments; you doubt the writers and their motives. You throw it all away and defy the canon to prove itself to you first. Dates are doubted, methods of copying are doubted, and so on. And indeed here we have the German and continental schools of biblical criticism: redactive, historical, and form criticisms. Academic criticism turns out to be a most effective means of frontal assault on the historic Christian faith. It is one way to get Christ to the make-up artist and extract his prophetic and judgmental aspects that so grate against the modern tempo.

Today, divinity schools, graduate departments of religion, and seminaries have taken the cue from the academic posture of doubt and used this as a way to reshape Christ to fit current fashion with a tolerant, leftward leaning, socially conscious, inclusive Christ. Once conformity-minded students take the cue that this is the only acceptable position among their fellow students and academic peers, it is a rare individual who will dare to step out of line. As someone said, they have come up with an emasculated Christ.

This Christ of academia is such a conciliator that he loses ground at every strategy meeting in which he is discussed. These days he is a champion of the lesbian/gay caucus and radical feminists. He is even pro-sodomy—as long as it is "responsible," "caring," and "safe" sex among "persons of alternate sexual preferences." This pallid invention of the academy is ready to fall right into line with the mystery Christ of the New Age. It is a rare faculty member who will risk tenure to stand against this wave. Each faculty member can grin knowingly—these doctors of knowledge—as they add the emperor's new clothes to their already considerable collection of vestments and tassels. They can still walk in ponderous academic lines with furrowed brows, borrowing from their lineage of intellectual profundity, while passing on the mantle to those whom they choose. Individuals, especially brilliant "individualists," who differ with their agenda are instantly "marked" for opposition. By conformity in the academy, Christ has been remade in a few generations. This is a remarkable pincer movement indeed—one of ponderous faces and furrowed brows, ambition, peer pressure, personal agendas in some and moral cowardice in others.

But there is an equally effective pincer movement composed of dizzyingly optimistic faces. These are the ones in touch with the cosmic Christ, and the messages that are coming in are compelling. Hundreds of thousands who attend New Age conferences and millions reading New Age books are feeling "confirmed" by these messages. Enter the cosmic Christ.

THE COSMIC CHRIST

Though Edgar Cayce died in 1945, the books concerning

this famous channeler still flood bookstores. They are top sellers among Bantam's "New Age" paperback series. Cayce spent years going into trances in which he claimed to gain access to the hall of records of the cosmic mind—better known as the Akashic records. He had the look and bearing of a simple Bible Belt Christian. His demeanor of kindly innocence made him believable. For years all he did was diagnose physical illnesses in this trance state. Even if the subject were halfway across America, the impersonal "we" voice would almost always accurately diagnose the problem of a subject whom he had never met, giving the method of cure. One day a wealthy Jewish theosophist in the Midwest paid for his trance time, but then started asking the Akashic mind questions concerning the nature of ultimate reality. The startling revelations that came through confused and even frightened Edgar Cayce. When he woke out of a trance he never remembered anything, nor had he "met" the "voice" that worked through his body, using it as a medium. When this groundbreaking channeler heard what he had said in his first nonmedical reading, he was almost undone, for he was revealing a cosmos identical to that of the theosophists, mystics, and Hindus.

The loving personal God whom Edgar Cayce had read about in the Bible as a child turned out to be a "myth of the dualistic mind." What Cayce's channeling revealed was the impersonal godhead, like an infinite ocean of consciousness, without attributes, yet composed of and beyond all qualities and forms of being. The cosmos was made not *ex nihilo*, out of nothing, but out of God. The pantheistic system was therefore the true one after all.

Along with reincarnation came the inevitable law of karma, the Akashic records simply being the records of all prior events and past lives. Cayce began to give "life readings" of past lives. Presto! What came out were accounts of Atlantis, the occult civilization that blew itself up. Now we learn that these same "evolved" souls who had perished in Atlantis were streaming into rebirth on "the earth plane." Though Cayce died in the forties, this would have been the sixties generation he was talking about. These same advanced souls had a mission: to restore to the earth the Atlantian spiritual secrets while taking civilization beyond Atlantis. Thus there would soon be a New Age with new powers unleashed. There would also be the return of the occult priesthood and adepts, oracles, psychics, astrologers, channelers, high mystics, and godmen who were here to change the "earth plane." (This revelation helped spur me to meet my spiritual destiny in India—at any price!)

Not just God, but the character of Christ changed as well. Christ was the perfect yogi, avatar/incarnation of the god-head, and god-man. He had already reincarnated on the earth a number of times to set up his messianic mission, perfecting himself even more each time. Melchizedek was but one embodiment in Christ's genealogy of past lives. In that sense he is a model for all men to follow in order to attain what is now called "Christ-consciousness." Strategically, the Akashic "voice" channeling through Cayce targeted the hidden years in Christ's life about which the Bible is silent. Now there was room to fill in the blanks.

With an elaborate explanation of astrological forces, the Akashic voice depicted the young "perfect master" traveling to Egypt to study at the temples of wisdom and beauty, where he learns certain psychic arts. Then the young Jesus goes on to India and Tibet to learn levitation and transmutation from certain Tibetan masters; while in India, he learns healing, weather control, telepathy, and ultimately reaches "at-one-ment" (the real meaning of atonement) with the cosmic over-mind. From there, at about age 29, he returns to the Holy Land as the fully promised Messiah.

Perhaps what initially bothered Cayce most about this channeled revelation was the fact that the apostles left all these critical bits of history out of the New Testament. Cayce knew that the Bible does not mention so much as a hint about any of these mystical sojourns. None of the historians of antiquity ever saw the dimmest traces of any of this nor, from all the hundreds of letters from out of the era of the early church soon after the life of Christ, was a word ever uttered about these trips to India. You would think someone would have gone along and written about it then. No, Cayce had to trust the invisible voice coming through him, and this took a certain leap of faith.

Thomas Sugrue, the major biographer of Edgar Cayce, in *There Is a River*, makes an observation about Cayce and all other channels of the cosmic Christ:

> The system of metaphysical thought which emerges from the readings of Edgar Cayce is a Christianized version of the mystery religions of ancient Egypt, Chaldea, Persia, India and Greece. It fits the figure of Christ into the tradition of one God for all people, and places Him in His proper place. . . . He is the capstone of the pyramid.[1]

But Edgar Cayce was by no means the first channeler to come up with revelations about the cosmic Christ. Another major source was Levi Dowling, a late nineteenth-century medical practitioner who traveled from town to town in the Midwest in a covered wagon. In the early hours of the morning he channeled and recorded through automatic writing the famed occult classic, *The Aquarian Gospel of Jesus the Christ*. Dowling records how he gave his body to a "higher force." Its purpose was to complete what the apostles had left out, updated for our coming "Aquarian Age." Dowling had already rejected the New Testament source. Dowling considered his channelings to be higher scriptures and numbered them chapter and verse like the Bible. One could almost lament at this point—oh, if only the scholars would bring their weighty redactive and critical methodology to bear on these channeled teachings from around the world, surely they bounce all over the map. What is a believer to do? Which channeled revelation do we trust?

According to Dowling's revelations, Christ learned herbal arts in Benares, India. The *Aquarian Gospel* reveals in chapter 23, verses 2-4: "Benares of the Ganges was a city rich in culture and learning; here the two rabbonis tarried many days. And Jesus sought to learn the Hindu art of healing, and became a pupil of Udraka, the greatest of Hindu healers.

Udraka taught the uses of the waters, plants, and earths; of heat and cold; sunshine and shade; of light and dark."

We also learn that "Jesus was accepted as a pupil in the temple of Jagannath: and here learned the Vedas and Manic Laws" (21:19). Yet the reality is this: The only Scriptures Christ quotes from in the New Testament are from the Jewish Torah. Not a breath about the Vedas, but plenty from the prophets, psalms, David, and Moses. Not a reference to Udraka or the Jagannath temple with its thousands of Hindu gods.

Perhaps in a pantheistic mood, the Aquarian Christ reveals: "With much delight I speak to you concerning life—the brotherhood of life. The universal God is one, yet he is more than one; all things are God; all things are one" (28:3,4).

At the feast of Persepolis honoring the Magician God, the Aquarian Christ has some good things to say at the invitation of the ruling magician: "Your purity in worship and in life is pleasing unto God; and to your master Zarathustra, praise is due" (39:5). When he goes on to Delphi, he has some great things to say about the oracle: "The Delphic age has been an age of glory and renown; the gods have spoken to the sons of men through oracles of wood, and gold, and precious stone. . . . The gods will speak to man by man. The living oracle now stands within these sacred groves; the Logos from on High has come" (45:8-10).

By the time Dowling's young master gets to Egypt he is ready to go through the seven tests of mystical brotherhood to become a full master. In the chamber of the dead he becomes a pupil of the Hierophant. Here he learns the mysteries of life and death and "the worlds beyond the circle of the sun." Faced with the body of a young boy whom he is to embalm, the cosmic Christ tells the boy's grief-stricken mother that "Death is a cruel word; your son can never die" (54:6,7). Indeed, these words can be found in the Bible, but are spoken by one other than Christ, to be sure: "Ye shall surely never die."

Today, we are 10,000 channels down the road from the days of Levi Dowling and Edgar Cayce and there have been a lot of history and words added to the cosmic Christ. It has been a most extensive and elaborate dress rehearsal. Currently, contemporary channels such as J.Z. Knight who channels Ramtha, Jach Pursel who channels Lazaris, and Elizabeth Claire Prophet, figurehead of the Summit Lighthouse, who channels multiple ascended masters, echo similar teachings to those of Cayce and Dowling. They have added sophisticated makeup to this cosmic Christ.

A COURSE IN MIRACLES

Now, in the last ten years, there has come a major new revelation to hit the stands and it has created a New Age furor. It is *A Course in Miracles*, channeled through a Jewish atheist—indeed, a woman in the department of psychiatry at Columbia University who even as an atheist took down what the voice told her. *A Course in Miracles* is one of the most-sought-after sources of teaching among New Agers and even some churches. Here too is an event, a phenomenon, that should not entirely escape our scrutiny.

In short, Helen Schucman, Ph.D., who in the midsixties was an associate professor of medical psychology at Columbia University's College of Physicians and Surgeons, worked in a department riddled with strain, tensions, and academic competition. This job stress ate into her personal life, creating anxiety and pessimism as it did also with her boss, Dr. Thetford. Department and faculty meetings were like war zones as medical egos displayed themselves. The two—at odds— made a joint commitment to straighten things out at almost any cost. One technique involved acknowledging and selectively seeing only the positive in the other person.[2]

Yet Helen Schucman, an avowed atheist, had always possessed a strange psychic faculty that she had only peripherally acknowledged. Her "mental pictures," which she had been seeing in her mind for as long as she could remember, changed from black-and-white to color, then they started moving, motion-picture style, and invaded her dreams. In the summer of '65 the psychic process heightened. Schucman got a flash of herself as an Egyptian priestess. Then in a "vision" she discovered a large black book in a treasure chest.

An inner voice began to accompany the moving psychic pictures. It told her that it was "her" book. Schucman told Dr. Bill Thetford that she might need to undergo a psychiatric examination herself, but that it might be pathological. Thetford was drawn to Edgar Cayce in looking for explanations. Cayce was a vital link, Thetford felt.[3] By September of '65 Helen had a premonition that something major was about to happen. The inner voice was appearing more and more.

Doctor Schucman finally phoned her boss, reporting that the inner voice would not leave her alone. He asked her what it was saying. "You're not going to believe me," she responded. Bill countered with "Try me." Helen announced, "It keeps saying, *This is a course in miracles. Please take notes.* What am I going to do?"[4] Dr. Bill Thetford encouraged her to take notes.

That night the voice came through loud and clear with the first words: *This is a course in miracles. It is a required course.* The atheistic scribe resisted but then followed her colleague's recommendation, skeptically doubting every word that came through. At first the inner dictation frightened her, but she went through with it anyway. This was in the fall of 1965. In seven years time, by 1973, the entire course was transcribed, resulting in a 622-page text and a 478-page workbook, as well as a short manual. Since then, the three-volume set has sold well over 500,000 copies. Years later her colleague, Dr. Thetford, described *A Course in Miracles* as "a spiritual document very closely related to the teachings of the non-dualistic Vedanta of the Hindu religion."[5] What was interesting about this was that the voice never divulged its identity. It stayed anonymous. Adherents of the course, however, have adopted Helen Schucman's hunch that the voice is really Jesus. It implies as much in the first pages of the course.

The emerging document produced by "the voice" was coherent and authoritative, but Schucman did not intellectually believe in its source. Should the dictation be broken at any point, when it was taken up again, hours or days later, it began exactly where it had broken off—like a computer modem, beginning again after a pause in protocol. A powerful intelligence was behind this event. Helen Schucman's biographer, Robert Skutch, observes with irony: "On the one hand, she resented the Voice, objected to taking down the material, was extremely fearful of the content and had to overcome great personal resistance, especially in the beginning stages, in order to continue. On the other hand, it never seriously occurred to her not to do it, even though she frequently was tremendously resentful of the often infuriating interference."[6] Skutch also observes: "Throughout the writing . . . the acute terror Helen felt at the beginning did gradually recede, but part of her mind simply never allowed her to get completely used to the idea of being a channel for the Voice."[7] It was only a matter of time before Helen Schucman surrendered herself to this unfolding revelation and became a believer.

When Dr. Schucman asked the voice why it was coming through her, it responded with the statement: "The world situation is worsening to an alarming degree. People all over the world are being called on to help, and are making their individual contributions as part of an overall prearranged plan. . . . Because of the acute emergency however, the usual slow, evolutionary process is being bypassed in what might best be described as a *'celestial speed-up.'* "[8] The coming changes were near, very near. World events meant that the crisis became a catalyst.

A Course in Miracles is not concerned with filling in the missing "bio" of Jesus. It is a spiritual teaching couched in Christian terms but giving them new cosmic meanings. As Dr. Thetford observed, it is essentially Vedanta. When Thetford gave the manuscript to Edgar Cayce's son, Hugh Lynn Cayce of the Association of Research and Enlightenment (A.R.E), Hugh Lynn became very encouraging. This was the same mystery Christos that his father, the famous psychic, had channeled.

Soon the guiding powers brought some key figures connected with the New Age movement into the lives of the two New York psychologists, and proposals for publication were well under way. The inner voice of Robert Skutch's wife, Judith, directed her to Helen Schucman. It knew about her inner voice. Judith's inner voice ordered her to commit to publishing the work before finances were even available.

Their foundation was already stretched to the limit in helping to fund ex-astronaut Edgar Mitchell's Institute of Noetic Sciences as well as Stanford Research Institute's breakthroughs in *remote viewing*.[9] When Judith Skutch first saw the manuscript she said to herself, "Finally . . . here's my map home."[10] In little time the Skutches published *A Course in Miracles*.

What new facets did it provide the cosmic Christ? None beyond a coherent supernaturally based document that itself was seen as a miracle and proof of higher guidance. Ironically, not far away in New Jersey, Seth had been dictating similar revelations through Jane Roberts.

The course is totally positive and totally reassuring— the kind of thing a self-described "mousy, anxiety-ridden" New York professional woman such as Dr. Helen Schucman needed for reassurance. It is a revelation that uses the Hindu concept of *maya* to dispel the threat of evil. Evil is an illusion, the projection of the mind. With enough positive thinking, it will disappear. In fact, we can reshape reality because we have the godlike power to govern reality through expanded consciousness because all that is, is spirit, and spirit alone. We get into trouble when we vacillate between the two modes of consciousness: the old and the new. If evil is not real, neither is any misguided sense of sin. In fact, as *A Course in Miracles* states, sin is the illusion that separates us from our own innate divinity, our own godhood. We are extensions of the "thought of God." So our natural inheritance is a state of pure love. The Hindu word for such cosmic bliss is *ananda*. One of the course's exercises in consciousness is to replace all fear and other such negative emotions with love.

Christ is our exemplar, model, and elder brother. But we are his equal, being already perfect like him. The course even claims that we are more powerful than Christ. Our manufactured illusions of sinfulness have made the world a prison for Christ. Thus we are the ones with the power to free Christ by perceiving the world in the higher mode—that is, free of all evil. The course encourages a person to say, "God himself is incomplete without me"[11]; and, "There is no difference between your will and God's."[12]

Clearly, if *A Course in Miracles* is right, Jesus is the most misunderstood figure in history. History for 2000 years has had it wrong, the church never even got off on the right foot, and the long-promised *paraclete*—the Holy Spirit, which was to guide the church through history—has not even managed to get through to Christians about their misguided understandings. They have uniformly—all of them—believed a counterfeit gospel for 2000 years. Christ's messianic act of sacrifice on the cross—that central historical fact of Christianity—was wasted blood and pain. In fact, he never even needed to come to earth if all he needed was a good channel, for there was no real sin to atone for, and our separation from God was just an illusion all along.

Of course, if matter is only spirit in high theatrical dress, then real history doesn't matter. If we wish hard enough, all the evils of the world will just go away! Just wish and meditate and concentrate, as they do in India where physical reality is just an illusion, and the illusion will improve—right? As we can see from India, consciousness has indeed overcome the evils of the world, for there is no travail, no suffering, no poverty and disease in India—right? Hindus have had three millennia to perform the grand experiment and reshape reality with their godlike feats of consciousness—behold. . . paradise on earth!

Yes, one must go to India and see how the millennial experiment has worked! Be amazed . . . and know that reality is merely an illusion of the mind. Walk through Calcutta and Old Delhi, as I used to, and perform the same feats of consciousness that I did. I reminded myself that it was only a test to take my mind off the reality of the perfection and bliss around me. Yes, the evils of the world were mere illusions that could be wished away. Prayer as mantra, and so on. Strangely, the harder I wished the more the evils didn't go away.

With such messages of hope coming from the cosmic Christ, one is tempted to quote the memorable words of Alfred E. Newman and say in all profundity, "What, me worry?" Or in the great words of Mr. Positive himself, Emille

Coue, echo: "Each day in every way I get better and better and better." Now look in the mirror and say it again, "Each day . . ."

Indeed, as the true mystical believer will tell you, the only real evil now is doubt, which prevents the miracle from happening. Something must be done with the doubters, for they are spoiling the harmony that the world is about to experience.

Who are the doubters? Among them are the orthodox Christians who do not recognize the new gospel coming from the cosmic Christ. They are still "hung up" over their carefully transmitted 2000-year-old canon that has survived the centuries intact. They claim it has already worked the miracle of grace upon their lives and does not need changing. They say they have encountered Christ personally, and when they read the New Testament, that it indeed describes the One whom they have encountered. Through the New Testament they claim that they have encountered the true historical person of Jesus Christ, and that he in no way resembles this new cosmic Christ others are channeling.

Between these two faiths the two paths, words, concepts, and traditions are at odds—irreconcilable odds. It is clear that something will have to give.

11

The Halls of Caricature

This was a day that I had dreaded facing.

Looming before me was a sight, a visage, too terrible to contemplate. It was a foreboding stone structure whose architecture carried the terrible essence out of which flowed the haunting memories of an event that blinds the mind in unspeakable paradox—an event such as a child being molested by a trusted parent and, in shock, being sealed into repeatedly reliving that event throughout life, forever crippled in soul by that event. I was near the concentrated essence of human evil, where in recreated images flowed the infinite sadness and outrage of a race. This event was only a stone's throw away in recent modern history. This was not distant ancient Rome. This was now.

I was standing before the Holocaust memorial—and multitudes of collective voices groaned through the rocks. Fittingly, it was a gray day in Jerusalem.

I was in Israel in the early spring of 1987, having just spent three weeks of exuberant exploration: I had witnessed wildflowers suddenly turn the fields and hills of Galilee into radiant canopies overnight. I had crossed the Sea of Galilee in silence as the sun burned away a strange gray mist and revealed stunning hills and mountains while the boat pulled into the port of Capernaum, its ancient synagogue standing as a reminder of an eternal moment. I had descended into the lush subtropical splendor of the River Jordan, traveled across the Negev, climbed Masada. Finally, I beheld the impressive sprawling Temple of Jerusalem from such vantage points as the souks of the Arab quarter to the Mount of Olives. But all the time there was a deep disquiet in my soul about the one dark reminder that lay ahead. I couldn't just lose myself in blissful ignorance. A terrible essence of history had been captured and bottled up for all the world to see.

In the Holocaust memorial I felt anguish and horror, as though caught in the middle of a Francis Bacon painting, as I walked down aisle after aisle. From picture to picture and in collected fragments oozed the terrible memories of Dachau, Bergen-Belsen, Auschwitz, Buchenwald and other concentration camps. Hitler had called it "the final solution." It involved gassing hordes of Jewish people with zyklon-b, performing shooting-squad mass executions of others, and torturing more people than you would care to count—many in the name of medical experiments. People with sensitive, intelligent faces stared out of pictures in pained bewilderment.

The Jews were a people whose ancient heritage perhaps made them a little different, but who were nevertheless the progenitors of countless historical giants from Einstein to Tolstoy, and Karl Marx to Sigmund Freud. As I moved silently and sadly through the museum, I studied face after face and I was haunted. There was Anne Frank in her pretty loneliness, a poet here, a violinist there. I felt it in my pores—a tragic, haunting melody. Here was a people who had wandered through an eternal diaspora as though searching for their soul, adapting here, adapting there—from high German culture to the ghettos of Warsaw. It was just a stone's throw away . . . a mere 40 years ago in modern history when it all happened—a systematic campaign to kill Jews.

Then there were the halls of caricature. Faded newspaper illustrations and cartoons and other captioned drawings lined the walls of a long exhibit. It represented the public opinion machinery of Germany where images of Jews were portrayed. The media, literature, newspapers, and textbooks wove a uniform theme, skewing Jewish faces into grotesque caricatures. The worst racial characteristics were exaggerated into deformed, treacherous, conspiratorial, hate-filled, arrogant faces. Some of it represented black humor, demonic humor.

In the halls of caricature, illustrated children's books depicted Jews as aliens who had infiltrated German culture, with no intention of fitting in, whose secret intention was to take over. Wealthy merchandisers, whose eyes were on acquiring and controlling wider domains, stared out from hidden vantage points. In other drawings, wealthy Jewish lenders ejected honest and hard-working Germans from their homes should they be late in their mortgage payments. They were as merciless as Shakespeare's portrait of the merchant of Venice. One picture series that I stared at for a long time, from some book or another, pictured a large, rotund, evil-eyed, bearded Jewish man with a hook nose and thick glasses following and then exposing himself to ("flashing") a helpless and innocent nine-year-old girl. He then abducted and raped her, getting rid of the evidence by murdering her and hiding her body. Quotes from Hitler's *Mein Kampf* put the blame for prostitution and immorality in Germany squarely on the shoulders of Jewish conspirators who wanted to wreck the moral fiber of the German people. Jews were depicted as an evil race full of hidden depravities.

When these images had gained permission from German society to emerge, they foreshadowed the coming persecution. They were a tool for blaming the collective ills of the German people onto a convenient scapegoat—in this case, a people who were "different."

The end result of this propaganda campaign of hate could be seen in black-and-white photographs of bone-thin bodies lying in heaps, like bundled wheat, waiting to be bulldozed into quarry-sized pits. Wave after wave of people were lined against walls and machine-gunned, while in the background chimneys belched the black smoke of their cremated bodies. Massive ovens were burning the evidence. These were scenes out of Hieronymous Bosch—grotesque, amazing. You wonder about the naive arrogance of the self-appointed cognoscenti of today who unilaterally affirm human goodness, forget history, and scorn those who might pinpoint the reality of human evils. Voices of peace on earth, they thrust open the doors of blind permissiveness and social experimentation without heed to the past, saying that there is no such thing as evil.

Today a wide range of "in" voices posture with an all-knowing arrogance as they proclaim the new dictums: Let the youth try pot and homosexuality. Let third graders learn about the occult. Let the youth of today overturn any and all institutions and traditions that have been around for millennia. Marriage is passé, so let's experiment with new alternatives. Let's switch sex roles. But don't inhibit human freedoms, for that is the only evil. Let's even open the door for a little healthy anarchy. Forget the Holocaust; forget the long history of human evils. The only freedoms these liberal voices would deny are those of disagreeing religious groups—these are the new bad guys. Ironically, if I can be quite pointed for purposes of example, one of the amazing things is that some of these permissive voices are Jewish! Though some are doing their level best to keep the Holocaust from ever repeating, others appear to be denying evil. With the latter, one should not be surprised, for this very defense mechanism appears daily in a thousand contexts: from ordinary people to such extreme examples as multiple personalities who cannot handle the ambiguity of evil, and so partition their nature.

Real evil is so terrible and threatening a void that to many it must be closed out and unmade, lest the mind go mad. It is too terrible to look at directly. When the prophets of Israel reminded the people of their folly and how it would summon the reality of evil and cause dire consequences, they scorned the warning. Such is the response of "enlightened" people of today who say, "Surely *that* cannot be real. We are enlightened, civilized folk and we will not entertain such things." Tangible evil implies a side to reality that people do not want to know. Few wish to face the implications of what it means if this is a part of reality. It is easier to remake the universe, to just think evil away.

Unfortunately, history could repeat itself. In another form the same evils of 40 years ago could return. The collective machinery of civilization could yet arbitrarily turn against some group, conveniently scapegoating them. Is the human race really less capable of evil than it was 40 years ago? Have we "evolved" so much in a generation or two as to have changed our fundamental human nature? Is that what the daily headlines show us, that we have changed as a race? Is that what we have concluded after viewing recent history from the pogroms of Russia where more than 60 million resisters were purged (many times the number murdered in the Holocaust) to recent Los Angeles gang slayings, cocaine wars, terrorism, and so on? In reality we must ask whether a campaign of image and innuendo could start up again, directed against those who don't go along with the consensus. Recent history resounds with a loud "yes." Depending upon the consensus, there are "in" groups and "out" groups. The consensus can easily change, as it has numerous times.

Nowadays in America, appropriately due to this recent "embarrassment" of history known as the Holocaust, we live in a time of pin-drop sensitivity to any discussion concerning Jews or Jewishness. This is such a taboo subject that any statement suggesting less than full-hearted support for Jews is instantly seized upon as being potentially anti-Semitic. The Jewish people are in an era of grace. They are above reproach— no ill dare be imputed to them. Reminders of their victimization are so great that never again will anything conspiratorial be imputed against them. The wrong public innuendo gets the full ire of the media, the ACLU, civil rights lawyers, the Antidefamation League, as well as other groups. Yet Jews are honest about their own human vulnerabilities and perhaps feel uneasy about "too much grace," for again it may mean being singled out as "different."

But if they are experiencing a time of grace now, as are other "minorities" such as homosexuals, women (if you can call them a minority), Hispanics, and so on, it seems to be open season on other convenient groups who are now seen as culpable for society's ills. Latitude offered one group does not stretch over to another, because they may not have experienced the same victimization and oppression level. That seems to be the criterion of special privilege: a history of past oppression—namely, oppression by someone else! Those who are viewed as previous oppressors are often candidates for becoming the newly oppressed. The grand cycle continues!

Increasingly, there are mounting attacks on Christians and Christian character—it is open season. This condition is like the creed in George Orwell's *Animal Farm* that says, "All are equal, but some are more equal than others." Strangely enough, it is a standard that we see applied selectively, as though some deserve special favor over others. People forget that this very condition might have helped bring about earlier instances of dislike between groups. Perhaps we are dealing with a sad fact of human nature.

Without doubt, if I were Jewish and had relatives who had died in the Holocaust, then when I detected any social currents mounting up that could start some of the same dreaded old prejudices, I would try to anticipate and head them off. I would protest, voice my views, use the media, and so on. That sort of well-warranted hypersensitivity is only normal. One learns to smell out potential trouble. That would also explain the perceived threat of Christian "right-wing" fundamentalist politics to Jewish groups who see embodied in them the possibility of a new fascism.

So here is the result: Several well-known Christian leaders are now on the receiving end of images and innuendo in the academy and the media. If "minority members" such as Professor Allan Dershowitz of the Harvard Law School, or Arthur Miller, another Harvard law professor, are on Ted Koppel's "Nightline," they are acutely sensitive to any number of civil rights, such as the rights of gays or the rights of vendors to carry all manner of pornography. But they cannot resist masterfully caricaturing Jerry Falwell through innuendo. It might come as a quick, offhanded reference, but there it is, as they use the full force of the academic and intellectual mystique of their office—they are, after all, Harvard law professors. They get equally emotional about other perceived threats, so there is almost a self-righteous outrage as these professors of law address feminist issues, women's rights, and public school prayer and why it should be banned. The audience tacitly absorbs what is acceptable, what is "in," dazzled in part by their brilliance, by their articulation and ability to frame thoughts and opinions.

Indeed, Dershowitz and Miller are on the forefront of fashioning what is acceptable legal opinion, thus shaping the future of the nation. With some, I imagine, this is almost a messianic task. Perhaps their vision is a safe secular state that is fully pluralistic, even "rabidly" pluralistic, if I might speak in irony. In ways I can identify with them supremely.

I am merely trying to reveal what may be some unanticipated outcomes. The downside to this is that Christians are now on the receiving end of liberal scapegoating. Another fact is that some of them deserve it, and that complicates the problem. There have been men representing Christianity in the media before the world who have been less than exemplary in every domain. They have caricatured the Christian faith. The backlash will be a rising mood of public contempt on several fronts.

Jesse Jackson will never be allowed to forget his anti-Semitic comment about New York City, calling it "Hymie Town." Can you imagine this level of concentrated outrage if some noted figure called Greenville, South Carolina, "Fundie Town"? No, not at all. It is almost to be expected. No one would blink an eye. Again, to repeat an earlier observation, are we dealing with arbitrary classes of privilege? If so, are they based on some arbitrary standard? If the "outs" are now "ins," by definition those that were "in" are being defined as "outs," and so continues the polarization. This can mean trouble because arbitrary tides can shift: That is my point.

Scapegoating is an ugly phenomenon. Psychiatrist Scott Peck deals with the harm it can wreak on individual lives in his book *People of the Lie*. Scapegoating is a dishonest way of dealing with the problem of evil. The common pattern is for two parents to scapegoat all their problems onto one child whose inner burden becomes intolerable and who winds up dysfunctional in life. On a broader level, when there are evils in history, some individual or group often ends up taking the blame. For Hitler, it was the Jews. With feminists, it's now men.

ANTI-SEX LEAGUES

The human tendency for an easy way out is to scapegoat. We see this in hardcore feminist doctrine where women are portrayed as having been "oppressed victims" from millennia of male rule and patriarchy. As victims they can do no wrong. They are above reproach. They are gentle victims of male barbarism, and obviously society's ills are from men's misgoverning of the affairs of the world. (Only a partial truth.) Today's evils thus are proof that men failed and are not cut out for the task. Implicit in this is that women would have done a far better job. They would have created utopia if given the chance. The new myth is this: Women's superior "caringness," "nurturingness," and "feminine intuition and attunement to earth rhythms" would never have allowed war or other forms of oppression.

So who is the source of history's evils? "Male chauvinist pigs" (See—they are free to name-call!), especially as embodied in masculine males. The safer, more tolerable men are the more feminized or effete males. They will go along with the feminist program, unlike the old-fashioned John Wayne types who are dangerous and will never change. Indeed, as a major Ivy League seminary deducted in a required theology class, the cause of societal evil can be boiled down to the patriarchal system, especially as seen with white men who are "chronic oppressors." The assistant professor of theology was one of the more nonthreatening effete males who disdained classic male traits and could be seen championing so many of today's gentler causes. He too had his own nonthreatening and gentle way about him as he glided harmlessly across campus— everybody's friend, especially to irate women who were forever vigilant for signs of threatening male traits. One gets the feeling that if these hyper-feminist women got control of the police, army, air force, and government, they would imprison any male whose attitude they found offensive. If it were possible outside of fantasy, in prison would be the founders of the nation, the framers of the Constitution, and 200 years of soldiers who have defended America's freedom. All but "safe" androgynous males would be put out of society's view. Enter the new ideal: feminist matriarchal culture.

Who in the name of the new fair-mindedness is being singled out? White males. Not just that, but white conservative Christian males. Show any number of groups a picture of Jerry Falwell, and he is hated. They jeer and scorn. He represents the strong, traditional, old-fashioned male who believes in God, country, and family with the man at the head of the family. Are we seeing shades of the new Holocaust memorial? I can see the halls of caricature: news photos of Jerry Falwell and other white males being shot and imprisoned; school books portraying drunk, irresponsible white male fathers leering at their young daughters and ready to molest them; white males abusing their wives repeatedly, etc. Creeping images are almost getting to this point, anyway.

The Christian academy has taken up the women's agenda. Yale started once as a divinity school, so did Harvard, and so did Princeton. These three schools have shaped the denominational church in America. Virtually every week the Ivy League's divinity schools and seminary host women's consciousness-raising events. It is their own tireless round of reminders of their own oppression. There are talks and films about wife abuse, films and seminars on domestic violence, films and seminars on fathers and stepfathers molesting their daughters. The family is a collapsing and inappropriate institution that must change or be abolished. There are seminars and planning sessions on totally egalitarian marriages. It should be a world of emasculated men submitting to assertive women. In such a world the gay caucus can announce homosexuality as the new virtue. It will be a golden age of lesbianism and homosexuality and perhaps the banning of such evils as marriage. God forbid that we ever see an era like "Little House on the Prairie" again!

There is a new ideal of androgyny. Self-described "minorities" (gay-lesbian task forces, etc.) have propounded this new ideal as the merging of male and female into one in which sexual differences would be minimized. Men would glory in their effeminacy, and women would become pseudomales. So many butch women have defaced what little genuine femininity they might have had. A British journalist described them as blockish or chunky, waddling in potato-sack dresses or trousers, with octagonal glasses and butch haircuts. To him nothing uglier or more unattractive to a normal man was conceivable. The allies of these women have become the whispering, effeminate males who are either attracted to other men or who have become ashamed of maleness and who have conceded defeat to the feminist and lesbian causes. Undoubtedly, androgyny in the future will further increase the split and alienation between the sexes. And this is what many homosexuals want! It is quite a campaign of recruitment and social change.

Times have changed. In the sixties I went to Franco Zeffirelli's movie *Romeo and Juliet*. I left with tears flowing down my face as I rode my motorcycle out into the Virginia countryside. I was overwhelmed by my longing for the beauty of the truly feminine, that allure that feminine women possess. When I fell in love in those days, I really fell in love. Girls from Hollins and Sweetbriar colleges with their pretty dresses and long hair would show up for dances at the University of Virginia and the attraction I felt was like a huge magnet. Girls in that era treasured the mystique of their femininity. I long to see such women again.

Let me engage in overstatement: Instead of lithe and feminine Olivia Hussey at 19 playing Juliet with her vulnerable eyes and beautiful face, we have "Ms. Betsy Gombler" waddling across the screen announcing her nonnegotiables to Romeo in that fascinating voice that some of them have (an imitation of the male voice just reaching puberty—not yet deep, but trying hard). Call it *Romeo and Ms. Gombler*, today's adjustment to an old story. Perhaps George Orwell was indeed a prophet of all these things with his "antisex league." With no opposites, there is no attraction—at least this is true between the sexes. When feminist linguists adjust all the great works of literature to their satisfaction, maybe they can insert into Shakespeare's great work of genius their own inclusive language as well as the new women's ideal, Juliet replaced by the androgynous person perhaps known as "Person 1" in the play.

On April 17, 1988, *The San Francisco Chronicle* reprinted a recent news story from *The New York Times* by Timothy Egan that highlights a significant national issue: the changing roles of women and the role of university campuses in this change. The article reported: "When Pete Schaub could not get into a crowded business course at the University of Washington last quarter, he signed up for an introductory class in women's studies, thinking he might learn something about feminism. What he learned was that when he repeatedly challenged course assumptions in class, he soon became the focus of the class itself. . . . Schaub said [about the class instructors], 'They ardently boast of lesbianism and deliver shallow sermons on socialism while making hate-breeding statements about men.' " He was dismissed by the two women instructors.

Schaub described his experience in this women's-study class: "But from the first day on, they started in about how all men are wife-beaters and child molesters and how the traditional American family, with a mom and a dad, doesn't work. . . . They classified everything I had to say as racist or sexist. Where's the freedom of inquiry?" A picture of a handsome, muscular blond athlete accompanied the article. Schaub, 20 years ago, would have been pursued by another generation of women in another way. He looks like an all-American football star at six-foot-one and 220 pounds. But he said that his size and business major made him the target of "everything that's wrong with men." Perhaps if he had been an effete ally and blended in, Schaub would have been tolerated. There are women's courses like this at every university in America, almost without exception. Invariably, only women attend them, and invariably, they start to change. Meanwhile, there is a new trend. Some men are flying to Asia to get mates to whom they are attracted—feminine women who want to be wives.

A backlash of male hostility could easily happen sooner or later. Things could get ugly. This might in turn justify the legal machinery of "the state" in defining the confines of male and female roles and what is acceptable. The State will "be forced" to monitor individual lives even more closely. There may even be legally enforceable code numbers for gender-related behavior, creating a gray conformity—premonitions again of Orwell's "antisex league." Many feminists would love to provoke some form of legal intervention upon men, where men's maleness would be curtailed. This trend is already happening as wife-abuse cases gain public airing. A case is quietly being built. There might come a genetic and cultural solution to manliness.

FROM GRIEVANCE TO CARICATURE

There is no question that women have legitimate grievances against male abuse. Fathers *can* be dictators, degrading their wives and hurting their daughters. Husbands can and do get drunk. Some even beat up their wives. Men (a small minority of them) can and do rape women. Some fellows will take out a girl, have sex with her, then leave her. Again, they represent some men. Life is full of heartbreaking examples; and indeed, mistreatment between men and women seems to be happening more as families fare worse. One expression for this is human depravity. There is no question that such abuse is wrong, but sometimes such instances can be used for propaganda with radical ends in view.

For example, imagine you are a college girl going to the campus women's center run by older women. Most universities have them. There are no men's centers. Women's solidarity is in view. The center shows an endless round of films and seminars on domestic violence and wife abuse, then films on fathers molesting daughters. After a while, your only perception of men will be a reductionistic stereotype that denies all differences among men as individuals. Suddenly all men will seem almost biologically predetermined to rape and abuse women. Marrying one of them would be like marrying a wild animal.

If the young college girl in question is truly hurting inside from a dysfunctional family, perhaps a remote or alcoholic parent, then she is even more vulnerable. But rather than being helped, in the long run she will be more alienated and angry. Women's groups use a legitimate argument that women are abused, then they engage in overkill. They fail to show the

20-to-1 other instances of homes in which men do *not* abuse women for each one they show that is abusive.

After this "consciousness-raising" process at the women's center, the average college girl will harbor such anger that her chances of a workable marriage are further lessened. If the man is less than perfect, it is almost doomed—especially if he has some anger of his own. The woman is now trigger-sensitive about male abuses and on the lookout for infractions. Rather than exhibiting trust, the relationship will be based on acute suspicion. The resolve, loyalty, and commitment that held together marriages of the old order have virtually evaporated from modern relationships, while polarizing alienation fares ever worse. It is a self-fulfilling prophecy.

"Consciousness-raising" or indoctrination? Women's centers do not show films and seminars about men as victims of women, such as men who are married for their money or manipulated for selfish ends, or where alluring women set one man up after another "for the kill." They do not show cases where a man's intimate vulnerability is betrayed, when he has opened up his heart to a woman he has trusted who then turns this against him to undermine and destroy him. To think that women cannot abuse men is pure blindness. No one gets out of this unscathed.

When women's groups recite the long litany of male inadequacies and abuses, the reality of such things cannot be repudiated, merely the editorial slant and solution they offer. Often the major women's voices are antimale and antifamily. Often they come from the lesbian viewpoint. Their solution is a feminist-controlled world, or lesbian marriages, or marriages with "changed" men. But this begs another deeper issue. Are women less bent than men, or are their dark sides merely expressed differently, as many ex-lesbians have admitted. A woman may not necessarily be physically violent with another woman, but she can be coercive, manipulative, treacherous, and jealous. She can oppress her fellow sisters as much as the most abusive of men. To use all the propaganda of feminist "consciousness-raising" to jettison the heterosexual family relationship, especially the traditional family, is to enter a greater unknown where the evils of abuse are by no means eliminated.

Let us ask the obvious: Would a mass reversal of sex roles have consequences upon society? Yes, most likely terminal ones, as would the final destruction of all evidences of monotheism. People know intuitively that there is a deep good to a loving, whole family. Latchkey kids and kids in homes torn by strife and divorce hunger for the ideal of the harmonious, integrated family as they look longingly at "Little House on the Prairie," "Father Knows Best," and "The Cosby Show." They see in a workable heirarchy a chance for love to operate. Dad is truly attracted to and protective of Mom; she wants to please him and is fulfilled. They get along, and they love their kids. They are not at war, but have joined in commitment to an ideal of love, mutual need, and clear understanding that their created differences are to be treasured!

The family is very much a part of the old world order, as are traditional roles of men and women whose differences are seen as being intentionally created by God. Different roles between the sexes are also seen as God-ordained. This is critical in the case of the family. A healthy Christian community will not be able to breathe in the kind of atmosphere the feminist/minority agenda has in mind.

THE CHRISTIAN HOLOCAUST MEMORIAL

Perhaps someday the entranceway to the Christian Holocaust memorial will chronicle "The Media, The Christian Money Changers, and The Televangelists." We will be painfully reminded of the fact that the public mind for decades was treated to an escalating spectacle, a rampaging burlesque. This left a bad taste in everybody's mouth, especially among nonbelievers who obviously showed more discernment than the more simpleminded believers who "will believe in anything if they believe in this."

On the one hand, as we saw with the Jewish Holocaust memorial, we will see the propaganda machinery of the collective at work. The movie industry will have spent years portraying Christians as bland, characterless wimps;

wild-eyed fanatics; small-minded bigots; and madmen who hear God's voice in their heads. There will be those cameo westerns—suddenly it is "The Christians." Here they are: wild-eyed, prejudiced hate-mongers ready to lynch and kill anyone who is not like them. In another film the Christians are superstitious rednecks, quoting King James Scripture in a drawl and seeing some prophecy come true in the full moon. They are ready to oppose the devil with guns and knives. More often than not, they will oppress women and minorities. If it is a program on the Salem witch trials, it is devils in the women that cause the Puritan divines to torture them endlessly. Innocent victims are killed while men with big buckles and hats rant and rave about demons.

If it is a father-and-daughter movie theme, he is cold, distant, suspicious, and unloving as his inflexible beliefs try to pin down her youthful soul which is crushed by his bigoted fanaticism. When the two have an encounter, he slaps her and calls her a whore. If her boyfriend shows up, he glares at him, shotgun in hand, while standing in the door in bib overalls held up by suspenders. Evening meals are oppressive events as the father mutters some archaic prayer of grace, while the other family members bow their heads in hushed fear. You can sense it: *Don't trigger him off; he might start executing God's judgment.* He is not loving, sympathetic, and understanding, embodying the true graces of the New Testament, but he is severe and accusatory. He represents the Christian man. If Hollywood had spent this much effort portraying Jews and Jewish families in this light, the outrage and litigation would be beyond belief. The Antidefamation League would have such films shut down on opening night.

At the same time, in the Christian Holocaust museum we would see how the national media biased public opinion. News programs would go out of their way to pinpoint embarrassing, deviant, and cultish fundamentalist incidents of any and all variety. Nothing would ever be shown in a positive light. A miniseries on Christian parents would portray them praying to God to heal their son who has diabetes. Naturally, God is never reachable and the parents finally withhold the insulin needle "in faith" while the boy dies. The picture portrays the tension between primitive superstition and a modern world. Ironically, two channels up the dial there might be a "positive" program about channelers and crystals and their healing effects, but that is unbiased and open-minded. Movies and the media, in the hands of the few, become irresistible propaganda tools over the minds of the many—the simple masses—and can create likes and dislikes by turning an image or innuendo.

Meanwhile, the world will have been treated to hundreds of thousands of television hours of believers who gloried in their own mediocrity or, in the world's eyes, boasted about their inferiority in everything as though it were a virtue. The public audience would see self-appointed representatives of Christianity on television who made a mockery of their so-called religion by their vulgarity; flippancy; and lack of awe, dignity, and integrity. When the personal lives of these media stars became revealed through scandal, the Christian faith was even more burlesqued as the world saw lifestyles no more worthy of merit than a scene out of "Dynasty." In the end this made Christianity a laughingstock of the world. One is reminded of the old aphorism, "With friends like that, who needs enemies!"

The non-Christian observes to the Christian, "If you have been so undiscerning and naive as to believe in that ranting idiot on the TV—a used-car salesman in polyester—then this Jesus of yours is to be equally doubted. By default, that Savior you believe in is no better than the vulgar idiot manipulating money out of you on the TV. You have shown blind judgment about the one on TV; why should I consider the one you have never even seen—this Jesus of yours! Neither you nor your Savior is to be taken seriously." It is guilt by association.

The money changers have done their job well. They have not attracted the world to Christ; they have made him a point of supreme derision. Not only that, but they have given all Christians a bad name. The noble sacrifices of 10,000 pious missionaries on the field are plowed under the rubble of a single garish mansion. The Jim-and-Tammy mansion, with its 2000-dollar air-conditioned doghouse and gold faucets in Hee-Haw city, auctioned off by escalating lewdness, is dragged over 10,000 missionary huts in jungles and villages. The world remembers the ridiculous and tasteless spending binges of the Bakkers, as they drew the world's eye to themselves. God in the Old Testament warned the Jews that his name would become scorned and jeered at by the unbelieving pagan world because of their own bad example.

Christians have become so simpleminded these days as to be blown around by circus sideshow doctrines that they inflict on the world. The world looks on as mass rallies claim prosperity. They think God will give them mansions and pink Cadillacs with rhinestones if they pray with enough fervency. There they are on TV: gobbling away, hands outstretched, eyes closed, and asking God for goodies. Kenneth Copeland, who claims to be a god, uses the words of Willow, telling a stadium audience that if they believe enough, they can have anything. The non-Christian skeptic looks on as these people confirm his suspicion about their powers of judgment. Here are people who cannot connect the fact that the very Christ they proclaim to follow told his followers that if he had been persecuted, so would they; if he had no place to lay his head, nor would they; if he had suffered hardship, so would they. They were told again and again that they would have their own crosses to bare—crosses, not Cadillacs. To the world these people are junk-food Christians.

The world turns on the TV set and looks on incredulously. On one channel we have Oral Roberts in his prayer tower telling "the faithful" that if they don't send in ten million dollars in the next few months God will take him home. Oral is crying on TV. The next shot is the faithful in tears. God's going to give Oral the death sentence if they don't cough up the cash. God is bankrupt is one implication. The other is that he is not too loving with his so-called servants; he kills them punitively for things over which they have no control. It is blackmail, extortion, a lie. The world knows it, and these people look like the fools that they truly are—right on national TV. A genius could not invent a more devastating scenario. It is a scandal for Christ, who never asked for money but made a point of warning of the dangers of the role of money. Paul the apostle never asked for money for himself—that is why he made tents. He did not forbid Christians to let their needs be known to other Christians, but this was to be done in private, in the family—not in a theater-in-the-round.

Paul warned the Ephesian elders at Miletus to look out for signs revealing false brethren, wolves in sheep's clothing—signs such as we see in empire building and private lust binges. If God has not sanctioned such ministries as we see embodied in these televangelists, who has? The blind and ignorant people who will believe anything? Those who don't believe?

An atheistic banker, hostile to Christianity, might do well to fund some outrageous and bogus ministers to represent and caricature before the world the faith he hated. He would not bankroll hero figures; he would bankroll antiheroes: vulgar, manipulative, crude, uneducated men without any social graces or dignity. He would bankroll the Jim Bakkers, Robert Tiltons, Ernest Angleys, and practically every other televangelist you see on TV—men in polyester leisure suits with phony mouth movements, unnatural and affected voices, who beg for money in the name of Christ. He would bankroll losers, not winners. This principle should be obvious in the world of corporate accounts where Wall Street advertisers go for the cream of the crop of the beautiful people—poised, healthy, articulate, radiantly good-looking people—to represent their products. Winners, not losers.

A billionaire who despised Christianity would never bankroll someone like Eric Lidell—the faithful, humble, intelligent track star from the University of Edinburgh who became a Scottish missionary and Olympic champion; the man whose life story was so stunningly portrayed in the academy-award-winning film *Chariots of Fire*. He would never bankroll a good-looking, self-sacrificing, principled believer, a man of character and humility who had a Cambridge University education, to represent the faith. No, he would get someone half a grade lower than a hog farmer to auction away Christ like a farm animal. He would bankroll people with inferior minds, inferior dress, inferior faith, who would stand before all the world as the clowns of Christ, laughable in the world's eyes. They would suffer persecution, but not because of their nobility of character or faithfulness to the gospel—but for the opposite reason. They would justify themselves with the Scripture that "God has chosen the weak to shame the wise," and then manipulate their followers with this, forgetting that God also chose Paul, Apollos, and Augustine—some of the greatest minds in the ancient world.

Perhaps the Christian Holocaust memorial will show that after the spate of scandals the faithful were in no way sobered by how easily they had been duped by their own appalling lack of discernment. They would blame God or the con artists, never themselves for poor judgment, poor taste, or their own shoddy knowledge of the true historical faith. Perhaps some future chronicle will show that what made them fall away from the Christian faith en masse was their own doubt when God refused to answer their prayers of positive confession for houses and Cadillacs.

When the social climate turned against them, when they were singled out by a hostile society at large, they just blended in with the woodwork. They had neither the guts nor the character to stand up. They had gotten aboard the train because it looked so inviting: the good life here and now for any and all. They did it for their own needs at the time. Being pragmatists, when dial-a-prayer did not work, they readily turned to something else.

These disillusioned followers would join the great apostasy, while God was held in derision by the unbelieving world whose only visions of Christians were the carnival sideshows on television and in the news. In the end most everybody would opt for the cosmic Christ. It was just plain easier, that's all.

12

Erasing God from the Universe

The course of the world has followed an amazing track. Unless this is seen in its great perspective, it loses significance.

What must be retraced are things that took place in a rather massive arena: the arena of world thought. Then we can see precisely why things have turned out the way they have, and we will have some clear indications of where things will be going. It didn't suddenly all magically happen. It has been centuries in the making.

Some of the most powerful minds in history have, wittingly and unwittingly, been caught in a chess game that for centuries has squeezed them slowly into a checkmate. It started out as a confident spree to arrive at philosophical certainty as to what the human mind could know. It ended up with the players not certain that they could even know their own names. One can easily imagine that this is what it would be like to play chess with or debate an immortal being such as Satan, whose IQ and experience are astronomically vast compared to our mortal limitations. It would take forever to see what lay behind every innuendo of thought and movement.

Philosophy over the centuries, has taken away man's certainty as to what can be truly known and what the nature of reality is. It has emptied our pockets and our minds. We are reminded of the famous sign outside the auditiorium of the Indian superguru Rajneesh, "Leave your minds and your sandals here." The rest of the human race has been like onlookers in a vast stadium looking down at the chessboard in the center of the field and believing their whole fate hangs on every chess move. The onlookers are powerless as they watch the game, knowing they are not clever enough themselves to figure out the next move. They are captives in a deadly serious game.

So far, philosophy is still searching for a clever rejoinder to the vast questions it has encountered in its search. Philosophy itself has been "waiting for Godot." It has become a player in the theater of the absurd.

Not only has there been a long-term chess game that the philosophers have been playing over the centuries, but each individual philosopher (or team player) has been tempted by lesser games and wagers that are quickly settled. We find that from David Hume on, some of the old sidewalk tricks have worked on some of history's greatest minds. The game looks easy for the confident intellectual at first glance. An ordinary street sleight-of-hand artist has a pea and three cups. He quickly switches them around. Famed British empiricist David Hume points to cup number three to reveal the pea. The pavement artist grins as he lifts the cup—behold, the pea is not there. It is under cup number two. Now consider the weight of David Hume's decision about where the pea is if all of civilization hangs on his decision. It would go from a lighthearted challenge to a distended moment of unspeakable horror. If Hume's mind fails to detect its location, all of history feels the consequences. This is not too far from what has been going on between the human race and the participants in the philosophical inquiry as philosophers have been gambling with the truth, from petty wagers to long-term chess games.

Charting the course of philosophy and its effect on world history clearly shows that the thoughts written on the philosopher's table in one century can rule another century. Karl Marx's *Communist Manifesto* was written in the last century. Today—a century later—its philosophical view of reality governs the lives of two billion people. Russia, China, and other Marxist nations would not exist in the form they do today if Karl Marx had never existed and if no one had ever thought of communism.

Indeed, it has been ideas all along, primarily coming from "breakthroughs" in philosophy, which have dethroned one age and thrust up another, altering the course of civilization. Far from being an innocuous ivory-tower pastime, philosophy has changed civilizations in the most concrete ways. Marx borrowed from Hegel and Feuerback, and so on, back through history. Meanwhile, most of the citizens of a given age have often been unable to articulate the forces that mold their lives—the ideas that lie behind the spirit of the age—but these ideas stir their thoughts all the same. Those that shape history have chosen to believe the supreme wisdom of the philosophers' stone. From political leaders, intellectuals holding the seats of learning, and artists and novelists, the newest ideas begin to pervade society—and the influence spreads.

THE CRISIS

Our spiritual crisis in the West has its roots in the Age of Reason, that seventeenth-century period out of which emerged the rationalists and the empiricists. In the 1600's and 1700's, strains of humanistic, man-centered thought came together and flourished, producing a widespread change in assumptions about reality.

The Age of Reason started with the assumption that the mind of man was an all-sufficient, autonomous agent for comprehensively understanding human nature and reality. Incredibly, it was no more than a small roomful of men who brought in the Age of Reason. This minority asserted that human intelligence could comprehend man and the world with adequacy. This was quite a heady assumption given the limited experience of man with his small allotment of time and space. It is an ambitious project to try to logically disassemble and account for the cosmos. Such a task requires an overview that is more than humanly derived, but the challenge of the game created a heady confidence.

A group of thinkers known as the Continental Rationalists, composed of Descartes, Leibniz, and Spinoza, assumed on faith the mind's ability to function correctly, independent of any external guidelines for thought and independent of God's revelations about his creation. The mind could build a sound, unshakable system of thought, they felt, by deductive reasoning from simple premises, reinforced by truths retained from the biblical worldview from which they could borrow for the sake of convenience. These biblical absolutes, after all, ensured ultimate meaning behind their endeavor. Leibniz and Descartes were theists. They did not want to dethrone God after all; they merely wanted to secure his knowledge within the bounds of pure reason. So they placed all the biblical absolutes within the mind as "innate ideas" so they would be unassailably safe, in a category where no other chess pieces could "check" them with skepticism—or so it seemed.

Descartes began building his rational philosophy from a single seemingly unassailable truth: *Cogito, ergo sum* ("I think, therefore I am"). This was the single fact upon which no doubt could be shed. Having established man as the ultimate fact in the universe, and the only unshakable fact, he proceeded to "prove" God's existence as well as the existence of the external world. God and the created universe were being rendered dependent upon man for authentic existence.

Then another group of philosophers known as the British Empiricists took things a step further toward modernism. This group, composed of Locke, Berkeley, and Hume, denied the existence of the "innate ideas" held by the rationalists. All that man can know, they proposed, must originate in experience. All "abstract ideas" such as God or truth must derive from some sense impression in order to be noetically valid.

Of the three philosophers, only David Hume explored the implications of a pure empiricism with unremitting vigor. All that man can legitimately know from experience, Hume concluded, is a succession of sensations. Therefore, since things like God, one's personal identity, and the events of life are not immediate sense impressions like pain or color or size, we cannot know that they exist (because of this observation by Hume, the philosophical category of metaphysics was effectively shut down and abandoned). Man experiences only a succession of events which habit and memory lead him to connect together into various unifying experiences. Our experience has no necessary connections with the future; therefore, no reliable knowledge is possible by empirical observation derived from experience if it is true that there are no real, necessary connections between events.

What Hume was in fact saying was that just because the sun has risen every day for thousands of years gives us no warrant to predict it will come up again. Hume had just declared the death sentence on what philosophers call causality—the very foundation upon which modern science is founded. Connections between things and events perceived by sense impressions could no longer be made. You can imagine how this notion shrank the field of acceptable knowledge. The world reeled from this proclamation of David Hume. The result of Hume's analysis left man without possibility of significant knowledge, without self, in a world without substance or structure. The scientific community of the 1700's was thrown into an uproar because, granted Hume's initial premises (which they did not dispute), they could find no flaws in his thinking. For Hume, knowledge became only possible in the most limited sense. Yet for Hume the practical demands of daily life still had to be assumed. You still had to assume that the sun would come up, that water would flow out of the faucet, and so on.

William Barrett in *Irrational Man*, captures Hume's absurd dilemma when Hume "in a moment of acute skepticism, felt panicky in the solitude of his study and had to go out and join his friends in the billiard room in order to be reassured that the external world was really there."[1]

When Hume finished his empirical analysis, the very possibility of true scientific knowledge was in question. Immanuel Kant, shaken by Hume, sought to extract thinking from the impasse into which it had worked itself, and his solution laid the groundwork for thought in the nineteenth century. Kant worked the chess pieces into a tighter situation, even closer to a final entrapment.

Kant's revolutionary move was this: In order to rescue science and philosophy from skepticism while at the same time preserving humanistic assumptions, Kant removed the form and structure of reality from their precarious place in a problematic external world and established them within the mind of man. The patterns that science studies, the dynamic orderliness of nature which rewards the efforts of science, are not the result of habit and custom as David Hume had proposed. Instead, Kant now argued, this order originates in the mind of the observer. This subjective ordering process is the condition for perception itself. Kant called this "the transcendental unity of apperception" (T.U.A.). All of a sudden the mind contained the creative power which produces what we know as "reality." This had vast new implications that would send philosophy reeling in a whole new direction, paving the way for Hegel and his concept of the evolution of history—with beingness mystically growing in the universe—and for the Romantics, who would delight in this breakthrough.

Suddenly, Kant's move of T.U.A. philosophically and epistemologically threw open the door not only for a knowledge independent of God, but it opened the way for mysticism, monism, and the pursuit of the occult. The nature of the mind, Kant argued, is to order the indeterminate stuff of sensation so that it can be perceived or known. This ordering takes place before the experience is possible. Therefore time, space, and causality are not "out there" in a real world; they are extended from the subject's mind for the act of perception. Science is successful in its generalizations about the normal relations between objects of experience because these relations between objects of experience are established *a priori* by what Kant called the forms and categories of human understanding which allow objective experience to occur. What reality is, what "things in themselves" are, cannot therefore be known. What we "know" is made possible not by God, not by the mind's penetration of a real world, but by the mind's projections of what we can know upon an essentially unknowable world. Kant placed God, the soul, moral freedom, and the like in the realm of the unknowable "things in themselves." This conceptual framework became known as phenomenalism, a foundation stone within the German school of idealism.

Needless to say, these "breakthroughs" spilled over from the philosophy departments to the schools of theology in

Tübingen, Leiden, Berlin and the other German universities, paving the way for the nineteenth-century German higher criticisms of Julius Wellhausen, Harnack, Ritschl, and many others. In turn, the theological left-hand turns within these schools of theology had an immediate impact upon other centers of learning outside of Germany, as well as upon the entire German Lutheran church, putting all the traditionally accepted tenets of the faith into total upheaval. By the early twentieth century, it would be a totally toothless church, incapable of voicing moral comment as the National Socialist platform rose to power, bringing in Hitler. A few individuals like Bonhoeffer were rare exceptions within the church and the academy. By then such opposition as his, during the era of Bergen-Belsen, represented little more than a twig trying to hold back the waters of a broken dam.

Almost immediately, Kant's thoughts in Germany hit the international intellectual community. Samuel Coleridge, the nineteenth-century English poet, could now say that we half create, half receive the world, so that what man fabricates in perception cannot be separated from what is really there. Man knows only experience, not "things in themselves." Walt Whitman, an American poet and a contemporary of Coleridge, elaborated on this by saying that man is like a spider who spins the world that he knows out of himself. For the world as we know it, as Kant had said, is a construct of our minds.

But now there is a terrible problem that the original quest of Descartes and Leibniz could not have foreseen a century before Kant. If one reasons earnestly about religious questions from Kant's philosophic position, one can only arrive at an agonizing agnosticism because God has been structurally removed from any relationship to existence—he has been erased from the cosmos. Even if he does exist, in the Kantian system men cannot know him. Proceeding from such assumptions, faith can never be more than a blind, desperate leap into the unknown. Faith can never be biblical faith rooted on the evidence that what is out there is real. In biblical epistemology you don't need to keep proving to yourself the reality of the external universe. It is a given that it is created by God, therefore real, and therefore has a purpose.

So what did the world lose when modernism disposed of biblical epistemology? It was a priceless treasure. In the biblical worldview, the significance of individual life was guaranteed. Time and history were intelligible and real. The fact that the universe exists was explained in a way that allowed for sustained, intelligent inquiry because the vast patterned structures and dynamic energies of the universe were seen as an outgrowth of God's wise and sovereign purpose. Form and structure were real and not Kantian projections from the mind of man; rather, they were inherent in the reality of a knowable world. When Isaac Newton wrote *Principia Mathematica* in 1687 at Trinity College, Cambridge, he rested on an intellectual assurance that the cosmos was trustworthy, and that his deep Christian beliefs were in no disharmony at all with the scientific task. Newton could be assured that Christianity links the world of the rational to the spiritual. It shows the harmony and continuity of all knowledge. There were physical laws such as gravity, and there were moral laws, each affecting different domains of God's creation.

But as the knowledge of God became suppressed through philosophy, these given and obvious truths became philosophically problematic. A hundred years after Isaac Newton, David Hume's *Dialogues Concerning Natural Religion* would be released posthumously in 1778, while Kant released his *Critique of Pure Reason* in 1781. By the time Immanuel Kant took his final bow on the world stage, the chess game was in full swing with nobody able to stop it.

Kant's influence on the modern world was immense, and it is no exaggeration to say that he dominated the nineteenth century. Some scholars argue that the nineteenth and twentieth centuries are footnotes to Kant. His epistemology laid the groundwork for an artistic and intellectual response, known as the Romantic movement, which swept the Western world. The Romantics too would open some terrible new doors, the implications of which they would not fully realize until it was too late.

13

Letting Mr. Gumby Control the Universe

The Romantics were a group of influential avant-garde thinkers, poets, and artists of the nineteenth century who strongly felt the diminished portion of reality with which they were left. They were given a reductionism coming from the eighteenth century that was antimetaphysical. Its hard, natural determinism and unfeeling, soulless universe left them with an impoverished vision of life. The Romantics did not question the humanistic and naturalistic assumptions of the Enlightenment. They merely sought to reverse the tendency toward impersonality by asserting the value of private experience over and above what was mere scientific fact. Hume had shrunken the universe with his unyielding skepticism. Mystery was gone. Now Kant was giving the Romantics new room to breathe. They loved Kant's idea about the mind creating reality. Hegel's influence after Kant marked the era of a new optimism, but this solipsism had not only an up side, it had a downside as well.

By the time Nietzsche entered the philosopher's chair, he took Kant a step farther and held "mere scientific fact"— indeed, the scientific undertaking itself—in complete contempt. Nietzsche was the one to rub the implications of what had happened over the past centuries into the faces of his contemporaries. He bemoaned the desolating universe that he and his contemporaries had inherited from his predecessors. It was Nietzsche who declared "God is dead!" Then he proceeded to show the dire implications of what this meant. However, the Romantics still had not yet caught on. They had not yet detected the inevitable despair and nihilism that lay down the road for them, rendering meaningless every Romantic undertaking to celebrate life. No, they continued glorying in the hopes and pleasures of private experience, but this required tunnel vision.

The Romantics no longer needed to worry about a sovereign, transcendent, and moral God looking over their shoulders. They gloried in their initial freedom. Now they could go on a binge and taste all of life's little delicacies. The English Romantics from Coleridge to Carlyle were swept up in this celebratory frenzy. Soon it spread from them to America, where it was seized upon by the New England transcendentalists: Thoreau, Emerson, and Whitman. Thoreau was to assert in *Walden* that "The universe constantly and obediently answers our conceptions. . . . Let us spend our lives in conceiving them." Man can create the universe he so desires simply by revolutionizing his thinking, Thoreau observed, marking the early beginnings of "consciousness-raising."

Mysticism attached itself to the Romantic quest. To penetrate the secret world of "things in themselves" required an occult approach. Many adopted the attitude that since by definition the rational, causal structure of the world is an aspect of man's consciousness, the rational faculties were merely an obstacle to true knowledge. Penetration to the true essence of things required deep intuition, mystical mind states, or some meditative epiphany. Ecstatic self-absorption into a mystical oneness with or through nature—most obvious in Wordsworth, Shelley, and Whitman—had become an almost conventional form of religious experience.

Nature began to be regarded as somehow divine. It was a tabloid for the sacred experience. Pantheism crept in. By the time the first translations of Hindu and Buddhist texts were made in the nineteenth century, there was an immediate influence on Western minds. Walt Whitman applauded these new mystical breakthroughs in his celebrated poem "Song of Myself." Whitman announced to the world: "Divine am I inside and out, and I make holy whatever I touch or am touched from."

Whitman's fellow transcendentalist, Thoreau, celebrated the occult potential in man with the help of the recently translated Vendantist Hindu texts, saying, "I have read a Hindoo book." Then he reveals the new teaching: "So the Soul, from the circumstances in which it is placed, mistakes its own character, until the truth is revealed to it by some holy teacher, and then it knows itself to be Brahma (God)."[1] The teaching that the soul is God is pure pantheism.

The Romantic movement introduced pantheism as a result of Kant's thought, and with that came the effort to lay aside traditional conceptions of good and evil. These categories were seen as limitations upon human consciousness and its quest for unlimited experiences. Besides, "sin" was never a popular word among artists, intellectuals, and the avant-garde. Blake, the English mystic poet, called this project on which he was embarked the marriage of reason and hell.

Later on in the nineteenth century, the very terms "good and evil" were made irrelevant by persistent reductive analyses of experience. The most famous and influential of these came through the Englishman Walter Pater in his critical work *The Renaissance*. Pater sought to isolate value judgment from experience. He extracted the teeth from moral judgment by saying that "not the fruit of experience, but experience itself, is the end." He said that we should quicken ourselves by intensifying our experience. "To burn always with this hard, gem-like flame, to maintain this ecstasy, is success in life."[2]

Moral questions are irrelevant to Pater who says, "The theory or idea or system which requires of us the sacrifice of any part of this experience has no real claims upon us."[3] Truth of any sort has no reference here and no normative effect. Truth is not true but useful, as long as it serves our interests. Man's own experience is the god for whom all is sacrificed.

Soon D.H. Lawrence and a host of other Romantics became champions of the pursuit of novel experiences and new pleasures, with no reference to morality. There was now a radical freedom to explore what used to be called "evil." Hosts of Romantics entered the forbidden and the occult. Any number of them tried opium, hashish, and other drugs as they broke through one morality barrier after another. Strangely, there are always some inevitable connections between serious pursuit of the pleasure principle and the occult. The nosedive into nihilism would not come until some of these Romantics put down their opium pipes and, with the help of philosophers such as Nietzsche who had far more intellectual insight and penetration than they, would realize the implications of the sort of universe with which they were left. There was a downside to living in a "godless universe." A child running away from home may feel an initial elation with the first temporary burst of freedom. The day is spent exploring and doing the forbidden, but by nightfall a terrible fear and loneliness takes over—there is no meal for the empty stomach, or nice warm bed and parents to tuck him in. Perhaps for the first time he becomes aware of freezing rain, cold alleys, and threatening strangers on the street. It's a whole new world.

The Closing of the American Mind, a *New York Times* bestseller by a former Yale University professor, Alan Bloom, addresses in broad scale what has been going on culturally in America as a result of postmodern philosophy. Bloom reveals something very telling:

> There is now an entirely new language of good and evil, originating in an attempt to get "beyond good and evil" and preventing us from talking with any conviction about good and evil anymore. Even those who deplore our current moral condition do so in the very language that exemplifies that condition. The new language is that of value relativism, and it constitutes a change on our view of things moral and political as great as the one that took place when Christianity replaced Greek and Roman Paganism. A new language always reflects a new point of view, and the gradual unconscious popularization of new words, or of old words used in new ways, is a sure sign of a profound change in people's articulation of the world.[4]

Those who dove headlong into the experiential quest, like

Faust, by disposing of the categories of "good and evil" as arbitrary and no longer binding, landed in a far different universe from the universe created and sustained by an infinite, loving, and transcendent God. It was a universe in which anybody could sit at the controls, like a Palisades Park bumper-car ride. Indeed, now Mr. Gumby could control the universe. Suddenly the romantic joyride was entering the house of horrors, as such twentieth-century intellectuals as Camus and Celine contended with angst and despair. Sartre could claim that "man is a meaningless passion." Having God dethroned and replaced with some mediocrity is a grim idea indeed to an intellectual who still prizes excellence, to a mind still aware of individual differences and hierarchy. Now the throne was up for grabs, like a lottery. As Nietzsche said, supermen were needed to replace God. Looking over your standard democracy of candidates from Nietzsche's perspective, it was slim pickin's indeed. There were a lot of toothless peasants out there, grinning idiots who would take the world for a madman's roller-coaster ride; incompetents who couldn't even take a left-hand turn from an intersection into a parking lot without taking the side off someone's car.

But Nietzsche's supermen, wherever they might be, look ridiculous in the role of pretenders to the throne which God has supposedly vacated. Humorous hyperbole here does not work, so vast are the differences between the size of the task and the participants. It vastly dwarfs, say, a man pitting the strength of his left arm against a nuclear aircraft carrier in a pushing contest. It enters the full incongruity of the absurd and, true to form, it was the absurd which became a literary genre of the nihilists and the existentialists.

There are insurmountable problems with the great philosophical quest to understand all of reality while declaring whether or not God exists, when the players in the game are merely men, merely mortals. If there is a purpose behind the cosmos, it is too vast for us to discover or comprehend by our own efforts. As we attempt this task from our own little square mile of land, limited by our mortality—a few sparse years—it seems like an ant trying to comprehend the rich complexity of a Beethoven symphony, or an ant walking over complex characters written on paper—characters that are in fact advanced mathematical equations in celestial mechanics. Such abstract calculations are infinitely beyond the ant's capacity. Yet the ant analogy doesn't approach the gulf of capacity between men and this philosophical quest, which only God is capable of performing. It would require a mind greater than the cosmos to reveal its true purpose to us. An intelligence of any less magnitude would not be equipped to provide an ultimate answer. Without revelation, we are hopelessly blind. There is no other way around this dilemma.

Yet in the Age of Reason men dismissed revelation as an unacceptable source of knowledge. Its statements about the nature of ultimate reality were thrown out. The transcendental, supernatural basis for existence was rejected. If, by rationalist criterion, God could not speak satisfactorily through revelation, the only alternative was for man to turn his faith toward himself as the final arbiter of existence and truth. If man could not have access to God on his own terms—either by his reason or direct sense perceptions—then God could be considered to be unknowable, if not nonexistent. That is quite a heady assumption for finite man to make, and he made it at a tremendous cost, as postmodern philosophers have articulated.

We find that the field of knowledge did not grow; it shrank. As the Age of Reason made pronouncements about the validity or invalidity of various approaches to knowledge, the arena of philosophic inquiry shifted from ontology—the study of the nature of being and reality—to epistemology—the theory of knowledge. Thinking shifted from the study of God to the study of the human mind and its capacities and limitations in apprehending reality. Kant posed the question, "What can the mind know, how does it know, and how does it know that it knows?" Then the field narrowed down even more as we entered the twentieth century, and the logical positivists such as Alfred North Whitehead and Bertrand Russell further limited the known. By the time Ludwig Wittgenstein of Cambridge University published his *Tractatus Logico-Philosophicus* in 1922, philosophy was virtually forced to limit itself to the field of philology—word definitions. Can language even be trusted? they wondered.

Diogenes Allen of Princeton, a professor of philosophy under whom I studied, commented on how the *Tractatus* of Wittgenstein radically narrowed what could be discussed in language:

> This very much restricted what we can say mean-ingfully. Not only are the concerns of metaphysics and theology unstatable, but so too are the concerns of ethics and aesthetics. Wittgenstein, however, was misunderstood by the logical positivists, who saw him as an ally. For Wittgenstein himself actu-ally believed that there was more than could be said, and he believed that what could not be said was far more important than what could be said.[5]

For a long time, philosophy students loved quoting Witt-genstein's famous comment, "What cannot be said clearly must be passed over in silence." After that, in most philos-ophy departments there was either silence or loud wrangling.

To see it in overview: Since the age of the scholastics, during the era of Aquinas, philosophy has gone all the way from the grand horizons of ontology to the ant-sized consid-erations of philology. Human hopes and dreams have trailed along—so have its rebellions. Civilization has been com-pelled to go along for the ride. In the meantime God has been removed from the dominion seat and replaced by your aver-age generic citizen. Mr. Gumby and anyone else walking into the video room these days can grab the dominion seat. It's really like standing next to one of those life-sized cardboard photographs of a celebrity or two in order to appear in the picture—and presto! There you are next to several faces nor-mally seen in the pages of *People* magazine—just you, David Bowie, the Dalai Lama, and Ronald McDonald leaning in with a wide grin.

Humanism becomes inevitably confronted with the despair of its own ill-fated project. Continental intellectuals like Sar-tre and Camus saw this long before their grinning American neighbors across the Atlantic. If reality cannot be grasped in any meaningful sense, then what's the use? they asked. It is really no exaggeration at all to say that purple mohawks and the punk-rock subculture with its heroin needles and "agro" are inevitable fallout from despair. What else can you expect in a society that has lost its moorings and thinks that life is a joke?

The academy on the American side of the Atlantic, of course, inevitably did start to ask the same despairing questions. Gunther Stent, a molecular biologist at the University of California at Berkeley, in his book *The Coming of the Golden Age: A View of the End of Progress* states that science is already on the decline because young students entering the sciences are no longer convinced that true knowledge is possible. Speaking as a secular observer, Stent feels that since God has been dethroned, there are no longer any clear-cut standards or values; and so feeling that correct discriminations are no longer possible with regard to human aspirations and behavior, the pleasure principle becomes the highest value in men's lives.[6]

Today, almost 20 years after Stent wrote this, the University of California at Berkeley campus continues to pursue the pleasure principle even more fully than in the sixties. Now the preferred highs are cocaine and designer drugs, different from the psychedelics of the sixties. Being a yuppie instead of a hippie certainly fits the pleasure principle. Material success is surely an anesthetic for the pain of poverty, which they see in so many of their sixties predecessors who don't have very much now as far as possessions go and yet still believed in something enough to search for it and make sacrifices for this search, however misguided it may have been. Today the remnant hippies from the sixties still sit on Telegraph Avenue as relics of a failed experiment. Insanity and poverty are their inheritance.

Older Americans have yet to face up to the despair faced by Europeans. Many are riding on a wave of philosophical naiveté, the false borrowed optimism of former eras, as Allan Bloom brilliantly articulates in *The Closing of the American Mind*. We have not fully faced our crisis. We are dealing with unbacked paper money in the realm of ideas. As MTV and statistics on teen alcoholism and suicide should illustrate, American youth are encountering whole new levels of meaninglessness and alienation. Naturally, much of the international rock scene ("We Are the World") comes out of Europe. It is truly an international enterprise—one whose perverse and defiant despair makes the rebellions of the Romantics seem naive and silly in comparison.

JUMPING OFF THE CHESSBOARD

A wide shift has begun among the public. Some are caught in the predictable meaninglessness and nihilism that has so benighted Europe. Others are taking a different turn. They are leaving the domain of the rational and turning to that other alternative: the extrarational, the intuitive, the mystical and occult. The present generation has become the inheritors of the belief that there will never be a unified field of knowledge encompassing the physical universe and the spiritual. They have been encouraged to take a leap of faith while believing the new creed that the only faculty for making judgments they have is their inner senses. Rejecting the revelation of God, the intelligent man has no standard, no basis in truth, from which to make intelligent moral and religious discriminations. Tolerance has become the only way of dealing with conflicting, even contradictory worldviews. Each is viewed as being equally valid and as a matter of mere private opinion. The "all is permitted" attitude really reflects a widespread loss of values, a moral and intellectual impotence which breeds pseudomoralisms for any sort of gratification people pursue. As Bloom observes, even the wildest of choices can all be included under the high-sounding banner of "lifestyle." Now it becomes a "cause."

Meanwhile, more and more people are gearing their lives by truly unprovable things. Syndicated astrology columns appear daily in practically every newspaper in the country. A growing din of spiritual voices fills the air, and every brand of teacher is available—from Ramtha, the self-proclaimed 35,000-year-old ascended master channeling through J.Z. Knight, to

Rajneesh, the Indian superguru and former owner of 97 Rolls Royces. New Age fairs fill huge civic centers of major cities, showing their wares. It is spiritual pluralism with no guidelines.

Once people have been seduced into abandoning reason, you can no longer reason with them. The concrete result is the New Age physicist, like University of California at Berkeley's Fritjof Capra, who consults the ancient Chinese book of fortune by throwing the I Ching, wooden sticks that are cast as lots. Once that has been taken care of and the physicist has been advised by the powers-that-be, Capra can then stroll up to the Lawrence Berkeley lab to resume some experiment in quantum physics. It is truly a picture out of C.S. Lewis' prophetic novel *That Hideous Strength*, where a postmodern agnostic science synthesizes with the occult—a strange grafting indeed. Former enemies of belief are now allies.

This is the irony. Philosophy has come full circle. Rather than establish the knowledge of God, it has erased him from the universe and replaced God with a range of things—from nothing or the void, to Mr. Gumby, Rajneesh, and your generic citizen on the street. Indeed, the West has regressed and reentered the forbidden land of occult practices which enlightenment rationalism once promised to abolish forever. Modern man has leaped from the checkmated position of rationalist despair to the extrarational free-fall of blind faith. Without any spiritual guidelines, man is now truly vulnerable in a wholly new way. He has returned to an inner-directed religious subjectivism—from New Age channeling and pantheism, to Satan worship. The equation begins to look more and more like some diabolical *tour de force*. It keeps suggesting that the opponent on the other side of the chess table, whom the philosophers have been playing over the centuries, may well be Mephistopheles after all. Revelation could have told them that all along, if only they had listened!

14

Bridges to the New Consciousness

At the turn of the century a small minority heralded a new consciousness. A key new freedom they needed was the freedom from moral restraint. They had the "right," after all, to do as they pleased as long as they did not hurt anyone, and the right to live without the constant fear of being stigmatized by the present social order. They wanted to be liberated from the Christian restraining force of morals and beliefs that had been a pillar to the West. They hungered for a changing of the guard.

The idea of "sin" was something repugnant to mystics and libertarians. They wanted it buried forever. Leaders of the new consciousness often crossed the boundaries of morality in their own private lives, and resented having to do this secretly. Madame Blavatsky, the founder of Theosophy who touted her freedoms, ate hashish and had countless affairs of all kinds. Such brashness would be nothing by today's standards, but in the late 1800's it stood out.

One way the new beliefs spread in the early days was through what we now call "consciousness-raising events." They were like energized particles colliding in increasing numbers prior to a chain reaction. The 1960's was that final chain reaction where the critical threshold was finally passed.

UNITING WITH THE EAST

One key early event, which took place in Chicago in 1893,

was the World Parliament of Religions, attracting 140,000 people. The speakers included Buddhist monks, theosophists, Shintoists, a token number of Christian modernists in search of a new ecumenism, plus several highly persuasive mystics. It was the mystics who stole the hearts of the audience.

The most articulate and brilliant of these speakers was Swami Vivekananda, an impassioned Bengali who was the premier disciple of Ramakrishna Paramahansa, who had recently died in India in 1887. Even today, the radiant face of Ramakrishna appears on Indian postage stamps, for he occupies a position of renown as great as that of Gandhi. He is considered one of India's greatest enlightened godmen.

At the time of the World Parliament of Religions, the spiritual force of Ramakrishna was lighting up India like lightning flashing across a night sky. The ancient gods of India were having a revival through their instrument. Ramakrishna's 12 top disciples were spreading his life story and teachings all over the land. With Vivekananda, the premier disciple, this revival of Indian mysticism was now reaching the West.

Vivekananda was an inspired orator whose pleas for unity became irresistible to the thousands attending the World Parliament of Religions. Anyone who condemned the spiritual treasures of this noble figure from the East was simply exhibiting those "narrow-minded biases" typical of Western "Christian" culture. One can almost hear the accusations of "cultural chauvinism." Take note: Here began the early traces of today's common cultural/anthropological argument which defines different religions as being universal spiritual truths filtered through variant grids of culture and tradition. Spiritual truths could now be seen as wearing the clothing of a given culture's language and imagery. So what the world needed were religious pundits acting as transcultural interpreters of religion. "Open-mindedness" became a key word.

Vivekananda had been a law student when he became enraptured with his guru. Now he was a renunciant in the ochre robe. His command of rhetoric and apparent nobility and virtue of character won his case time and again. Beneath it all was the admonition: "All roads lead to God."

Vivekananda's guru, Ramakrishna, was the syncretist's saint: He had studied the scriptures of each of the major world religions, verifying each of them by claiming to reach "samadhi," or enlightenment, with each one of them. Whether it was by meditating on Christ, Buddha, or Krishna, Ramakrishna claimed he was taken to the same godhead. Each world faith took him back to the pantheistic One of the Vedantic godhead. Westerners loved this romantic imagery— God as the ocean of being and infinite bliss, the static eternal, the oversoul ("paramatma"), and so on.

Vivekananda, like his master, used the following illustration: The faiths of the world are like five blind men trying to describe an elephant. One describes the trunk, another grasps a leg, another the ear, and so on. They all seem to contradict each other until their reports are unified into a whole—then one sees the whole elephant. Vivekananda was not shy in stating that the most complete description of the whole shape of spiritual reality lay in India's ancient storehouse of revelations given by its "seers," "rishis," "mahatmas," "avadhuts," and "avatars." India was portrayed to the World Parliament of Religions as a land on fire with spiritual truth. India's role among the nations was to enlighten them with its spiritual wealth.

The cardinal Vedantic truths are that the soul is eternal and divine and part of the godhead. It keeps evolving through reincarnation after reincarnation until it rejoins the impersonal godhead. Life is merely an illusion, sucking us all in with its sensualist pleasures and pains that deny the underlying unity of all existence. The dualisms of sweet and sour, light and dark, and good and evil, are two sides of ultimate unitive reality, like light coming out of a prism and breaking into colors. All reality is composed of consciousness. Existence therefore is the "dream" of the godhead. It is Vishnu lying on the thousand-petalled lotus forming the phenomenal universe out of his undifferentiated being. Only when the droplets of consciousness merge back into the primal ocean will this illusion of separateness end. A godman such as Ramakrishna claims to be none other than this—one who has sojourned the grand circle from eternity to eternity. When he speaks, he claims it is the voice of the eternal coming through a human frame. Exquisite indeed.

Mysticism had the ability to use sentimental feelings within people to capture their allegiance. Ramakrishna won people's hearts by his apparent selflessness, sensitivity, and tenderness. What an overwhelming ace card to refute any attack of deception on his character—he seemed primevally innocent and sweet. Indeed, he oozed with love for his young disciples, transmitting the voltage of his possessing force to their foreheads with a single touch. Therefore, when men such as Ramakrishna seemed to embody such goodness, they were above reproach. The power of this sentimental goodness cannot be underestimated.

What drove me to India initially was the lure of Ramakrishna combined with a number of mystical experiences. The power of this hook of sentimentalized Vedanta must not be underestimated.

WESTERN ADEPTS OF THE EAST

Another group of players on the world stage at the turn of the century were the early figures of the Theosophical Society. The most notorious of these was the founder of the Theosophical Society, Madame Blavatsky, a strange Russian noblewoman who had been into the occult from her childhood. The headquarters for this society, which started in 1875, was in New York. But within a few years, Blavatsky moved it to Madras, India. She died two years before the World Parliament of Religions, choosing as her successor Annie Besant, a member of the British Fabian Society, the top of the pyramid of Britain's left-wing intelligentsia. Besant was a suffragette, most likely a lesbian, as well as a former member of Parliament.

Another member of this occult triad was Alice Bailey, whose writings as much as any have directed the course of the New Age movement. She later branched off from the theosophists, forming the Arcane School, taking with her the Lucifer Publishing Company of the theosophists which she renamed the Lucis Trust. The main remnant of her organization is now headquartered at United Nations Plaza.

These turn of the century occultists pieced together a body of beliefs that look like a constitutional charter for the entire New Age movement. Where did they get these ideas? From Indian mysticism and from their own spirit guides! Before the term "channeler" was ever popularized, replacing the older term of "medium," they were channeling down "higher" revelations from the "masters."

James Webb in *The Occult Underground* states that the early theosophists felt themselves "specially chosen to bear the light to the newly evolving global society."[1] Those who had "chosen" the theosophists claimed to be superhuman Tibetan spirit masters whose disembodied presence was in the Himalayas. They were setting up the world for "global evolution" and "the appearance of a messiah." One plan was that "Lord Maitreya" was to possess the body of Jiddu Krishnamurti. Webb comments that his body "was to become the vehicle of the 'Lord Maitreya,' the coming 'World Teacher' of the new age . . . preaching the Theosophical message of love, brotherhood, and the unity of all religions."[2]

Krishnamurti renounced this role in 1929 and became a guru in his own right. Krishnamurti claimed to lose all memories prior to 1929. A little before then, Alice Bailey split away from the theosophists, and a disappointed Annie Besant died in 1933. Who was this Lord Maitreya? The "Master who had inhabited the body of Jesus in ancient Palestine, and who would take possession of the body of Krishnamurti in the same fashion."[3] Bailey again predicted Maitreya's return to establish a one world order and that this cosmic messiah was above all religions and all faiths. Bailey, like the others, got her revelations from forces outside of herself, namely, from "the masters."

Blavatsky revealed in a letter: "All I can say is that someone positively inspires me—more than this, someone enters me. It is not I who talk and write: it is something within me . . . that thinks and writes for me. . . . I have become a sort of storehouse for somebody else's knowledge. . . . Someone comes and envelops me as a misty cloud and all at once pushes me out of myself and then I am not 'I' anymore . . . but someone else."[4]

In the *Mahatma Letters*, which are purported writings from the masters to Colonel Olcott, a theosophist leader, one master referred to Madame Blavatsky as "it, and the brother inside it." Olcott stated that no one knew the real Blavatsky since she was possessed and they "just dealt with an artificially animated body."[5] With Blavatsky, this began at an early age. Indeed, the "masters" that channeled through Blavatsky, Bailey, and Besant formulated an intricate and far-reaching occult revelation.

THE EARLY CREED FOR
THE NEW AGE MOVEMENT

This occult revelation showed that man's problem is that he has fallen from his previous status as part of the divine godhead into material existence, and that he has been deceived into doubting his oneness with the godhead. Only the hidden truths can set him free. Sin is nothing but ignorance. The theory of evolution, now applied to spiritual existence, was used to show that beings evolved as they reincarnated. The Hindus, of course, thought of this centuries before theosophists used Darwin. Resembling gods, the ascended masters, en route to the godhead themselves, could extend a hand down to help those beneath them on the ladder of spiritual evolution. The hierarchy was there to help us. And who was Jesus Christ? Again he becomes the New Age cosmic Christ.

Jesus was simply an occult adept, one of many masters, who the "Christ consciousness" possessed. His teachings needed to be rescued from Christianity. Extracanonical sources were needed, from early Gnostic heresies to revelations from the masters. The culprit hiding the esoteric truth was Christianity. Blavatsky's *Isis Unveiled* is one long 800-page attack on Christianity, anticipating today's now-familiar posture of moral outrage at any biblical or moral judgmentalism (which itself is judgmentalism—against Christianity). The council of Nicea was attacked for supposedly throwing out reincarnation along with other secret teachings. Christianity seemed to be nothing but a cover-up campaign lasting 2000 years. And its great adversary was really man's greatest ally—Lucifer.

ENTER LUCIFER, VANQUISHED
HERO AND SAVIOR

Blavatsky launched a stinging attack on the God of the Bible calling him "capricious and unjust,"[6] "a tribal God and no more."[7] Blavatsky then reveals that the biblical account is reversed, that Satan is the victim of Jehovah. She says:

> The appellation Sa'tan, in Hebrew Satan, and Adversary . . . belongs by right to the first and cruelest "Adversary" of all other Gods—Jehovah; not to the serpent which spoke only words of sympathy and wisdom.[8]

Madame Blavatsky declares:

> Once the key to Genesis is in our hands, the scientific and symbolical Kabbala unveils the secret. The Great Serpent of the Garden of Eden and the "Lord God" are identical.[9]

Satan, indeed, is viewed as the savior of mankind, freeing men from ignorance and death. He becomes the creator of divinized man. Blavatsky says:

> Satan, the Serpent of Genesis is the real creator and benefactor, the Father of Spiritual mankind. For it is he . . . who opened the eyes of the automaton (Adam) created by Jehovah, as alleged. And he who was the first to whisper, "in the day ye eat thereof, ye shall be as Elohim, knowing good and evil," can only be regarded in the light of a savior. An adversary to Jehovah . . . he still remains in Esoteric Truth the ever loving messenger . . . who conferred on us spiritual instead of physical immortality.[10]

Lucifer becomes the greatest initiator. Churches that oppose this savior "are fighting against divine truth, when repudiating and slandering the Dragon of Esoteric Divine Wisdom."[11]

It is only a small step from this to Alice Bailey's talk about a "Luciferic Initiation of Mankind." The road was well-paved. Nor was Bailey the only one to say this. A hundred years ago General Albert Pike, the top Masonic leader of the Scottish Rite of Freemasonry in Charleston, South Carolina, anticipated a global Luciferic initiation in his letter to Mazzini in Italy.

Blavatsky calls Christ "the first born brother of Satan." Christ too becomes a great initiator who brings in the hidden light. "Atonement" is now seen as "at-one-ment" with the divine inner self. It reverses the fall of divinity into the realm of matter. Blavatsky and her masters hate the biblical view of the Fall and speak of this with considerable emotion:

> Finally, it has created the god-slandering dogma of Hell and eternal perdition; it has spread a thick film between higher intuitions of man and divine verities; and, the most pernicious result of all, it has made people remain ignorant of the fact there were no fiends, no dark demons in the universe before man's own appearance on this, and probably other earths.[12]

What is the Second Coming of Christ? Theosophists precede New Age beliefs by more than half a century: "The coming of Christ means the reawakening of the Christ spirit in mankind or in as many as are able to receive it. . . . For man, essentially divine, having wandered away from the knowledge of his own divinity, has to regain it."[13] The Second Coming of Christ is now reinterpreted by theosophists: It is the descent of a massive "Christ consciousness" upon the inhabitants of the earth. It becomes a global transformation through consciousness-raising as the human race reclaims its lost divinity. To most New Agers, this best explains the Second Coming. In reality, their scenario provides for what the Bible calls the Great Lie, on a massive level. In that light it is a vehicle for the delusion of the human race. Even the blessed hope becomes disfigured by occult spell-weaving. To those who reject the truth, who are hostile to it, it is an attractive alternative to Christ's visible return.

"Lord Maitreya" on April 25, 1982, was announced in newspapers around the world in a full-page ad predicting his return as the global messiah. The ad proclaimed at one point: "What is the Plan? It includes the installation of a new world government and new world religion under Maitreya." Benjamin Creme, who placed these paid ads, claims to be Maitreya's channeler. Creme is the founder of the Tara Association. So far there has been no appearance, and the blame invariably falls on the lack of spiritual consciousness in the world.

MAKING EARLY CONTACT

Both Annie Besant and Alice Bailey claimed to be channels for a number of ascended masters including "The Tibetan," or Djwhal Khul. Today, Elizabeth Claire Prophet claims to be a channel for the ascended masters spoken of by the theosophists.

Alice Bailey knew she had been marked for a task. There is no greater way to increase feelings of self-worth than to feel that you have been chosen for a major cosmic task. She might have secretly gloated that she was now light-years ahead of her better-looking sister.

This same entity entered Alice Bailey's life in seven-year intervals. It was not until 1915, when she was 35, that she finally discovered that this turbaned visitor was "Master Kutchumi."[14] In 1915 in Lucknow, India, Bailey was close to a mental breakdown from overwork and mental exhaustion. Then a master appeared:

> Suddenly a broad shaft of brilliant light struck my room and the voice of the Master who had come to me when I was fifteen spoke to me. . . . He told me not to be unduly troubled; that I had been under observation and was doing what He wanted me to do. He told me that things were planned and that the life work which He had earlier outlined to me

would start, but in a way which I would not recognize.[15]

Then in 1919 two things happened to Alice Bailey. She met her first husband, Foster Bailey, an officer in the Theosophical Society, and she met her highest Tibetan master, known as "The Tibetan," or Djwhal Khul. The Tibetan would be the true author of her many books. It was her moment to enter the world stage. How could she say no?

Little did Alice Bailey know at the time that the organization which she and her husband would eventually found would be in United Nations Plaza in New York City by the 1980's and that "The Plan" dictated to her by "The Tibetan" would be something held up by world leaders of the New Age movement as the most comprehensive overview of the New Age agenda. Bailey had taken her dictations from Djwhal Khul word for word. She notes, "After all, the books are His, not mine, and basically the responsibility is His. He does not permit me to make mistakes and watches over the final draft with great care."[16] It is hard to resist the notion that because of the great logistical and strategic effort focused on Bailey, Blavatsky, and Besant by the masters, something dealing with world events was critical to their agenda. The masters had a vested interest in the destiny of the human race apparent in their concentrated efforts.

For almost 30 years Alice Bailey became the mouthpiece of "The Tibetan," producing 19 books in the process. Probably the most powerful revelation, the one containing "The Plan," was *The Externalization of the Hierarchy*. All of these revelations went from "The Tibetan" to Alice Bailey to the world-at-large. But what if "The Tibetan" is not who he claims to be?

It's a ploy as old as the Trojan horse of the ancient world. The Trojan army did not have the power to batter down the huge stone wall and gates of the enemy, so they presented the enemy with a "present" that was wheeled inside the heavily fortressed gates. Inside of this colossal carved horse hid an army waiting to spring out at night and slay the slumbering inhabitants of the kingdom. It worked, and the Trojans destroyed their enemy without losing a single man or battering down the gate.

The FBI will sift every nuance of detail concerning the private lives of public officials of national importance, such as a member of the cabinet or a Supreme Court justice. Supreme Court nominee Robert Bork got knocked out of contention over opinions in articles he had written for law journals years earlier. Though an official can affect our lives in a given context, none of them claim to be channels of divine truth. During the era of the Old Testament, a prophet was ruthlessly scrutinized. But "The Tibetan" and similar entities have been accepted by millions of people who don't even question their credentials or their origin. They stake their eternal souls on some voice wired to the other end of the universe. It is a strange double standard: The same people who rattle off minor points about the Bible that they think will dispose of its validity and hence its authority will offer their souls to some channeled revelation or godman without hesitation. Their focused skepticism is selective and self-serving. It's as if they have already made up their minds. Herein lies a deep mystery—it is the mystery of the human heart.

By the 1960's America passed through the rainbow bridge as many decided what sort of "truth" they wanted. What a handful had experienced at the turn of the century was commonly being experienced by an entire generation. The youth of the sixties started reveling in the delicious newness of something that held great promise and unlimited horizons. Indeed this was a rainbow bridge for the New World Order.

15

Going Beyond Good and Evil

The Romantic movement, beginning in the last century, opened some interesting doors in our world. Its tremendous artistic output has been a lure for generations of university students who have pored through its literature during their most formative years. They have felt the delicious taste of various wild freedoms dangled before their eyes. Imagine the student away from home for the first time, free of supervision, and thrust into a unique permissive egalitarian atmosphere. What a time to be tempted by the Romantic challenge that exalts human experience! The Romantic ideal was Faustian: Human consciousness was seen as a deep ocean of mystery with unlimited potential. Experience was the vehicle for opening up this consciousness—the wilder the better. Critical in this process was the casting aside of the old religious and moralistic paradigms of good and evil that limited this new freedom to experience all things.

When Goethe wrote *Faust*, that is exactly what he was opening up—a Pandora's box of consciousness-expansion through experience. The Indian Tantrics taught the identical thing for centuries—that one must go beyond good and evil, that adepts must become infinitely wise in both. Then, and only then, can they transcend the false duality of both good and evil and merge with God. The Indian guru Rajneesh borrows from this Tantric teaching by saying that by exhausting the experiences of pure evil, one can truly know good and one can truly become God. Experience is the key.

There was a time in the Western civilized world when nobody would have believed the level of immorality—indeed, evil—that society has opened itself up to and permitted. As we saw from examining the philosophers, certain doors had to open first. Humanism was one of the outcomes of this, but it is only a halfway point. It allows you to say that good and evil are relative, but unlike the Tantrics, unlike Faust, unlike the New Age movement, it does not really believe in or understand the supernatural. What humanism does is blur distinctions of good and evil; relativizes them. It says that the old traditional understandings no longer apply, that they don't really matter. Now classrooms in the public sector teach "values clarification." Peer groups decide what is okay and what is not. The distinction between good and evil has been powerfully neutralized over the past five decades. There are a number of indicators that tell just how much good and evil have been neutralized. Once humanism has performed this task in America and in Europe, a new brand of supernaturalism can use humanism for a surprising turn of events.

One area where good and evil have been blurred has been in the field of entertainment. The audience gets dull to heightening thrills, then in turn wants to see more. It keeps feeding like a fire. Now young children can become more jaded than middle-aged adults of several generations back through a corruptive voyeurism as films take them to forbidden areas.

Indeed, movies are a very powerful index of this blurring process. They are a formidable cultural reality, whether on TV or at the movie theater. Films have changed drastically. As we shall later see, particular films have stood out as major trend-setters of public thought. In that sense, they are tools of propaganda and behavior modification. Some films are landmarks of conscience-searing—they push the mind to new boundaries, sometimes morally, sometimes conceptually. What would have been terribly bizarre or shocking at one time can later enter the realm of the ordinary. Increasingly movies have abolished distinctions between good and evil. They have offered to millions in the general public what only a handful of outrageous Romantics would have pondered in the last century. The Marquis de Sade was among this handful within the French Romantic movement. But what was true of a handful then, has become common reality for the masses today.

What happens is that we become more experienced in knowing evil, never in knowing good. It never works the other way around. It is like most compromises: One side usually gives more than the other. What is really happening is the invasion of evil. We become more and more curious and knowledgeable about evil.

How much have films really changed? There is an experiment that would be very revealing were it possible—for instance, sending a few movies back in a time machine to the old Ziegfield Theater of the 1930's to see how the audience might react to several powerhouse conscience-searers of our era, and then interviewing the audience to see if things have really changed that much. Tell them that it is an experiment in intracultural appreciation, from the future to the past. Tell them our "cognoscente" have appreciated some of their old black-and-white movies, things like *Petrified Forest* with Leslie Howard, and films with Lombard, Barrymore, Mary Pickford, and Douglas Fairbanks all playing noble souls whose virtue, integrity, and humanity always manage to stand them in good stead against the dark forces. When they fall in love, it is believable. Men are still men and women are women. Their words are deep and sincere, their eyes searching and vulnerable as they speak to one another with endearing respect. Nary a crudity passes their lips. Such are the old celluloid heroes. They still believed in good and evil in those days.

Now, in our experiment at New York's old Ziegfield Theater, have the house packed from stem to stern with the good old folk of the 1930's, the solid citizens. Maybe include a representative sample of rural folk from all over—from the Midwestern Iowa corn belt to citizens from quiet towns in New England and the deep South. Then do a triple-header: Imagine their gasps as beak-face appears in *Clockwork Orange* with a bowler hat, mascara highlighting a single eye, a false genital strapped to his nose, and holding a cane, acting out

Gene Kelly just "singin' in the rain" while dancing on somebody's face. By now they will need to be strapped in their
seats. Then imagine Bob Guccione's *Caligula* with the Roman
emperor, played by Malcolm McDowell once again, ranting in
an effete, androgynous, blood-drenched orgy, with scenes of
bestiality, sodomy, and dismemberment. Then end it up with
something like *Blood Simple* or Clive Barker's *Hellraiser*, where
none of the characters are either remotely likable or human,
everyone plotting against everyone else in vulgar stupidity—
black humor at its most sardonic. Finally, conclude the gala
occasion with an ensemble of rock groups sent down from the
future: for instance, The Talking Heads singing "Burning
Down the House," David Bowie as Ziggie Stardust, and Billy
Idol singing "Whiplash Smile" in leather and chains, while
standing in the middle of a pentagram and sneering at the
audience with the most defiant smile you've ever seen.

Most probably the outraged audience would literally tear
down the movie house, and repent that they could ever be the
ancestors of such a future world only 50 years down the road.
They would wonder in stunned horror how we got so evil.
How did beliefs so disintegrate? How did our relative innocence so completely go down the tube? They would probably
suspect they had just seen some collective Antichrist.

Then, while they were all raging or beating their breasts in
despair, now show them what has become of the television
gospel message to meet such horrific needs. Send them "The
Man with the Answers." Have Ernest Angley or Smopper Bob
the Evangelist slide across the stage in a metallic polyester
leisure suit while putting on the barnyard growl, shaking
with sweat, and howling into the mike—guttural slang as
gravelly and cacophonous as a chicken yard during an earth-
quake, morphemes and phonemes coming out at ten per
second in a drawl as thick as molasses and with as much
content as an idiot without novocaine in a dentist's chair.

Perhaps it takes such editorial overkill to make a point.
There are indeed disturbing signs in our culture that we just
cannot brush off. It is like a sleeping giant. Bonhoeffer in pre-
Nazi Germany saw the writing on the wall. By the time of the
Barmen Declaration, others agreed with him. The irony was

that Bonhoeffer would die in one of Hitler's death camps. He spoke then of "the world coming of age" in a darkening sense.

Malcolm Muggeridge, Britain's former liberal, intellectual media commentator and writer turned Christian convert, succinctly pinpointed the self-destructive tendencies at work within our world system. Muggeridge observed:

> It is difficult to resist the conclusion that there is a death wish at work at the heart of our civilization whereby our banks promote the inflation which will ruin them, our educationalists seem to create the moral and intellectual chaos which will nullify their professional purposes, our physicians invent new and more terrible diseases to replace those they have abolished, our moralists cut away the roots of all morality and our theologians dismantle the structure of belief they exist to expound and promote.[1]

The answer for why the liberated West is in a process of self-destruction is coherently explained by the biblical view. Its clear teaching is this: Sin and evil will take down individual lives as well as entire civilizations. The process and the answer serve to become, in the end, a kind of validation of the Bible and biblical truths which emphasize that good and evil are real. From Sodom of antiquity to Los Angeles today, a Pandora's box is opened when evil is allowed free reign. When the language of value relativism replaces clear statements about good and evil, it becomes that much harder to back out of the trap. Good is mocked at and people become trapped. As people lose their God-guaranteed dignity and their value in the eyes of others, then literally anything becomes possible with them.

Elie Wiesel, a Jew who survived the Nazi experiment, has become a voice to the West so that it will never happen again. His books, for which he recently won the Nobel prize, have been a crying reminder. Wiesel shows what can really happen when a society becomes seduced by a lie—that men are

186 • *Tal Brooke*

capable of anything. He reminds the world again and again that during the reign of Hitler, people—human beings!—were put by the millions into ovens and first gassed, then burned. Today, the potential options are even more frightening.

To our 1930's film audience in the Ziegfield Theater, certain basic givens of life seemed unshakable: things like the family, the dearness of human life, and men and women being truly different and unique. Pregnancy and birth were still precious then. Abortion was still seen as an inhuman act. It was, quite simply, the killing of a human life. Nothing justified it. It was evil. They had not learned Weber's language of value relativism.

The astronomical level of abortions today would have been beyond their wildest nightmares. Abortions today have become matters of cold decision—almost on the level of buying a kitchen appliance. They are done on mass scales supported by the strident, moralistic-sounding slogans of the women's movement demanding their rights. That someone would have to die in order *not* to "oppress them" or disturb their comfort zone is something so inhuman as to defy imagination.

So often feminists and homosexuals are seen lining the mall of Capitol Hill to protest their "rights," to champion their freedoms—to abort fetuses, to perform sodomy—things that were barely mentioned above a whisper during our Ziegfield era. Recently half a million of them displayed a quilted tapestry signifying the thousands who had died because of AIDS. At the same time with angry indignation they demanded that antisodomy laws across the nation "limiting freedom" be repealed. With one foot in the grave, they still want to engage in sodomy.

This crusading coalition will lead you to believe that they are "caring" and "nurturing" and oppressed victims as they murder infants, commit anal intercourse, or engage in lesbian acts. Imagine our audience at the Ziegfield Theater seeing a news special on some of these mass rallies, then with hidden glimpses of the camera seeing the acting out of what is being spoken of with such noble language. They would be assaulted. If only we could see it from their perspective, but it is too late.

The Nazi atrocities showed us something: People hide the horror by removing the evidence. Occasionally by accident someone will be overwhelmed by the spectacle of seeing a mountain of dead infants stuffed in a trash incinerator, but this is a rarity. On the evening news of May 20, 1985, there was an embarrassing story about the discovery of thousands and thousands of dead "fetuses" in California. A growing mob of protesters waited to hear if the court would rule the babies as human or as products, and whether they would be buried or cremated. Collagen from such flesh is used in certain cosmetics. Those who encountered the rotting flesh were struck with the reality of abortion as opposed to tame descriptions of it. Perhaps they briefly came to their senses and were forced to deal with what was being done, but only briefly.

Peter Adam, an associate professor of pediatrics at Case Western Reserve University, within only six months of the *Roe v. Wade* decision, joined some of his medical associates conducting experiments on 12 babies: "These men took the tiny babies and cut off their heads—decapitated the babies and cannulated the internal carotid arteries (that is, a tube was placed in the main artery feeding the brain). They kept the diminutive heads alive, much as the Russians kept the dogs' heads alive in the 1950s. Take note of Dr. Adam's retort to criticism: 'Once society's declared the fetus dead, and abrogated its rights, I don't see any ethical problem.... Whose rights are we going to protect, once we've decided fetuses won't live?' "[2]

The news media, like in the above case, occasionally digs up some chilling artifact that signals new dangers. Different aspects of our social cancer come to light. For instance, 14-year-old Marcy Conrad of Milpitas, California, had been raped, strangled to death, and left lying off the road in the hills outside of town. According to the local paper, at least 13 students went out to look at her body. One girl picked up the murdered girl's jeans, cut off a patch, and threw the jeans down along the side of the road. One student tried to cover the body with leaves. Another took his eight-year-old brother along to see the body. One boy went twice. Those who saw the body went back to class or to the pinball arcade. One went home to bed. Another student said he only cared about collecting the marijuana cigarette he had won on a bet that the body was real. As the newspaper reported: "The shock is the shock of the encounter with icy indifference, the indifference of the kids in the first instance, but much more importantly, of the culture that produced them. . . . The depersonalization did not begin yesterday; it is not unique to this moment, yet it seems more complete—and they seem more alienated and isolated—than we have ever known before."[3]

Walker Percy dwells on an alarming pattern of statistics in his *Lost in the Cosmos*:

> The suicide rate among persons under twenty-five has risen dramatically in the last twenty years. . . . The incidence of drug use in teenagers and pre-teens has increased an estimated 3000 percent in the last thirty years. On a recent talk show on "tough love," it was claimed that about one-third of all teenagers were depressed. Of the one third, as many as 75 percent were on drugs.[4]

Walker Percy continues to shine light on another sacred institution—marriage and the marriage bed:

> Of all sexual encounters on soap operas, only six percent occur between husband and wife. In some cities of the United States, which now has the highest divorce rate in the world, the incidence of divorce now approaches 60 percent of married couples. A recent survey showed that the frequency of sexual intercourse in married couples declined 90 percent after three years of marriage.[5]

Walker Percy goes out of his way to show that there is a worldview operating behind these strings of statistics. It is a relativism of values, that there are no absolute truths, thus making all moralities impotent in the end. They have no teeth—they are not able to make any real judgments or say "no" to evil with any authority.

In Germany in the late 1930's the state became open to killing undesirables. This could be justified if men have no intrinsic value—then it becomes okay to kill the mentally handicapped and others who would biologically pollute the species. It makes sense for the state to abort babies that might be inferior, whose parents have low IQ's. If the state decides that a certain group is detrimental to it, then racial genocide becomes the solution. Ironically, Hitler's term for the racial extermination of the Jews was "The Final Solution." By then, Weberian value relativism had sunk its teeth into the German mind, and all things became possible.

Perhaps the most frightening artifact that the news media has unearthed in the last decade is the reality of satanic crimes and abductions. It is a phenomenon more sobering than anything that happened in Germany before Hitler took full control.

The San Francisco Chronicle, one of the most prestigious papers in the United States, had the following headline on Thursday, November 5, 1987: "SATANISM LINKED TO SCORES OF U.S. CHILD ABUSE CASES." Edward Lempinen's article stretched to a third of the back page. The front-page section summarizes this frightening reality:

> Children as young as 2 and 3 years old have come forward with harrowing tales of drinking blood, animal sacrifices and sexual abuse as part of the rituals, according to law enforcement investigators, child abuse experts and parents.
>
> Others have even talked of cannibalism and ritual sacrifice of children.
>
> After hearing similar tales over and over from people across the country, many investigators and child abuse experts have come to believe in the unbelievable.

The article discussed the latest horror involving 58 children who attended the U.S. Army Presidio Child Development Center in the San Francisco area.

Ted Koppel, the popular moderator of "Nightline," said something quite profound when he was speaking at Duke University in the fall of 1987. Koppel left the standard posture of so-called objective impartiality that the media is supposed to embody and spoke from his heart. He portrayed the bankruptcy of the permissive liberal approach to morality, saying: "We have actually convinced ourselves that slogans will save us. Shoot up if you must, but use a clean needle. Enjoy sex whenever and with whomever you wish, but wear a condom. No! The answer is no. Not because it isn't cool or smart or because you might end up in jail or dying in an AIDS ward, but no because it is wrong. . . . In its purest form, truth is not a polite tap on the shoulder. It is a howling reproach. What Moses brought down from Mount Sinai were not the Ten Suggestions."

But humanism, unfortunately, is just that—"the ten suggestions." It can never be God's revelation. It can only be man's revelation and, as such, it can change from day to day, from consensus opinion to consensus opinion. Writing in *The Humanist* magazine, Paul Blanshard confesses a perspective not uncommon among the educational elite. The title of his article is "Three Cheers for our Secular State" (March/April 1976):

> I think that the most important factor moving us toward a secular society has been the educational factor. Our schools may not teach Johnny to read properly, but the fact that Johnny is in school until he is sixteen tends to lead toward the elimination of religious superstition. The average American child now acquires a high school education, and this militates against Adam and Eve and all other myths of alleged history. . . . When I was one of the editors of *The Nation* in the twenties, I wrote an editorial explaining that golf and intelligence were the two primary reasons that men did not attend church.

Perhaps I would now say golf and a high-school diploma (which has evidently replaced intelligence).

Humanism is the grandchild of the Age of Reason. What is it exactly? *The Glossary of Humanism* defines its position:

> Humanism subscribes to a view of life that is centered on man and his capacity to build a worthwhile life for himself and his fellows here and now. The emphasis is placed on man's own intellectual and moral resources, and the notion of supernatural religion is rejected. One of the most important trends in modern Humanism is its reliance on the application of scientific enquiry and its evaluation of truth, reality and morals in purely human terms.[6]

These are pretentious words indeed in light of the disintegration of society. Indeed, the humanist must avert his eyes from seeing the world he is passing on to others. It is infinitely more sinister and hopeless, full of despair and alienation, than the Christian alternative he so greatly seeks to replace.

A doctrine of meaninglessness has real consequences. Our latest example is the novel/film *Less Than Zero*, where life meant less than zero. This problem has grown acute in the twentieth century, stretching from the Dadaists of Berlin in the early twenties, to the existentialists in Parisian cafés on the banks of the Seine coolly planning suicide in the thirties and forties, to the multicolored punk rockers in London and Merseyside slashing and kicking one another as they dance, to the Los Angeles school kids OD'ing on cocaine. They are the products, the unwilling participants, of a world in which they found themselves. Their lives are the echoes of postmodern thinkers such as Ibsen, Ionesco, Beckett, Camus, Sartre, Kafka, and Henry Miller, plus a host of nameless humanists and social engineers of every hue conceivable.

The price of present-day denials of biblical truth is different from what it was in the past. Once people could bury themselves in the myth of human decency and respectability.

Complacency masked over any deep sense of spiritual need. Michel de Montaigne could ignore spiritual questions because he was able to lose himself in easy, affluent diversion. The same kind of mood prevailed in America during the Roaring Twenties when the ideal of many liberated secularists was to kick up their heels and drink mint juleps under colonnades while talk was light and frivolous or pretentious and daring. Most still retained their traditional rules of decent conduct. The invasion of the demonic was completely unforeseen. Now it is sitting on our doorstep. Imagine an old Model T ride from the Colonnade Club of the 1920's right into a 1980's satanic mass where an abducted child is being sacrificed to Satan—a child whose face might well appear on some Safeway milk carton.

In the 1980's we have gone way beyond moralistic posturing to appear decent. There is little pretense of innocence, especially in the youth. The writings of Henry Miller 25 years ago typify America's awakening into continental nihilism and despair:

> It may be that we are doomed, that there is no hope for us, any of us, but if that is so then let us set up a last agonizing, blood-curdling howl, a screech of defiance, a war-whoop! Away with lamentation! Away with elegies and dirges! Away with biographies and histories, and libraries and museums! Let the dead eat the dead. Let us living ones dance about the rim of the crater, a last expiring dance. But a dance! . . . A fatuous, suicidal wish that is constipated by words and paralyzed by thought.[7]

Soren Kierkegaard, the postmodern philosopher of the nineteenth century, articulated the basis of our nihilistic crisis a century ago:

> If there were no eternal consciousness in a man, if at the foundation of all there lay only a wildly seething power which writhing with obscure passions produced everything that is great and everything

that is insignificant, if a bottomless void never satiated lay hidden beneath all—what would life be but despair?[8]

Kierkegaard himself saw the route out of this terrifying despair within the pages of the gospels. He saw Christ as providing the only hope in the world.

When belief in the reality of good and evil really ceases, you are left with a world that either has a sense of hopelessness and meaninglessness, and people exist in a state of despair or defiant hedonism, or else a new kind of mysticism enters their midst. When either of these happen, the doorway for the pursuit of evil can really open up and almost anything can happen. Humanism is only a halfway point. There is another specter further down the road.

16

An Agenda for New World Globalism

What is the scenario for a one-world religion that can break down transnational religious differences while at the same time banning such "exclusive" religions as Christianity which stand in its way? And what if that one-world religion is a revival of ancient occultism? And what if it is totalitarian in power? If it is all these, it has fulfilled all of the requirements of an ancient prophecy.

The following argument shows how things are intricately set up to do what was just described. This scenario was predicted 2000 years ago by the New Testament writers. Before writing the Book of Revelation, the apostle John had a vision on the Island of Patmos. In it he saw world history ending in a battle between good and evil. He described how a one-world religion was due to come on the world scene, destroying all rivals. It would begin as a sweet enticement and end as a brutal dictator. He would describe it as *Mystery Babylon* revealed, likening it to the ancient occult system that the biblical God abhorred in the ancient world. That system would return with fierce power. C.S. Lewis portrayed this in his novel *That Hideous Strength* 40 years ago. There have been numerous apocalyptic novels. Now there is a very real possibility that the real thing is unfolding.

What are the stepping-stones for this to happen? Without sensationalizing history, how can we see this possibility? It is not at all hard to envision. In fact, you have to be blind to miss it. The first step is to limit the religious freedoms of the one

196 • *Tal Brooke*

faith that predicted this eventuality and that claims to have the unrivalled truth. Like it or not, that is what the "good news" of the gospel is—the exclusive truth. It does not parade as broad-minded and tolerant of counterfeits or evils. For the above agenda to unfold, the Christian faith must be silenced and suppressed. There are a thousand ways for this to happen. One is through the legal and political system.

"RIGHTS" AS A LEGAL AGENDA

Our world has many examples of the limitation of religious freedom. Mainly we think of the Communist bloc as the prime example of this, but there are now a growing number of examples in the United States of America. It was the atheist Madelyn Murray O'Hair who in 1963 won a landmark Supreme Court decision barring religious practices—specifically prayer—from all public schools. Why? Here's how legal experts defined the problem: The atheistic viewpoint of the O'Hair family, including that of her son, was being violated due to the fact that public schools allowed and practiced Christian prayers. These violated her son's rights because he had to suffer hearing these prayers, and there were no atheistic ceremonies being given on his behalf. What if he were a Hindu or a Jew—would he not also require that these religions be given representation as well? Therefore the state was showing one-sided favoritism toward Christianity within a system that was supposed to be pluralistic, since public schools were a branch of the state. O'Hair won and Christians ever since have been literally prohibited by the state to practice their religion in America's public schools.

What concerns us in the O'Hair decision is that we have here a legal precedent for how a pluralistic state system is supposed to function when those of many beliefs are involved: The religious practices of some are not to infringe upon the religious rights and freedoms of others. This can have far-reaching permutations.

If it seems irrelevant and futile to speculate about a developing trend, one only needs to recall Bonhoeffer's efforts to put together the Barmen Declaration as the church in

Germany succumbed to an antihuman and anti-Christian system. What had seemed fantasy suddenly became reality.

For Americans who celebrate religious freedoms, the curtailment of such freedoms may seem remote—until we contemplate one blatant thing: our own public school system. Pretend that an average public school in America were suddenly to engulf the nation in size and in operations. All of a sudden voluntary Bible studies and prayer, revivals and church meetings, and all manner of religious activities would have to be prohibited and frozen for the good of all. Those who wished to engage in such practices would have to sneak across the border—that is, if America were run along the lines of *one of its very own public schools*. This is an interesting thought.

To a future world-at-large that is without the legacy of a United States Constitution or Bill of Rights, the same kinds of limitations we put on those people in our public schools might seem quite reasonable in a globalist-pluralist atmosphere. Religion would be fully privatized. Certainly our legal system is busy trying to do just that—limit religion entirely to the private sphere. Courtesy of the ACLU, numerous displays of the nativity that since the inception of this country were displayed openly in public parks, etc., have been banned, and cities across the country have been forced to take nativity displays down. Isn't it interesting what gets these lawyers all full of self-righteous rage—nativity scenes and prayer in schools. Nowadays you can get by snorting cocaine in a public school without raising the ire of these crusaders for justice. With drugs they seem tolerantly understanding. That's not a major problem. But try praying in the name of Christ. Angry ACLU faces will fill the nightly newscast of whatever locale this grievous event happened, and multi-million-dollar lawsuits will begin. Are we seeing a social agenda being inacted?

Let us proceed with more examples of state and secular interference. It is common knowledge that missions work is very much affected by the political situation in Tibet (as well as in neighboring Nepal). Quite simply, there is no missions work. And that is because the political system will not tolerate it. The same situation is paralleled in Rumania, Albania, and Hungary. Communism has become a political reality in these countries, and it has completely affected the religious rights of the individual. These are only a sample of all of the countries under similar communistic rule. This is what can happen to religious freedoms when a political system becomes the arbiter of religious rights—often, there aren't any rights. Those in Russia or Albania engaging in house churches and prayer meetings can be legally arrested by the state police. They are imprisoned. Americans don't know what this is like.

Meanwhile, we greet the subtle disappearance of these freedoms naively, unlike immigrants who have come here from Eastern Europe who nod with grim understanding. They have seen what an all-powerful state can do; they have gotten their hands dirty in the pits. They have seen their neighbors carried off at midnight. There are no choruses of wimpy humane voices in the world they left behind. Now their warnings fall on deaf ears of the all-knowing liberal elite in America who have substituted the knowing smile for real experience. The students of Harvard loved to patronize the alarming words of Solzhenitsyn when he spoke at their commencement, because he was their new radical chic *cause de celebre*. But the words of warning of this great Russian author went right over most of their heads. Many still touted their leftist lapel buttons because they have learned the language of role-modeling—that's what "intellectuals" do. They protest only the most vogue causes, and in fact can be identified as intellectuals by sporting all the right causes and paraphernalia. It's known as the liberal mystique: People role-play and posture themselves into intellectual status. It is unearned and cheap imaging that the truly gifted usually see through at a glance. This is the power of consensus. Few individuals can rise above it.

There are other kinds of examples of the state blocking religious freedoms. During India's recent state of emergency, the Indian parliament was about to enact a law that permanently prohibited Christian proselytizing, evangelism, and foreign missions because such activity was perceived as interfering with the rights of Indian nationals. India, using its state of emergency situation, had already banned a range of these Christian activities. This act would make this ban permanent law. Already thousands of missionaries had their missionary visas revoked and were due to leave the land permanently. Conversion was seen as denationalizing and anti-Hindu. Yet since India is a secular democracy, its line of argument followed a clever argument propounded by the United Nations. Alger Hiss, who helped formulate the United Nations charter in San Francisco in 1948 with the help of his Communist bloc comrades (he was convicted as a traitor), based the document on the Soviet charter (left-wing media commentators and academics have always downplayed such connections).

What is the United Nations' line of reasoning?—that it is a religious right of every follower of a given religion not to be aggressively proselytized by those of another religion. Mission boards across the world knew immediately what it would mean for them if this became law in countries such as India: They would be forced to leave, and those caught engaging in missionary activities would be prosecuted, even jailed. We have in India, then, a type of precedent that we have already seen at work. In the name of the religious rights of one person, the rights of the adherent of another religion could be legally limited. Specifically, if an aspect of being a Christian is to obey the command "to make disciples of all nations" in order to spread the gospel, this religious mandate can now be legally restricted in the name of the greater rights of all the collective religions and faiths. There is a darker aim beneath this line of reasoning. What is planned if the world becomes a federation of global states, whether loosely or tightly structured?

THE NEED FOR GLOBALISM

As we have seen, in recent history there have been an interesting array of devices used to close the doors on religious freedoms. Under the banner of human rights, we have seen a line of thought which has been a supremely effective device in curtailing these freedoms. This argument is tailor-made for a pluralist and globalist situation.

The United Nations itself was founded upon a well-thought-out globalism. Indeed, if we suddenly submitted to the decrees of the United Nations General Assembly as law, then America would operate very much like our example of the extended public school. We would submit to doing this "for the benefit and out of respect for all world citizens."

Globalism has been a growing trend. In 1973, many famous and influential people signed the Humanist Manifesto II as a virtual collective of academics, lawyers, financiers, and politicians whose names read like a *Who's Who*. They declared:

> We deplore the division of humankind on nationalistic grounds. We have reached a turning point in human history where the best option is to transcend the limits of national sovereignty to move toward the building of a world community...a system of world law and world order based upon transnational federal government.

If this roster of experts feel this way, then maybe globalism is not just idle speculation. However, what concerns us the most about their global vision is the framework of laws and decrees that these experts intend to draw up which will affect each of us. Could we use United Nations law as a conditional model for what we might expect? Many of these experts have done just that, forever throwing their support behind the United Nations. What does the United Nations provide for world citizens desiring religious rights? If you consider the following, George Orwell could not have done a better job had he included the following in his novel *1984*.

In the 73rd plenary meeting of the 36th General Assembly, on November 25, 1981, among the resolutions adopted by the Third Committee was #36/55—"The Declaration on the Elimination of All Forms of Intolerance and of Discrimination Based on Religion or Belief." Should the world's nation-states come under the umbrella of the United Nations, this will become inviolable law. Under Article 1, Sections 2 and 3, it states:

2. No one shall be subject to coercion which would impair his freedom to have a religion or belief of his choice.

3. Freedom to manifest one's religion or belief may be subject only to such limitations as are prescribed by law and are necessary to protect public safety, order, health, or morals or the fundamental rights and freedoms of others.

These same words have appeared in another context. In the United Nations Covenant on Human Rights, Article 15, Section 3, it states: "Freedom to manifest one's religion or beliefs may be subject only to such limitations as are prescribed by law."

Some years ago George Orwell wrote a brilliant satire on twentieth-century collectivism entitled *Animal Farm*. It is the story of a revolution staged by animals on Farmer Jones' place. As with all revolutions, there were leaders and there were followers. In this case, the pigs became the leaders since they were, through no fault of the others, a little smarter than the rest.

One of their first official acts was to draft a statement of seven principles which were then painted on the back wall of the barn for all to see. These principles became the basis of the new order and were designed to protect the animals from any future injustice or infringements on their rights. There were noble pronouncements as "No animal shall drink alcoholic beverages"; "No animal shall sleep in a bed"; and "No animal shall kill another animal." But the greatest and wisest of these was, "All animals are equal."

As the months became years, however, things did not turn out quite the way the "workers" had expected. They were working twice as hard and eating half as well as they had when they were "exploited" by Farmer Jones—all of them, that is, except the rulers, the pigs, who were now drinking Jones' ale and sleeping in his bed. When the puzzled workers tried to figure out how things turned out this way, they went to the rear of the barn to see if there was not something in the seven great principles prohibiting this kind of injustice. They found, instead, that the principles were now worded slightly differently. Indeed, just a few words changed here and there completely changed the picture: "No animal shall drink alcoholic beverages... *to excess*"; "No animal shall sleep in a bed... *with sheets*"; "No animal shall kill another animal... *without cause.*" But by far the worst shock of all came when the poor creatures turned with hope to the seventh principle guaranteeing their rights but which now declared, "All animals are equal... *but some animals are more equal than others.*"

Before we examine the spiritual arms of globalism, let us again remember the resolution from the above United Nations declaration: "Freedom to manifest one's religion or belief may be subject *only to such limitations as are prescribed by law and are necessary to protect public safety, order, health, or morals.*" With enough legalese, word games, and elastic redefinitions of concepts, the above limitations could be instituted at the drop of a hat. Christians, should they ever fall under the United Nations World Court, might well look to the back of the barn one day and ponder these words.

17

Building the New World Temple

Those who want to abolish national boundaries and cement the nation-states together still face one of the great obstacles to this: namely, religious differences. They can be heard decrying the polarizing force of Islamic fundamentalism. But imagine how secular globalists greet Christianity when it becomes inspired by evangelical fervor. This clashing of beliefs must be dealt with by a cunning backdoor approach.

Here is one such backdoor argument: If Western countries are going to initiate globalism, they need to set the precedent for a new unitive generic religion, since religion itself is an enormous factor in creating lines of demarcation and thus preventing transnational unity from happening. Therefore, a new type of spirituality is needed: one that disavows the old order, one that can synthesize the beliefs of both East and West. This is not easy, for no one will ever be completely satisfied, especially that conservative minority of the three major monotheistic religions. But there is a movement afoot that attracts increasing numbers of educated, globally minded people in the West. You guessed it—it is the New Age movement. This has enormous implications for the direction and even the survival of religious freedoms.

As has been said, in the last ten years the New Age movement has emerged as a self-conscious spiritual/political movement with its own proselytizers and speakers; its own agenda, philosophy, and worldview; as well as its own insiders' vocabulary. Overall, this movement might best be summarized as a form of post-Christian cosmic humanism dedicated to global spiritual transformation by means of consciousness-raising. They want to install the New Age. Theirs is a prototype for a global religion, being a syncretism of Eastern and Western religions fused to modern and postmodern thought. As such it is an ideal generic global religion.

Perhaps the most significant publication to alert the public to the reality of the New Age movement, and which was on *The New York Times* bestseller list for the year 1980, was *The Aquarian Conspiracy* by Marilyn Ferguson. This book suddenly announced with unrelenting optimism that the New Age had officially had its genesis. It expounded the agenda and beliefs of the New Age movement, its leaders, its influence, as well as from whence it came and where it would be going.

None other than respected sociologist Virginia Hine defines the New Age movement in one of its own magazines, *The Networking Newsletter*. In it she says:

> In the *World Issues* article entitled "The Basic Paradigm of a Future Socio-cultural System," I suggested that a radically new form of social organization is emerging at all levels of the global system. . . .
>
> What we are reaching for here is the outlines of an emergent cosmology, the mythology of the NEW AGE. The "de-mythologizing" that is supposed to have occurred over the last two or three hundred years was in fact a replacement of earlier medieval and primitive cosmologies with what Jose Arguelles calls the Faustian myth of scientific humanism, a conceptual paradigm which now, in its turn, is falling before its successor. If we are to clarify the wide variations in NEW AGE ideology, we must seek the core tenets of the emergent paradigm.
>
> . . . I would suggest that out of the welter of current ideological variants three basic tenets have emerged and that these constitute the NEW AGE answers to basic human questions. These answers, the core of the NEW AGE paradigm, stand in clear

opposition to those that guided the evolution of the Faustian era of the industrialized nation-state.[1]

Hine hints in passing that the core of the religious transformation is to be found among pioneers of consciousness not wholly unfamiliar these days, ". . . mystics who have been illuminated by an actual experience of the Oneness of All and try to communicate the ineffable."[2]

Hine's words are recognizable rehashes of statements made by New Age advocate Marilyn Ferguson of *Aquarian Conspiracy* fame, who says, "Aquarian Conspiracy is the term I have coined for the network of people working for social transformation based on personal inner change."[3] She continues, "These people, who are advocates of what I call the 'Aquarian Conspiracy paradigm shift' are formidable."[4]

To Ferguson, we have reached the catalytic point of critical mass. We have reached "cultural dislocation" (a term used by historian William McLoughlin):

> All extensions of democracy and of human rights have been preceded by a period of spiritual awakening, according to historian William McLoughlin. These periods of cultural dislocation, he says, are not periods of social neurosis, but are times of therapeutic and cathartic renewal. Awakenings occur when we lose faith in the viability of our institutions and the authority of our leaders. Religious and spiritual awakening gives people a new vision of themselves which is then transplanted into social action.[5]

Clearly, they see the impediments to this transformation as coming within the old established social order, especially the traditional and mainline religions. Ferguson says that anthropologist Anthony Wallace "concluded that when a culture can no longer tread its customary paths from birth to death, when these are suddenly blocked, stress in that culture will be so great that some of the fringe people will begin to crack under the strain. About that time the people he refers to as the 'new lights' will propose alternative paths. As they begin to attract more attention, this process sets in motion what we call a 'backlash' by those people he calls 'nativists.' "[6] Ferguson goes on to define and rout the anticipated enemy of the cause, the nativists:

> They ask for a return to the good old ways as a solution to all our problems. Their battle cry is, "Back to basics," "Back to God," or back to whatever. Eventually, however, no matter how loud the voices of the status quo, the culture breaks through what McLoughlin calls the "crust of custom" and finds new avenues of expression.[7]

The Christian faith is a central part of that nativist crust.

Ferguson admonishes that the New Age path of salvation is the discovery that "the myth of the savior 'out there' is being replaced with the myth of the hero 'in here.' Its ultimate expression is the discovery of *the divinity within us*. Out of our evolutionary consciousness will emerge the end of our illusion of separateness."[8] Our own divinity is a key reason for global unity. We are united anyway—divinely.

This message is broadcast far and wide at all of the New Age symposia and conferences across the country. Hospice pioneer and author of the bestseller *Death and Dying*, Elisabeth Kubler-Ross predicts, "In the decades to come we may see one universe, one humankind, one religion that unites us all in a peaceful world."[9]

Robert Muller, assistant secretary general to the United Nations and author of the key New Age book entitled *New Genesis: Shaping a Global Spirituality*, is a key voice among the political VIPs of the New Age movement. The United Nations is portrayed by Muller as a key catalyzer of globalism and a special friend of the New Age movement.

In August 1983, Robert Muller was the main speaker at the Ninth Annual Mandala Conference at the Town and Country Convention Center in San Diego. To the 2200 present, Muller presented a familiar message, that "the earth and, ultimately, the cosmos are becoming self-conscious through Networking and the evolution of humankind."[10]

Of course there is a catch to this. Muller was asked by a reporter about exclusive religions such as Christianity (Mc-Loughlin's "nativists") and their role in the New Age. Muller replied, ". . . they try to be exclusive, but I think there is no religion that can win. What they should do in my opinion is get together and define the principles they have in common."[11] Muller's provisional solution is a generic religion based on a mosaic of syncretisms. Ironically, the anthem of the conference was the national anthem, but with the words changed. You might call it a generic New Age anthem. To the tune of "The Star-Spangled Banner" came the words, "O say can you see, by the One light in all, A New Age to embrace, at the call of all Nations."[12]

FORCING THE NEW AGE TO HAPPEN

Muller uses an argument of moral need: "The next stage will be our entry into a moral global age—the global age of love—and a global spiritual age—the cosmic age. We are now moving fast towards the fulfillment of the visions of the great prophets who through cosmic enlightenment saw the world as one unit, the human race as one family, sentiment as the cement of that family, and the soul as our link with the universe, eternity, and God."[13]

New Agers project a positive spirit, proudly rising above contemporary despair. In both Marilyn Ferguson and Robert Muller this mood of optimism is almost a reckless glee, a manic expectancy. Muller exults, "If Christ came back to earth, his first visit would be to the United Nations to see if his dream of human oneness and brotherhood had come true. He would be happy to see representatives from all nations."[14]

Evil is conveniently redefined as ignorance, and not as sin against a personal God. Evil is our failure to see the unity that is already there, thus forcing us to succumb to the "myth of separation." New Agers thus anticipate the collapse of the old age and the birth of the New Age by means of the *paradigm shift* in the way reality is perceived. Monotheism and ration-alism will be supplanted by mystical monism. This is all "positive."

Mark Satin in his book *New Age Politics: The Healing Self and Society* goes so far as to label the mind-set of the present age as an obsolete "Six-Sided Prison." When this mind-set is changed, the world of "Little House on the Prairie" will be demolished, along with a million and one other wholesome and good things. A homosexual teacher in public school can tell the kids about "safe sodomy" in "open-minded" state-funded sex-education classes, but he'd better not find them praying to God. Sound alarmist? Listen to some of Satin's ideas.

Imagine advocating the following to that 1930's audience in the Ziegfield Theater in our earlier conceptual time-travel experiment. Satin advocates overthrowing such things as patriarchal attitudes in which women are the victims of the male psyche with the societal consequences of a male social order resulting in an overbalance of rationality, competitive-ness, and independence;[15] and egocentricity—the false pride and selfishness stemming from the view, grounded in dual-ism, that we are our bodies. Satin (and historian Theodore Roszak) observe that this mentality can be blamed on archaic Jewish and Christian beliefs;[16] scientific single vision, the analytical scientific viewpoint which breaks things down to analyze them, failing to see their unity—therefore, "a male trait" that alienates us from "mother nature";[17] and finally nationalism—that archaic mind-set that keeps us from world-citizenship and that is grounded in territoriality and dis-trust.[18]

Satin's alternative to this "Six-Sided Prison" is a New Age society that is androgynous and feminist,[19] neo-occult and paganistic,[20] tribal and cooperative,[21] and both localized in a feudal sense as well as fully and globally planetized.[22]

New Agers hold that the dark and foreboding horizon of impending nuclear war is an important catalyst that will help force the planet into a new awakening, breaking down walls of resistance. Such things as the atomic threat raise the global temperature to the boiling point in the manner that hostages trapped in an airplane are willing to make desperate sacrifices. Outward necessity forces the dire realization. The media is a powerful instrument in harping on the crisis of our atomic and ecological time clock.

The pressure can also come from another direction. Many New Agers believe that the crucial triggering mechanism for this global event will be through the appearance of a world messiah such as Maitreya who will establish the New Age— that it will take such a one to raise the temperature high enough to create the change. Even visiting Princeton University professor and United Nations consultant Johannes Galton has expressed the view that the world was waiting to be unified, and that this would happen through the appearance of a messiah.[23] Professor Galton ventured the notion that this messiah would be triggered by science but did not elaborate beyond this.

The Los Angeles Times of September 3, 1978, stated that none other than Aurelio Peccei, founder and driving force behind The Club of Rome and one of the first endorsers of the United Nations-based Planetary Initiative project announced: "I think mankind is building up something within itself whereby it will be able to make a jump." And what will trigger this? Peccei named the two-pronged New Age apocalyptic agenda: a disaster and a messianic savior. "One disaster, one charismatic leader" could trigger this transformation, Peccei claims.

The United Nations-related group called The Planetary Initiative for the World We Choose was conceived in January 1981. According to its *Organizing Manual*, its cosponsors were from the Association for Humanistic Psychology, The Club of Rome, Global Education Associates, Planetary Citizens (a United Nations group whose honorary chairman is Norman Cousins), and the United Nations Association of New South Wales.

The wording of the *Organizing Manual* of The Planetary Initiative is noteworthy. Well-known writer Dave Hunt has seen the manual and cited it in his writings. This manual divulges: "The Planetary Initiative project will develop . . . an enduring network of individuals, local groups and global organizations . . . for contributing to the creation of a peaceful, just, and humane world order."[24] Does this sound a little like Orwell's doublespeak? Dave Hunt observes that the names associated with The Planetary Initiative read like a *Who's Who*. Its newspaper-periodical, named *The Initiator*, bears a name not without potent import according to New Age terminology.

David Spangler, a Planetary Initiative board of directors member like Muller, as well as a New Age leader, has said something rather revealing about his idea of spiritual initiation and its eschatological role in the New Age. Not all New Agers will agree with or even know about Spangler's definition of initiation when he says:

> Lucifer works within each of us to bring us to wholeness as we move into the New Age . . . each of us is brought to that point which I term the Luciferic initiation. . . .
>
> Lucifer comes to give us the final . . . Luciferic initiations . . . that many people in the days ahead will be facing, for it is an initiation into the New Age.[25]

How can women help push for a New Age? By getting angry and becoming a political force, as our media constantly remind us. Women must see themselves as oppressed, and then make sure to blame it all on men and patriarchal society. Then they can attack it from another direction: They can elevate their self-esteem by remembering who they really are. Who are they really? Goddesses who have been forced into amnesia by primitive men trying to keep them from their true potential.

New Age feminist and conference speaker Charlene Spretnak in her book *The Politics of Women's Spirituality* (New York: Anchor Books/Doubleday, 1982) teaches that, according to one reviewer, "Goddess worship, paganism, Wicca, and witchcraft are all names for a form of natural religion that is centered around the mystery, sexuality, and psychic mysteries of the female. The book is a clarion call to women to regain their natural power and to overthrow the global rule of men. The author's starting point for the re-establishment of female dominance is *in bringing an end to Judeo-Christian religion."*[26]

Charlene Spretnak was a key speaker at an event that *The Los Angeles Times* on March 16, 1982, billed as "Goddesses of Coming New Age Probe the Meaning of It All." This New Age feminist conference resolved that churches should either adopt New Age beliefs or be shut down. One backdoor approach in bringing this about is to give New Age definitions to Christian doctrinal terms (i.e. atonement means at-one-ment with the divine). Can this backdoor approach work?

There was a recent Presbyterian Congress on Renewal that took place from January 7-11, 1985, in Dallas, Texas, entitled "The Five Year Plan for Evangelism in the Presbyterian Church—The New Age Dawning." The amazing thing is that the keynote speaker, Bruce Larson, is a self-confessed evangelical, touted as a shining light of faith in his shrinking, politicized, and intractably liberal denomination of Presbyterianism. Bruce Larson has gone on record as saying great things about the coming "New Age." The words by now might begin to have a familiar ring as Larson says:

> I had and have now a growing belief that we are in the beginning of an exciting new age . . . which I believe is already imminent . . . (and will) change life for all people upon this globe . . . inner space and inter-space will become just as important, if not more important than outer-space.
>
> Mine is not an isolated hope. Carl Jung stated that in Jesus Christ there is made possible a new rung on the ladder of evolution. Pierre Teilhard de Chardin talks about his dreams for the evolution of a new being and a new society. . . . My dream is that we are on the verge of such a discovery.[27]

Larson's naive concesssion illustrates the power of the backdoor approach. The denominational churches especially are being caught sleeping. Just when the church in Nazi

Germany should have been waking up, it too had been falling asleep. When it came time to take a stand, they couldn't, as the German evangelical movement found out. In little time, they lost their religious freedoms and the church became a mouthpiece for the state, as it now is in Russia. What happened to those individual Christians who did take a stand? To use an Orwellian term, they were disposed. No one could see the writing on the back of the barn. Are people now any less naive or blind? Hardly. Again, consider the United Nations' declaration: "Freedom to manifest one's religion or belief may be subject only to such limitations as are prescribed by law." The New Age has an underside that nobody wants to see. Its words are sweet and its promises are full of utopian optimism, but it has all the weaponry in place for an awesome coup.

The changing of the guards of key conceptual *paradigms*—to use this seemingly harmless term—will squeeze the life out of the church, while the laws of the state, by the presently emerging agenda, could close down Christian functions overnight. Meanwhile, New Age "Christian" churches would flourish like state churches today in Russia. They would slip right into gear with smooth compromises, along with everyone else, and slide into a post-Christian neopagan era, intractable and totalitarian. It just might be *Mystery Babylon* revealed. And on the horizon could well be a "final Luciferic initiation" that would open new gates for all concerned, as we shall see.

18

From the Abyss to the Light of Day

I could not escape the terrible screen before my eyes. No matter what, I had to keep looking on as I pressed myself down into the thick burgundy chair in horror. Vivid impressions of the ancient Roman world penetrated my five-year-old mind. The horrifying scenes before me depicted real events, true history, and that was the shocker.

I looked on helplessly from the balcony of one of Washington's grand old cinerama movie theaters as the colossal power of the emperor Nero was being portrayed. In his eyes was a perverse cruelty, a concentrated evil given to arbitrary whim. He seemed a law unto himself as he played with people like a bored child plays with helpless insects, cutting off this and that bit to see what happens. This emperor was so hard that no pleading would get through to him. The fact that such a dehumanized figure could exist baffled my young mind. What power could bend such a soul so grotesquely? How could someone choose evil over good? He was a human monster without an atom of sensitivity, goodness, or compassion, and he ruled the entire world! There was a reality behind this that I would learn of much later in life. Nero, in truth, was a vehicle for something else. He was a representative and a type among a very select group.

Contrasting with this terrible figure was a group of people who stuck in my mind as the supreme embodiment of good. In one scene they were in the center of the huge Colosseum of Rome. They were being persecuted because they would not

213

214 • *Tal Brooke*

pay homage to Nero. They were loyal to Christ alone above any state or emperor, and for that they would die. The crowds in the Colosseum roared. They wanted entertainment. Christians by the hundreds were spread across the arena. Nero was outraged, for rather than begging for mercy, renouncing their Christ, or running in terror, they sang these powerful hymns to their God while looking skyward. Peace radiated from their faces. Nero could not stand it. Finally he gave the thumbs down. Huge iron gates into the arena opened as scores of lions entered the stadium. The lions left some of the Christians alone as they sang and stared fearlessly into the crowds and at the emperor. Others were mauled while still singing. In the end, all died with dignity, leaving the Circus Maximus in an eerie silence. The emperor's desire for a blood orgy was completely frustrated, but only for the time being.

My terror increased as I saw the city of Rome all ablaze. I recall asking my parents to take me out of the movie theater. The face of Nero grinned as it flickered with a scarlet light radiating from the enormous flames. Perhaps he was punishing his subjects—mere insects to him—or seeking new forms of entertainment. He sang mad, intoxicating songs. Massive crowds of the populace wailed in the background as they ran in helpless terror to escape falling columns and collapsing buildings. Nero ranted and laughed. How did he of all people end up with so much power? Why this evil creature among men?

After the fire of Rome, Nero blamed the Christians. Waves of persecution rolled on even more grotesquely. It was an affront to everything I instinctively felt, to see that evil and falsehood could hold such power. This situation cried out to be judged. As the mobs of Rome went wild in the streets looking for Christians, believing their emperor's lies, the powerful figure of Paul the apostle reassured the believers in the catacombs of Rome of ultimate hope. Nothing could quench their hope or their goodness. I sensed something far mightier in the Christian martyrs than the despotic evil that Nero embodied.

Three decades after seeing this movie I was able to glimpse

this era once again through the eyes of such ancient contemporary historians as Pliny, Tacitus, and Suetonius, whose eyewitness records of the Roman era were brought to vivid life in a course by Dr. Bruce Manning Metzger, a member of both Princeton Seminary as well as Princeton's Institute for Advanced Study. Dr. Metzger, a man with five Ph.D.'s and one of the world's most brilliant evangelical scholars, was a key reason I was at Princeton during the last years of his tenure. There was no question that the Neronic persecution was real history—that this all happened in Rome. Indeed, the mortar of the early church was persecution.

It was incredible what the ancient Christians suffered—and did so time and again without God invisibly removing them from the scene! That is history. Like their Christ, they too suffered martyrdom, and they expected no less. Christ himself had told them: "If they persecuted me, they will persecute you" (John 15:20 RSV); "Blessed are you when men revile you and persecute you and utter all kinds of evil against you falsely on my account" (Matthew 5:11 RSV); and "If any man would come after me, let him deny himself and take up his cross and follow me" (Mark 8:34 RSV). Paul had followed suit, saying, "When reviled, we bless; when persecuted, we endure; when slandered, we try to conciliate" (1 Corinthians 4:12,13 RSV). And Paul knew from experience what this was like. Paul was stoned at Lystra; he and Silas were beaten by a mob in Philippi, then with lacerated backs sang hymns to God; he had experienced the near-lethal 39 lashes on various occasions; and he had a long imprisonment in Caesarea, was later sent to Rome as a prisoner, and died a martyr. He says to some of the slow-witted believers in Corinth: "Five times I received from the Jews the forty lashes minus one. Three times I was beaten with rods, once I was stoned, three times I was shipwrecked, I spent a night and a day in the open sea, I have been constantly on the move" (2 Corinthians 11:24,25). Paul's litany of trials goes on and on.

If God could allow such trials to happen to the apostles and early Christians without removing them from the scene, should modern and postmodern Christians count on any less? The wrath of man should not be underestimated. As we see in the Roman era, it can seem almost as bad as the wrath of God from the receiving end—almost.

The ancient Roman historian Tacitus, who like most of his contemporaries did not sympathize with the Christians, describes what he saw after the great fire of Rome in his *Annals*, XV, 44:

> Therefore to scotch the rumor [of his starting the fire], Nero substituted as culprits, and punished with the utmost refinements of cruelty, a class of men loathed for their vices, whom the crowd styled Christians. Christus, from whom they got their name, had been executed by sentence of the procurator Pontius Pilate when Tiberius was emperor; and the pernicious superstition was checked for a short time, only to break out afresh, not only in Judaea, the home of the plague, but in Rome itself, where all the horrible and shameful things in the world collect and find a home. First, then, those who confessed themselves Christians were arrested; next, on their disclosures, a vast multitude were convicted, not so much on the charge of arson as for hatred of the human race. And their death was made a matter of sport: they were covered in wild beasts' skins and torn to pieces by dogs; or were nailed to crosses and set on fire in order to serve as torches by night when daylight failed. Nero had offered his gardens for the spectacle and gave an exhibition in his circus, mingling with the crowd in the guise of a charioteer or mounted in his chariot . . . it was felt that they were being sacrificed not for the common good but to gratify the savagery of one man.

This happened in A.D. 64, around the time that the apostle Paul was martyred.

Sixty years later, Pliny, governor of Bithynia in A.D. 112, wrote the emperor Trajan describing his manner of dealing with the Christian problem. By then, the church had endured well over 60 years of persecution. Pliny tells the emperor in his *Epistles of Pliny, X, 33 & 34*:

> So far this has been my procedure when people were charged before me with being Christians. I have asked the accused themselves if they were Christians; if they said "yes," I asked them a second and third time, warning them of the penalty; if they persisted I ordered them to be led off to execution. . . . An anonymous letter was laid before me containing many people's names. Some of these denied that they were Christians or had ever been so; at my dictation they invoked the gods and did reverence with incense and wine to your image, which I had ordered to be brought for this purpose along with the statues of the gods; they also cursed Christ; and as I am informed that people who are really Christians cannot possibly be made to do any of those things, I considered that the people who did them should be discharged.

Pliny's letter to the emperor Trajan describes the reality of emperor worship and the very real fact that Christians lost their lives for refusing to engage in this brief act. One wonders how many Christians of today could face death with anything approaching this degree of raw courage and faith. The governor knew of no true Christians who had tried to spare their lives by resorting to this brief idolatrous act—no exceptions! Imagine instead the well-earned image of so many modern Christians, who to the world are a great host of butterballs and couch potatoes sitting at their TV sets and flipping through channels to view their modern "Christian" leaders. And who do modern Christians follow? People whose faith has been borne out by suffering, whose purity and strength of character have shone through even to the death? Unfortunately, not at all. They remain the ignorant faithful even after these leaders have been caught repeatedly with prostitutes, homosexual lovers, and after they have built up private, luxurious estates with Rolls Royces and mansions from good-faith money that these leaders have pilfered by graft and sham causes.

What would these modern "Christian" leaders of today do in the face of the emperor Nero or Trajan? I believe they would do anything to hold onto their lives and estates. They would jump through any hoop—including burning incense to an altar and uttering a quick one to the emperor. They have already done as much to stay on TV. All these voices would beg the emperor just like they beg their TV audiences. Don't they ever fearfully wonder whether they might be among that massive crowd of false believers who hear the stinging sentence of Christ uttered after they implore him, "Lord, Lord, did we not prophesy in your name, and in your name . . . perform many miracles?" And Christ will respond, "I never knew you. Away from me, you evildoers!" (Matthew 7). Rather than awe or reverence, they tout God's name with the cheap flippancy of game-show hosts.

Christians of today, alas, have no idea how much harm these "Christians" have done. What is incredible is that they would dignify them with even a moment's airtime. Paul had well warned the Ephesian elders at the port of Miletus, on his third missionary journey, that the church would be inundated with false Christians throughout the ages, coming both from within and from outside the church. The epistles warn that such false teachers would ply people for money, exercise their secret lusts, introduce false doctrines, and seek personal glory. The condition of the church today reflects this very spiritual cancer. The church is flaccid, ignorant, and unprepared. It has subsisted on a diet of candy and junk food. If most of the contemporary church were somehow able to change places with the early church, it would be in dire straits, capitulating its beliefs instantly at the first moment of discomfort before it got even within earshot of Rome's Colosseum.

Had the apostle John, who saw and recorded the Book of Revelation, been sitting by my side when I saw Nero in action on that movie screen, he would have told me that I was sensing the spirit of Antichrist filtering through this Roman emperor. John wrote in his first epistle to those under his leadership that the spirit of Antichrist who will come in the end was already at work in the world in his forerunners (1 John 2:18).

Like mounting refrains in a symphony, Nero foreshadowed the climax. He was but one of many antichrists. John lived to see Nero. By the time John recorded the Book of Revelation in A.D. 92, Domitian sat on the throne of the Roman empire. By then, many Christians had been martyred and the imperial cult of emperor worship was fully enforced. The caesars, who were considered to be "vehicles" for the Roman gods, by the time of Domitian's reign claimed to be fully god incarnate. Until that time they were given the title of gods posthumously.

The line between life and death for early Christians was the following: The test of fidelity to the state involved public ceremonies before altars of Caesar across the empire. Subjects were to proclaim Caesar as Lord and offer incense to his likeness at the altars. Subjects referred to Domitian (A.D. 81-96) with the words *dominus et deus noster*: "our Lord and God." Those who refused this test of loyalty to the state were seen as "haters of the human race," a term we saw in the account of Tacitus. Josephus and others revealed that Jews, as subjects under the empire who had a long-established religion, were exempt from this. Not so with Christians. It was before these Roman altars that Christians were rooted out repeatedly. Christ was their Lord, not Caesar. They could not with integrity utter the words *Kaisar est Kurios*, "Caesar is Lord," while offering incense to an idol of Caesar. They recognized what spiritual powers of darkness worked through this system of tyranny, where the emperor sat in the seat of godhood demanding to be worshiped by his subjects. It was an ancient theme that would reappear across history during that span of time between the first and second advents of Christ, but this span would not endure forever. God had placed an upper limit on it.

The Bible spoke emphatically of a final day. Evil would have its ultimate unleashing in a shocking escalation at the end of history. The final denouement of evil would be so great that God himself would have to intervene in the affairs of the world.

When asked about the world conditions before his return, Christ told his apostles that these future days would be more wicked than the days of Noah. How evil were those days? They were sufficiently wicked for God to send a global flood! The biblical record in Genesis mentions that virtually the entire human race mocked and defied God. The common picture we have is that the race engaged in various perversities and occult-sexual practices in a hedonistic feeding frenzy. The lid had been blown off. If they retained a patina of spirituality to justify it, it required removing the knowledge of God and replacing it with some kind of sorcerized nature religion. We are certainly crossing taboo barriers today. The definite picture we do get of Noah's day is that all moral restraint was broken so that "all flesh," except for the family of Noah, was now rotten beyond restoration. "The Lord saw how great man's wickedness on the earth had become, and **that every inclination** of the thoughts of his heart was only evil all the time" (Genesis 6:5). Like Sodom, it required a total purge.

Such was the antediluvian world before the flood. Interestingly, New Agers believe that an advanced occult civilization named Atlantis in prehistory was totally destroyed, leaving only a handful of survivors. Now they believe its secrets are being rediscovered. How ironic if this is in reality the Noachian age, and a foreboding sign indeed if such "secrets" from Noah's day are being rediscovered in today's occult revival. It is not impossible.

The era of the Roman emperors was a major refrain in history's vast symphony. Christ spoke of many antichrists that would come. Some would be miracle workers. They all would claim to be divine. Jesus spoke of this in Matthew 24:24: "For false Christs and false prophets will appear and perform great signs and miracles to deceive even the elect—if that were possible." Their effect would be to delude and deceive masses of people, counterfeiting themselves as the Messiah. The concluding climax would be the final Antichrist—one figure over the entire earth. He would come as an eschatological personage, not a collective symbol (as the Reformers viewed the papacy), though he would have human forerunners, other antichrists. To the world he would be the Messiah.

In the Old Testament, Daniel describes the Antichrist at the close of his vision of future things. Daniel 11:36,37 (KJV) gives the profile:

> And the king shall do according to his will; and he shall exalt himself, and magnify himself above every god, and shall speak marvellous things against the God of gods, and shall prosper till the indignation be accomplished: for that which is determined shall be done. Neither shall he regard the God of his fathers, nor the desire of women, nor regard any god: for he shall magnify himself above all.

Indeed, he will "honor the God of forces" (v. 38)—or Satan.

Paul further focuses in on this eschatological personage in the second letter to the Thessalonian church:

> Now concerning the coming of our Lord Jesus Christ and our assembling to meet him, we beg you, brethren, not to be quickly shaken in mind or excited, either by spirit or by word, or by letter purporting to be from us, to the effect that the day of the Lord has come. Let no one deceive you in any way; for that day will not come, unless the rebellion comes first, and the man of lawlessness is revealed, the son of perdition, who opposes and exalts himself against every so-called god or object of worship, so that he takes his seat in the temple of God, proclaiming himself to be God (2 Thessalonians 2:1-5 RSV).

The early church knew that the church era existed during the period of time known as "the last days"—that spanned between Christ's first and second advents. Now they learned from Paul that a general apostasy, a falling away or rebellion, needed to come first before the Lord would return. Evil would increase, while the scaffolding of the nominal church-at-large would collapse. The world would rebel against God and his truth. They also knew that the final Antichrist had to come not as a collective symbol, but as a man, "the man of sin." Paul reveals the source of the Antichrist's power: "The coming of the lawless one will be in accordance with the work of Satan displayed in all kinds of counterfeit miracles, signs and wonders, and in every sort of evil that deceives those who are perishing" (2 Thessalonians 2:9).

THE BOOK OF REVELATION:
THE ANTICHRIST AS "THE BEAST"

As we have seen, the Antichrist has been called the "man of sin," the "son of perdition," and "the lawless one," as well as other descriptive terms. In the great apocalyptic book of the New Testament, the Book of Revelation, he is called "the beast." The most extensive New Testament description of his activities on the earth at the time of the end is documented in the Book of Revelation. These descriptions are couched in apocalyptic imagery and language, giving a very vivid sense of the outrageous reality of this being. He may use the body of a man, but we are admonished that he is far more than a man. A massive, ageless power is occupying a human body to fulfill a deadly agenda centuries in the making. The trick is not to be fooled by the illusion of a man's body operating like a puppet.

Why is "apocalyptic language" used? Apocalyptic imagery and language is needed when mortal minds are grappling with dimensions of reality that go far beyond the senses, such as the spiritual dominions and realities so out of the reach of most men. Add to this the fact that these unreachable spiritual realities are to be described operating in the distant future, and the challenge of communicating this becomes incredible. Apocalyptic language is the only conceivable medium to say anything at all.

God, using the apostle John as his instrument, would not invent some Aramaic or Greek word for "holographic laser scanning" that by its own future context could not possibly have any meaning at all in the ancient culture of 2000 years ago. John the apostle cannot say, "Oh yes, it was a laser operating at a billion joules of power," or "After they achieved nuclear fusion . . ." or, "Particle beam weaponry in advanced satellites . . ." He could only describe things with available imagery. Even in the 1920's these same terms would have no meaning. Even as recently as the early seventies, people would be baffled by a statement like, "I booted up my IBM 386, but since it was MS Dos and operating at 17 megahertz, there was no way it was compatible with the old CPM disk I was trying to open up."

Now imagine suddenly being able to glimpse into the far future from the ancient world, then being told to describe that utterly different world 2000 years ahead. Add to this an ability to discern spiritual realities at work, and the job of communicating this to contemporaries and others across history is titanic. Only God can find a linguistic medium to do this—apocalyptic language: visual and symbolic metaphor that describes spiritual and concrete realities intersecting and acting in concert. There will be lessons in apocalyptic descriptions applicable to any era, such as the ageless struggle between good and evil, but only when outward conditions approximate the time of the prophecy do things really pop into view. That is why Luther and Calvin almost gave up on the Book of Revelation!

The Book of Revelation is like a four-dimensional moving hologram. Daniel was told when he asked God the meaning behind his baffling vision of the future, which seemed to carry the symbolism of a dream: "The meaning of these things will not be shown until the time of the end." So too with the Book of Revelation. It unfurls like a massive master plan or blueprint opening into view as the calendar of world events progresses.

It is a tough book to deal with. It has carried multiple levels of meaning. Below are the main ones.

For one thing, the Book of Revelation had a message to the early believers of its day about the real powers at work behind

Rome and the caesars. It provided a context for their persecution, spiritual insight regarding the source of this adversity. It encouraged the efforts of the early church to maintain the faith against immense opposition. All this helped the church survive this first wave of persecution (the preterist view).

Revelation also portrayed the rising and falling tides across history, the patterns and interplays between good and evil, the kingdom of God versus the principalities and dominions of Satan (the idealist view).

Many suggest that Revelation also showed the shifting stages of church growth versus church decay and apostasy throughout history (the historicist view).

Finally, the Book of Revelation showed the supreme blueprint of history and the outcome at the end, prophesying the last days right up to Christ's return (the prophetic futurist view).

What all this means is that the Book of Revelation provides ultimate meaning to history and portrays ultimate hope no matter to what heights evil arises. It also predicts the end of linear history with its grand conclusion as well as its cyclic movements. We see that history is indeed "his story" (from where the term "history" came)—and nothing can thwart God's plan.

As has been said, the Book of Revelation gives us a glimpse of the Antichrist, also known as the beast, who is to come in the final days before Christ's return. This is by far the most complete revelation of the Antichrist, adding further detail to all the other prior biblical sketches. Revelation, chapter 13, describes this future reality:

> The dragon [Satan] gave the beast his power and his throne and great authority. One of the heads of the beast seemed to have a fatal wound, but the fatal wound had been healed. The whole world was astonished and followed the beast. Men worshiped the dragon because he had given authority to the beast, and they also worshiped the beast and asked, "Who is like the beast? Who can make war against him?"

The beast was given a mouth to utter proud words and blasphemies and to exercise his authority for forty-two months. He opened his mouth to blaspheme God, and to slander his name and his dwelling place and those who live in heaven. He was given power to make war against the saints and to conquer them. And he was given authority over every tribe, people, language and nation. All inhabitants of the earth will worship the beast—all whose names have not been written in the book of life belonging to the Lamb that was slain from the creation of the world (vv. 2-8).

Then another powerful figure emerges two verses later:

Then I saw another beast, coming out of the earth. He had two horns like a lamb, but he spoke like a dragon. He exercised all of the authority of the first beast on his behalf, and made the earth and its inhabitants worship the first beast, whose fatal wound had been healed. And he performed great and miraculous signs, even causing fire to come down from heaven to earth in full view of men. Because of the signs he was given power to do on behalf of the first beast, he deceived the inhabitants of the earth. He ordered them to set up an image in honor of the beast who was wounded by the sword and yet lived. He was given power to give breath to the image of the first beast, so that it could speak and cause all who refused to worship the image to be killed. He also forced everyone, small and great, rich and poor, free and slave, to receive a mark on his right hand or his forehead, so that no one could buy or sell unless he had the mark, which is the name of the beast or the number of his name. This calls for wisdom. If anyone has insight, let him calculate the number of the beast, for it is man's number. His number is 666 (Revelation 13:11-18).

The beast, or Antichrist, and the second beast, or false prophet as he is sometimes described, form an awesome

226 • *Tal Brooke*

power. They are directly empowered by Satan himself, who is called "the dragon" in the Book of Revelation. Satan gives a human agent his throne and his powers for the first time in history.

John has just revealed in the prior chapter, Revelation 12:9, that "The great dragon was hurled down—that ancient serpent called the devil or Satan, who leads the whole world astray. He was hurled to the earth, and his angels with him." It is the dragon that seeks out and establishes the beast. In the very first verse of chapter 13, the chapter about the Antichrist, the dragon initiates the process: "And the dragon stood on the shore of the sea. And I saw a beast coming out of the sea." Again, the sea represents the endless masses of humanity from out of which the beast emerges physically. That is the physical shell, the body, but what about his soul?

Indeed, what about the soul of the Antichrist? Here is another deep mystery. Those who have read my book *Riders of the Cosmic Circuit* will see far more completely the dynamics of demonic possession as it takes place with the heaviest of today's New Age emissaries in India. There is an ancient and secret path for this mystery initiation to unfold. I myself felt these ancient forces in south India beginning to unravel my soul. My former guru—India's greatest miracle-worker, Sai Baba—had totally undergone this possessive transformation. As with all "enlightened" masters, we used the term "there's nobody home" inside the shell of the body—meaning there is no human ego. We, his disciples, assumed it was God inside. It turned out to be something else. This is deadly serious stuff, and the following gives us a further hint about the Antichrist.

We now discover that the soul of the Antichrist has another source. In Revelation 11:7, we are given a hint: ". . . the beast that comes up from the Abyss . . ." The abyss is that shaft of infinite darkness which is the holding place and gateway of the demonic powers and principalities. The beast does not have a functioning human soul, but is in a state of total possession. A spirit being from the highest of the demonic hierarchy, if not Satan himself, enters the body of the beast. At last Lucifer walks the earth as "the god of this world."

What God prevented from happening at Babel when the world spoke one language—a unified world system under an earlier prototype of the Antichrist, Nimrod—is finally allowed to happen. For only once in history a one-world system, with Lucifer at the helm empowering and working through his Antichrist, is allowed to take place. It is the crowning abomination, the completion of the prophet Daniel's "abomination of desolation."

In the Book of Revelation we gain an interesting glimpse of the Antichrist. He is inspired and empowered by Satan while the hidden powers and kingships of the earth provide the floor plan for his emergence. The kings surrender to him their dominions. It is a reemergence of the former great empires, embodied last of all by Rome, but it stretches beyond them. The territory of Europe today comprised the central corpus of Rome. This revived Rome is to reappear again. It is interesting that 1992 is being pinpointed for a united Europe, commercially and otherwise. Nations must surrender a degree of sovereignty for this to happen. One highly placed international banker remarked to an acquaintance of his that a shadow government of ten or twelve men in international finance would be the true rulers of this merged Europe in 1992. One could almost think of them as the true invisible kings, the banker kings, who would pull strings while almost no one would know who they were. The 2000-year-old Book of Revelation continues to unfurl.

The beast will be in the control seat of an awesome power: the world's military arsenal. This will give him direct powers over life and death—the life of every citizen on the earth. He will be feared the way the Roman emperors were feared. We see this with the words, "Who is able to make war with the beast?" The rhetorical answer is clearly, "No one on earth."

U.N. leaders since Alger Hiss have talked of a global military force policed by the United Nations. Leaders in high places, such as Brzezinski, who wrote *Between Two Ages*, have spoken of a simultaneous surrender and merger of American and Soviet military powers to enforce world peace. It would be run by a third force, a "neutral" force. This has been a long-term goal of the Trilateral Commission, the Bilder-bergers, as well as the Council on Foreign Relations (the CFR), among a number of elitist groups. This shadow government, in place for some time, will be waiting in the wings for the switchover and surrender of powers to take place. These are the real movers and shakers of history. Once the global police force is in place, there will be no turning back, no divvying back the chips to once-sovereign nations.

Picture, therefore, a global umbrella of Star Wars technology—satellite-linked supercomputers communicating in gigabytes, total-eye satellites, lasers, particlebeam weapons platforms, ICBM's—now under centralized control once the merger of Soviet and American military arsenals has taken place. Orwell's Big Brother, portrayed in the novel *1984*, did not approach this kind of supreme power. And come to think of it, what better imagery could the apostle John 2000 years ago—indeed, a thousand years before the Dark Ages—use to describe the reality of some futuristic laser and Star Wars technology than the descriptive phrase "fire coming down from heaven"? No better metaphor was available in the ancient world. Like his predecessors the Roman emperors, the beast will indeed have life-and-death power over every inhabitant of the world. For good reason they will ask, "Who can make war on the beast?"

The beast and his ally are also empowered with enormous spiritual powers directly from Satan. They are able to work deceiving miracles. The beast is at the axis of the world's new religious system, which in reality is a revival of what the Book of Revelation terms *Mystery Babylon*. The second beast is his high priest.

In the ancient world, the source and root of the various occult mystery religions was Babylon, founded by Nimrod soon after the Great Flood. From there its metaphysical system moved into culture after culture. But Babylon's secret mysteries are due to revive as a world religion. Every evidence today seems to point to the fact that this is happening right now. The beast, like his predecessor Nimrod, is to be the messiah of this global religion, receiving worship from the inhabitants of the earth who will also worship the dragon.

The mystery of Lucifer will finally be unveiled—"They will worship the dragon." Foreshadowings of this have recently appeared. Blatantly, there has been the rapid appearance of the phenomenon of satanism. On a subtler level, Alice Bailey pointed to a coming Luciferic New Age initiation, as has David Spangler, a major New Age leader. New Age events dotting our horizon form a rising aggregate of voices speaking of New Age initiations. The spirit beings in the channelers echo the teachings of *Mystery Babylon*, with its divine within and its expectation of the coming world messiah. So who are they and where are they from? Couldn't they be from among the host of "the dragon and his angels," these entities ranging from Ramtha to Lazarus?

The third global domain that the beast has total control over is the world's banking and economic system, which is now finally centralized. He is the mystery banker as well as the messiah. This reality has been foreshadowed by the Roman emperors whose images appeared on ancient coins accompanied by words proclaiming their deity. The imperial cult and commerce were interlinked. This ancient link will be forged once again. A surviving structure of this has existed in recent centuries in the Masonic orders where commerce and an occult brotherhood form a secret link.

But there is yet another detail that alarms us. It is a prophetic detail that comes to us from 2000 years ago. Keep in mind that computer chips did not hit the world scene till the 1970's, and Norbert Weiner at the Massachusetts Institute of Technology (MIT) did not talk about cybernetics till our era. Yet the apostle John describes a reality that has only recently come into focus: global banking, laser scanning, and the universal computer bar code. As was recounted earlier, John recorded the following 2000 years ago on the island of Patmos: "He also forced everyone, small and great, rich and poor, free and slave, to receive a mark on his right hand or on his forehead, so that no one could buy or sell unless he had the mark, which is the name of the beast..." (Revelation 13:16,17).

It is a tiny step to go from using a Visa card or a bank card on the Plus System and other ATM machines, in which the electronic strip is attached to the card, to putting that same strip of information on the human body so that it can be laser scanned. This has already been done with laser tattoos and implanted microchips. It is only since the advent of networked supercomputing (we are close to fifth generational autonomously intelligent machines, as we saw foreshadowed in Arthur C. Clarke's computer HAL, who appeared in the film *2001*) that the hardware is now in place to easily track economic and other profiles of every citizen on earth. Again, what better descriptive term could John have found in the ancient world than "the mark," which would enable every citizen to buy or sell who had it? The Plus System is now global—with instantaneous satellite interlinking and global identity marks on the horizon. The building blocks for a one-world economic system are already in place—colossal power in the hands of a few.

What we see in the Book of Revelation is that the beast is the military commander of the world, the messiah and object of worship of the world's unified mystery religion, and the supreme banker. These three headships (or heads)—military, religious, and economic—give him virtual control over the inhabitants of the earth. He wields totalitarian and undisputed military, religious, and economic powers over a one-world system. Finally "somebody gets it all," and it is the beast. After all these centuries and plans for one man to master the earth, it finally happens. The dreams of Alexander the Great, Napoleon, and Hitler; the dreams of hundreds of ambitious men of power through the centuries who would have given anything to achieve this end (and many have) are finally achieved. The Antichrist is light-years beyond Nero, and only God can defeat him. Literally no one can stand up against the Antichrist. The world hands him its soul on a platter. It is like Esau selling his soul, his birthright, for a meal—and this taken to cosmic proportions. It is the guaranteed welfare of socialism traded for the price of freedom—that's the barter of the whole earth.

As under Orwell's Big Brother in *1984*, there is barely

freedom to think. The mind dares to move beneath the surface, but that is all. In the end, all who differ with this agenda will be found out and exterminated. Like the pogroms of 60 million in Russia, or the millions of political prisoners killed in Cambodia, or the tens of millions in China, or the millions and millions of "political" prisoners killed during our present era, so too this genocide—which is by no means too fantastic to conceive of since it has already happened— will happen again. But with the beast, this killing of dissidents, with Christians as the primary target, will be open season. The Christian holocaust will become a reality. In the words of Revelation 13:7, "He was given power to make war against the saints and to conquer them"—but only for a brief season.

The final emperor, like his predecessors the Roman emperors, will rise to world power. He will claim to be divine, and his vehicle to this divine claim will be a mystery religion. His aim will be to usurp God, have the full powers of the world and the full collective of human souls under his dominion. To achieve this, he will try to totally abolish any evidence of the knowledge of the true God from the face of the earth. Appearing to be good at first, he will be vastly more demonic than any of his Roman predecessors such as Caligula, Nero, or Domitian. He will be a hollow shell, a human body, in a state of total possession by perhaps no less a spirit being than Satan himself. He will enforce his religion with the death penalty.

We know from history that the earth has seen such emperors before in the flesh, and it will see one again. If Christ came in the flesh, so will Antichrist. The groundwork for the appearance of the man of sin will be incredible, beginning centuries before his time. By stages the world will fall into line with this secret agenda. It will welcome this seduction as it comes riding atop *Mystery Babylon*.

When I saw Nero on that movie screen as a small child, it was little wonder that my skin crawled and I felt horror in the pit of my stomach. Perhaps I was sensing the spirit of Antichrist which was at work even in the apostle John's day. Something far more foreboding than the celluloid images pierced my soul. I didn't know then that I would one day be under an antichrist myself for two years in India, nor did I know that a far greater one has been on the way, from out of the abyss and into the light of day.

19

The Great Lie

A single thought has danced as a whirling dervish across history, seducing millions in its path. Indeed this very thought seduced the highest created intelligence in the universe. It was also great enough to cause the fall of the entire human race. It has invaded culture after culture, each time captivating the hearts and minds of the people. People find it infinitely desirable and beautiful, its promises irresistible, as it seems to hold such great promise. This thought seems to answer our greatest hopes and longings, our deepest struggles with our identity in the cosmos, and our quest for ultimate meaning. It is the Great Lie. It is the foundation stone of Hinduism, Buddhism, Sufism, Jainism, Sikhism, Taoism, the Kabbala, the Greek Hermetic and Eleusinian Gnostic beliefs, Neoplatonism, all the occult creeds from Theosophy and the Masonic orders to the Rosicrucians, as well as too many cults to mention. It is the central foundation stone of the New Age movement.

The tenets of the Great Lie have been chanted on the banks of the Ganges since time immemorial. Weather-beaten sages have uttered secret syllables and mantras in caves to invoke its powers. Modern meditators have sought to plumb its secret depths as they have gathered in intimate meetings from MIT to Esalen, from Greenwich Village to Marin County, from the west bank of the Seine to Cambridge, England.

The Great Lie is quite simply the belief *that man is God*, that his true identity is the immortal self that is ageless and eternal, and that *as God he will never die*! Death is merely a veil through which we pass—it is not real. Sin and depravity are therefore illusions since this inner divinity is at man's core. Sins and imperfections are passing blemishes clouding the effulgence of the eternal Atma. The outward drama of the world can be used to beckon us back to our ultimate self if we know the secret wisdom.

The Great Lie promises delicious temporal rewards. Oh, to be divine and do anything we want, whenever, wherever! To sin and do it divinely, to paraphrase Rajneesh. What outrageous freedom! It is behind the knowing smile at the Rainbow festival. It is behind the body language of the outrageous and autonomously defiant Berkeleyite cruising down Telegraph, or the straight yuppie in the corporate world waiting to run a line of coke and then go to a wife-swapping party cum seance. Now all those wild little desires can be acted out without real risk because it is God playing the game with himself. The Hindu term for this is *Maha-lila*. One can sin without consequence since it is all a cosmic game of hide-and-seek anyway. In mainline Hinduism this does not apply, for karma hangs over the head like a mountain. But many Westerners use the guru's argument from the *Bhagavad Gita* that any action is permissible if done in the right consciousness, even killing. Rajneesh cites this all the time.

Thus part of the Great Lie involves blotting out the reality of the consequences of our actions. People hate to acknowledge them anyway. It is like the odd defiance, the turning against reality that we witness in the homosexual underworld now that AIDS has killed hundreds of thousands. Now many are even more profligate, swapping partners like they are on a merry-go-round. Yet the whirlwind of self-destruction follows along behind—as real as a tornado uprooting a Texas ranch house.

Genesis 3 recounts the fall of man through the Great Lie. Satan, speaking through the serpent, promised Adam and Eve that they would become like God. In the same breath he assured them that there was no death—that death is an illusion. " 'You will not surely die,' the serpent said to the woman.

'For God knows that when you eat of it, your eyes will be opened, and *you will be like God*, knowing good and evil' " (Genesis 3:4,5). Here it is: "You will not surely die" and "You will be like God." It is a direct contradiction to what God had told them and what Adam and Eve knew in their consciences. In Goethe's masterpiece *Faust*, the question is asked Mephistopheles, "What is the fastest thing in the Universe?" The answer is that it is a thought, "when the will turns from good to evil." How great the plunge! Adam and Eve fell for it and fell from a vast summit, taking all of the human race with them. It was a cosmic event.

Originally Adam and Eve were exemplars of everything we long for. At the height of their created powers, these federal heads of the human race had the full capacity of immense intellects and clear consciences—without taint of original sin. They had original righteousness. Their senses were razor-sharp. This was human potential at its best; nothing dulled their vital intimacy with their Creator. If we believe the biblical record, these two foundational heads of the race were created perfect. With all their faculties operant, living in paradise, the ideal environment, experiencing deep fellowship with the living God, they fell for the Great Lie. It was the unhindered human will without the environmental argument of: "I grew up in a poor family in Detroit and was abused as a child, and that's why I did it." There were no excuses. The will alone was accountable—the naked will. Under these conditions they chose evil, and their choice flew in the face of both reason and reality. That alone illustrates both the potency of the lie and the human vulnerability centering around the self, the "I."

The lesson is this: If our two perfect federal heads of the race succumbed by their wills, can we be so confident that we ourselves won't fall as they did? We have so much less and are but blemished images of these original paragons. If they fell in paradise, how are we supposed to fare in a corrupt world inundated with evils of all kinds? In God's great salvation plan, only the doors of grace can free us, and such grace can only come through the mystery of the Messiah's atoning act. God's counteroffer of grace has been on his terms, not on the serpent's. Unfortunately, multitudes have opted for the latter's offer because it felt good, it seemed right. Playing God with their own wills, many have declared it the more desirable choice.

But the Great Lie did not originate in Eden. It came through one cosmic being far superior in capacity to the two perfect humans who were later seduced. The most endowed created being ever, who witnessed the creation of the physical cosmos before time began, wanted to become God and ascend above the throne of God. Isaiah 14:12-14 (KJV) recounts this pivotal cosmic event:

> How art thou fallen from heaven, O Lucifer, son of the morning! How art thou cut down to the ground, which did weaken the nations!
> For thou has said in thine heart, "I will ascend into heaven, I will exalt my throne above the stars of God; I will sit also upon the mount of the congregation, in the sides of the north; I will ascend above the heights of the clouds; I will be like the most High."

The fall of Lucifer heightens the issue of what took place in Eden. In deep heaven, the will embodied in Lucifer existed in the most-exalted spiritual regions, unlike Adam's physical existence. For in the midst of heavenly splendor, bathed in the love of God, the unimaginable *Viseo Dei*, free of any possible influence or pull of physical existence (the Gnostic excuse), and with the most lucid of intelligences imaginable, the will still chose evil. Cambridge philosopher Austin Farrer pinpoints Lucifer's perversity of choice as that of "preferring the sterile satisfaction of pride and self-will to the inexhaustible wealth of a participation in the life of God." This becomes the most monstrous of imaginable sins. To Farrer, this incident depicts "without obstruction what perversity is—the perversity expressed in any and every sin." Human perversity "can do all the devil can do in making an absolute beginning of evil; this at every moment in time."[1]

Lucifer fell and became Satan, the father of lies. The very pride that ensnared him—the desire to become God—he turned against the human race. When absolute greatness corrupts and then falls, its evil is beyond estimation. Satan became the spiritual equivalent of a black hole. His evil became all-consuming and his hostility to God, after he transformed, became total. No *Star Wars* imagery can depict this complex and fallen being. His footprints, however, can be seen across time, across human history, as the great adversary of God who is the architect of the Great Lie, and the secret mystery religion upon which it rides.

The almost 2000-year-old Book of Revelation, the last book of the New Testament, summarized and distilled over 1500 years of Jewish prophecy in its far-reaching vision of ultimate one worldism. Brooks Alexander comments on this future global empire involving economic, political, and military forces under an occult *gnosis* which appears in a single unified system of oppression and delusion known as *Mystery Babylon*. Ten years before the term "New Age" appeared, Brooks Alexander, founder and director of Spiritual Counterfeit Projects, wrote in the early seventies: "The Bible gives us a clear, if unpleasant picture: in the last days of history as we know it, our race will be brought together in a common expression of cosmic humanism. This coming great world religion will offer itself to us as the ancient wisdom and hidden truth underlying all the religious forms of history."

Why "Mystery" Babylon? Something is a mystery as long as it remains secret and hidden from public disclosure. Yet the Book of Revelation says that the mystery will be revealed. The public proclamation of the mystery only takes effect when the prophecy becomes activated at the critical historical moment. As Brooks Alexander notes, "Mystery Babylon is a spiritual system that is founded on the widespread public disclosure of previously concealed information." Keep in mind that Hinduism has both exoteric and esoteric knowledge. There is a polytheism-pantheism for the general masses, and there is a high level "advaitic" monism for the higher initiate. Tantra has always been extremely secret, though gurus like Rajneesh are starting to popularize it in ever-widening circles.

Why does the Book of Revelation pinpoint Babylon? What can we glean from Babylon-of-old if its mystery is to be revealed?

Isaiah warns God's people of Babylon's deadly delusion. God reminds them, "I am the Lord, and there is no other. . . . I did not say to the offspring of Jacob, 'Seek me in chaos' [or the formless void]. I the Lord speak the truth, I declare what is right" (Isaiah 45:18 RSV). God is the great "I AM." He is transcendent. He is not the impersonal Brahmin of Hinduism or the void of Mahayana Buddhism. Only He claims the title of the "I AM." But what of Babylon? Did it not seek the divine within while living by the hedonistic pleasure principle? Again, that same pattern keeps appearing—a society given over to the hedonistic pleasure principle, shattering moral laws, while teaching the divine within. That was Babylon-of-old, and it seems to be resurrecting in our day—in Europe and America as well as other places.

In Isaiah 47, God exposes the spiritual realities of the Babylonian religion as he addresses Babylon: "Now therefore hear this, you lover of pleasures, who sits securely, who say in your heart *'I am and there is no one besides me'* . . . [God's judgment] shall come to you in a moment . . . in full measure, in spite of your many *sorceries and the great power of your enchantments*. You felt secure in your wickedness, you said, 'No one sees me'; your wisdom and your knowledge led you astray, and you said in your heart, 'I am and there is no one besides me' " (Isaiah 47:8-10).

Babylon embraced the Great Lie. Its inhabitants claimed the title of "I AM" and identified the human self with God. They were also earmarked by their sorcery and their hedonism—that was the essence of Babylon. Their occult practices, such as astrology and channeling, undergirded this. God was not denying that such occult pursuits gave them experiences and powers. After all, God said "in spite of your many sorceries and the great power of your enchantments." But the root source of this occult power was the dragon himself, never God. God abhorred these practices. Israel was warned with drastic words to stay away from Babylon's occult practices, the way a parent warns a child to avoid an electric power line that has fallen and could kill the child with a touch. The presumed wisdom, like the child with the parent, is that God knows some things that mortals don't. His warnings then were against the same occult practices that are surfacing today. They could equally apply to every New Age holistic fair where hundreds of booths are selling crystals, pyramids, and so forth while live channelers are opening the doors to the void. Apart from a miracle, it is hard to deny that *Mystery Babylon* is resurrecting again.

What does God say about the Babylonian channelers as he warns Israel to avoid contamination? And what do we gather about the "familiar spirits" that work through their human vessels? God by no means denies the reality of "familiars" or "familiar spirits," but we learn that they are demonic and not to be trusted—that these spirits teach the Great Lie, just as they are doing again today through J.Z. Knight and Jach Pursel. They are enemies of the one true God. Indeed, as we saw in the first contact in this book from the number-one bestseller *Communion*, Whitley Streiber even speculated that his otherworldly visitation might have been the ancient goddess herself—none other than Astarte. Modern author Streiber himself used this very name of the goddess! Yes, even the gods and goddesses are demonic, or maybe I should say *especially* the gods and goddesses are demonic.

God from the beginning warned of the Babylonian/Canaanite/Chaldean sorceries. Here are some clear scriptural examples—again, think of a parent warning a child of a downed power line which is arcing thousands of volts:

> And when they say to you, "Consult the mediums and the wizards who whisper and mutter," should not a people consult their God? Should they consult the dead on behalf of the living? (Isaiah 8:19 NASB).

> There shall not be found among you any one who burns his son or his daughter as an offering, any one who practices divination, a soothsayer, or an augur, or a sorcerer, or a charmer, or a medium, or a wizard, or a necromancer. For whoever does these

things is an abomination to the Lord (Deuteronomy 18:10-12 RSV).

Regard not them that have *familiar spirits*, neither seek after wizards, to be defiled by them: I Am the Lord your God (Leviticus 19:31 KJV).

If a person turns to mediums and wizards, playing the harlot after them, I will set my face against that person, and will cut him off from among his people (Leviticus 20:6 RSV).

A man or a woman who is a medium or wizard shall be put to death; they shall be stoned with stones, their blood shall be upon them (Leviticus 20:27 RSV).

To put it simply, the Babylonian occult arts were an abomination so serious that they were a capital offense among the Israelites.

Remember Jane Roberts and her pluralistic entity, Seth and Seth II, recounted in our first chapter of contacts? How would that fit into the rubric of biblical explanation? We see a perfect example of a pluralistic entity when Christ confronts the Gadarene, who when asked his name responded that it was "Legion." Why was that his name? The demons in the man responded "for we are many" and then they begged not to be sent into the abyss when they were exorcised.

As an illustration of the concrete reality of these demonic possessing spirits, Christ sent them into a large herd of pigs nearby. The pigs charged off a cliff and into the sea, killing themselves—not at all normal behavior for a pig. The man "Legion" had in his possessed state exhibited a sufficient range of superhuman and paranormal feats to scare everyone away. Among other things, he had the physical strength to snap heavy chains. But when Christ appeared, the demons trembled in horror.

Legion was demon-possessed. After he was exorcised, his countrymen were awed when they found him fully clothed and in his right mind. Somewhere in his past he had opened the door for these "familiar spirits," just as Jane Roberts had when she played with the Ouija board and got Seth. She hooked a spiritual manta ray. Yet Roberts was only too accountable, for at a specific time in her life she turned her back on the God of the Bible. She refers to that era scornfully, making sure to give us all the caricatures. She says that as she grew older she found it increasingly difficult to accept the God of her ancestors. "God seemed as dead as they were." But what is interesting is that this modern and liberated woman, after caricaturing God, confessed to being ignorant about the Bible. Instead, she turned to the revelations of Seth.

Channeler Jane Roberts chose to follow the one who bears the same name as the Egyptian god of evil, Seth, the ancient twin of Osiris—Seth, whose image is carved in the dank, musty descending corridors of stone beneath the Valley of the Kings, whose huge stone colossi lean against the bulbous pillars of Karnak, a subterranean god from the ancient past of Egypt. This multiple entity, Seth, claims to have never been enfleshed. Little wonder—this being from the void existed before the foundations of our world. It floated across the ancient world, maybe even into Babylon, for it is a spirit; it has always been a spirit, and there are others. As we saw, the Old Testament calls it or them "familiar spirits."

Paul reveals still yet another mystery—that these spirits can even stand behind idols, like the idols of ancient Babylon or of modern India. Paul says, "Do I mean then that a sacrifice offered to an idol is anything, or that an idol is anything? No, but the sacrifices of pagans are offered to demons, not to God" (1 Corinthians 10:19,20). He calls them "elemental spirits."

Paul also says, "Now the Spirit [of God] expressly says that in later times some will depart from the faith by giving heed to deceitful spirits and doctrines of demons" (1 Timothy 4:1 RSV). Such was the story of Jane Roberts, who fell away from the faith to pay heed to doctrines of demons. Channeling is by no means new at all. As we plainly saw in the Old Testament, it came right out of Babylon.

The Babylonians also had a radically different view of reality compared to Israel, another reason they were declared off-limits.

NIMROD—AN EARLY ANTICHRIST

The Tower of Babylon, its founding edifice and spiritual center, observes Brooks Alexander, "was an astral temple representing the structure of reality. As the 'cosmic mountain,' it tied heaven and earth together. It was the all inclusive image of the totality of the universe." Alexander adds that "in the ritual act of ascending the astral altar, the priests acted out the stages of god-realization and the inner meaning of mankind's oneness with the cosmos. The Babylonian monarch was the focus of the occult power channeled through the activities of the priesthood. He was regarded as a divine being, a god-man."

The monarch was also the one through whom the gods spoke. He was the initiate who could travel to the realm of the gods. He was the mouthpiece for the gods and goddesses of Babylon. The secret wisdom of Babylon is a direct ancestor of India's mystical system, from its hidden wisdom of man's inner divinity and its priestly class, to its gods and goddesses. Pantheism fuses with polytheism, just as in India.

How did Babylon's mystery religion suddenly appear in the ancient world? The Book of Genesis informs us that before the flood, the world was in a frenzy of "wickedness." God's wrath fell, while a remnant was preserved in the ark.

But scarcely had the waters of the great flood abated when, sure enough, the Great Lie appeared again. Nimrod founded the city of Babylon centered on the tower, that temple of man rising to the stars. He appointed himself as its savior, and again the mystery religion rose from out of the floodwaters. If some sorcerized hedonism caused the whole earth to fall away from God, bringing on the flood, then that handful of survivors would have been very aware of it. Noah's sons had very long lives and very long memories, and Nimrod's father (Cush) was a son of one of Noah's sons—"Cush begat Nimrod" (Genesis 10:8 KJV).

Nimrod's father caused the first great apostasy in the post-flood world, then Nimrod was able to introduce the ancient mystery religion. It appealed to his lusts, his vanity, and his ambition. He was feared and adored. Later he was killed by those who understood the nature of this ancient blasphemy. His almost preternaturally beautiful wife, Semiramis, was pregnant and she bore him a child, claiming that it was her husband, Nimrod, coming back as the godman Tammuz. Reincarnation appeared and formed a building block for the mystery religion. It enabled the divine family to reach god-hood, as it does in India today.

Likenesses of Semiramis and her son have appeared on coins, statues, murals, and in all manner of temple icons. She is the great goddess—from Diana of the Wiccans and neo-pagans of today, as well as of the ancient world (one thinks of the great temple of Diana in Ephesus), to the great goddess of India, Shakti. Her name has changed many times through history, as has that of her avatar son. She was heavenly Venus or Cybele, Jove's wife, mother of Janus, the god with the all-seeing-eye. She was also Minerva, Europa, Ceres, and Ash-toreth. In India she appears in many forms.

Noted English archeologist and antiquarian Alexander Hislop says of this goddess and child:

> The Babylonians, in their popular religion, su-premely worshipped a goddess mother and son [Semiramis and Tammuz]. From Babylon, this wor-ship of the mother and child spread to the ends of the earth. In Egypt, the mother and child were worshipped under the names of Isis and Osiris. In India, *even to this day*, as Isi [or Parvati] and Ishwara [The Indian God Ishwara is represented as a babe at the breast of his own wife Isi, or Parvati]. . . . [Hislop says] . . . the Hindu mythology, *which is admitted to be essentially Babylonian, could not have been subdued.*[2]

The mystery religion of Babylon is the root of all mystery religions, the secret initiations, the exalted priesthoods and, above all, the secret knowledge. It promises the keys to the tree of life, immortality, as well as divinity. A fully functional flow chart of this whole process is most clearly seen in the world's greatest reserve of this belief system, India. India has been the place where the mystery religion has taken root unhindered. It has distilled over the centuries into a refined wine—the Chateau Rothschild of religious wines. Revelation reports that the whole world becomes drunk on the wine of Babylon.

BABYLON'S GODS AND GODDESSES TODAY

India's sages (from Shankaracharya to Patanjali) became over the centuries the think tank for Babylonian mysticism. In India we see the crossover, from the dualism of village idolatry to the monism of the sage claiming to have merged with God. India takes us from the Vedas of the dualistic gods to the Upanishadic breakthrough. Village India worships the gods on the lower strata, till the villagers realize that the self is embodied in those gods and, through them, transcend all and become the one god, Brahman. Such is the refined Brahmanism of the yogis and rishis.

A supreme moment of crossover was illustrated when nineteenth-century Ramakrishna identified with the Bengali goddess Kali and, once becoming her, destroyed the illusion of separateness by destroying the image of the goddess on a shard of glass. Then he experienced enlightenment and claimed to become Brahman. Ramakrishna reported that he became the overmind, and entered Nirvikalpa Samadhi. He did it through Kali, through the doors of Babylon, in the arms of Semiramis. He adored his goddess Kali, also known as Durga, also known as Siva's consort, Shakti—Sacta, the tabernacle, the goddess of Babylon. It was through the spiritual system of Babylon that Ramakrishna became enlightened—that is the link.

Ramakrishna became possessed by his cosmic goddess and joined the cosmic aristocracy. He claimed to become God through the yoni of the goddess, and that is the next secret doorway through which to merge with the goddess. This mystery path is highly developed in India's Tantra. It is sex with the goddess through a woman as a vehicle—that is why the temple of Diana in Ephesus had temple prostitutes. Sex through them was a way of worshiping and touching the

goddess herself. That was why Venus was known as a goddess of lusts. The goddess behind *Mystery Babylon* in the Book
of Revelation is called the "whore of Babylon." There is
double entendre—it is both spiritual harlotry as well as physical harlotry. The temples of India to this day have temple
prostitutes. *Mystery Babylon* dances through history, but her
garments and dance remain the same. It is a forbidden fruit
that men and women crave: sensual fulfillment and godhood,
a hard combination to beat. This shiny apple of Tantra is what
Indian superguru Rajneesh holds out to his tens of thousands
of Western followers. But his secret ceremonies of true Tantra
are even more amazing, as I point out in *Riders of the Cosmic
Circuit*.

Modern feminists are rediscovering the great goddess. Certainly nothing can seem to lift a woman's self-esteem more
than becoming a goddess. That indeed appears to be one
solution to "problems of self-worth and identity." To them it
vindicates the feminine in a universe where too much male
principle seems to be operative. An injection of the cos-
mically feminine is required. If the goal is judicial equality in
society, then the same alternative must be applied to the
cosmos. Followers of the goddess say that a male deity must
be counterbalanced with a female counterpart. It only makes
sense in an era of judicial egalitarianism. It also brings back
androgyny. Margot Adler, a modern witch, points out in
Bringing Down the Moon that it is now time for the sisters to go
out and do the magic circle and summon the goddess. Such
"consciousness-raising," suddenly a reality in our modern
world, was unforeseen by humanist intellectuals who thought
they were moderns who had left the supernatural behind. But
then again, they wouldn't have recognized *Mystery Babylon's*
attire if it were dancing before their eyes. The mystery danced
right by them.

The goddess of Babylon even dances across the TV screen.
Joseph Campbell, whose book *The Power of Myth* has been the
number-one *New York Times* bestseller, has done a noteworthy
job in service to the goddess. Indeed, through the insights of
Joseph Campbell, Semiramis and Tammuz have returned

once again to the modern world as inner mythological figures. They are archetypes of the self, the heroes within. The gods are the gateways to one's own godhood. If one does not worship the goddess outwardly like the Wiccans, one can still encounter her as an archetype within. For neopagan "advaitins," she helps them realize their true identity, *The Hero with a Thousand Faces* (also the title of Joseph Campbell's book). This too fits the secret gnosis of the mystery religion. There is a goddess for intellectuals as well as sensualists. It is an uncanny fit, a supreme work of genius. And if you have discernment, you can see the handprints of its architect and his mystery religion.

Today's Tower of Babel, using the building blocks of ancient Babylon, will be forged into a supreme edifice syncretizing all the world's mystery paths. Babylon-of-old provides the clue to this all-encompassing system which the apostle John saw in an immense vision.

20

The Hidden Aristocracy

As the massive pieces of this emerging global order fit into place, it must be emphasized that by no means are all the pieces just airy "spiritual" abstractions creating the mere illusion of globalism. Very tangible forces have been at work.

It must also be emphasized that we are not dealing with some prophetically speculative or futuristic fairy tale, but with a real flesh-and-blood plan. It is important that we glimpse this enormous piece of the puzzle to appreciate the reality behind what has been going on. Gears and levers of history have been moved and adjusted, and a large-scale game of Monopoly has been played, with real currency and real assets shifting hands—a game with very real winners and losers. It is not at all out-of-the-question that such "players" would finance the New Age movement with their publishing and broadcasting monopolies using it as the religious arm for this plan. We have seen what the New Age movement has been able to do in the changing of the guard from the old world order to the New World Order.

The New Age piece of the puzzle is by no means the dominant one, as so many have thought. The New Age movement may have its very greatest role in influencing free and affluent nations such as America to go along with the global plan for a New World Order. People operating out of self-interest do not surrender their freedoms and heritage unless they are persuaded that there is something better ahead. Meanwhile, there are quite a few already-socialistic European nations who will be more swayed by the outward promises of a socialist political agenda than by some New Age vision. The seduction of a world takes supreme pragmatism—literally whatever works is permitted. Many Europeans are far less spiritually motivated but much more motivated by security and pleasure than Americans. Not that this can't change—they too will eventually embrace the final religion.

If it takes communism to get the Eastern bloc and Asia in line, fine. Or if it takes some varied socialism for modern Europe, fine. If America needs a New Age bromide, no problem. The meshing of the net of steel to capture the world has been a quiet conspiracy out of public view. Its big events, as we shall see, have taken place at quiet meetings where an elite few move enormous amounts of capital. The superrich and the superbrilliant have teamed up while the masses watch television and eat at McDonald's. Their small, dull, prosaic worlds never embrace the truly colossal perspective around them. And should one of the masses look up for a second, there is always an army of experts, intellectuals, and skeptics to ridicule any suspicions. It is the "complexity of life" argument tied in with the "random forces of history" argument that sages of today use to numb a public deeply preoccupied with their own immediate problems.

The world has had an elite few operating in the shadows of history and far from public view. These insiders have avoided the spotlights flooding the main stage of history. Other actors have been thrust onstage, but the ones directing the drama have been backstage. This fractional minority of people can only activate their plans of power and affect millions and millions of lives if they remain out-of-view and beyond suspicion. It is a dangerous and risky undertaking, for they are vastly outnumbered. Secrecy is critical.

To someone who is an atheistic materialist, this idea seems preposterous. People have but one life to live, so what would inspire loyalty in or sustain any participant in some grand-scale conspiracy to take over the earth, if those who finally benefited were not even on the scene for another few hundred years? How could anyone, fired with ambitions for the moment, be made to sacrifice his life for a long-term plan?

What human channels could carry the flame of such complex and deliberate planning that spans beyond their individual lives?

The supernatural dimension is the one that gives the puzzle meaning. How else can you explain a master plan that has existed for hundreds of years? If there is a spiritual dimension guiding the insiders, a messianic plan, then it makes sense. Like a chess player who is seeing 30 moves ahead, the present sacrifice of a pawn or a rook makes perfect sense in light of the coming checkmate. Each player in the game can feel the impending victory when he manages to reach some remote crank or dial and turn it while out of public view. He becomes a cosmic player in history. He feels as if he is in the body of some corporate messiah. He can feel a kind of transnational allegiance to a higher cause, not to speak of the extremely generous temporal rewards of wealth and prestige he will usually accrue as part of the plan. The lesser players in the game can continue to be motivated by the rewards of the moment. There are benefits at every level.

Almost 200 years ago, in 1797, one of the most respected scientists in the world wrote a book entitled *Proofs of a Conspiracy* (London: Creech, Cadell, Davies Publ., 1797). He was John T. Robison, secretary general to Scotland's prestigious Royal Society and professor of natural philosophy at the University of Edinburgh. He was considered to be one of the truly great intellectuals of the day. Science was called "natural philosophy" in that day. Robison was also a high-degree Mason. Whenever he traveled to Europe from Scotland, he always attended the Grand Orient Masonic Lodges. But when Robison had recently been in Europe on a sabbatical, he detected a new element in the Grand Orient Masonic Lodges. More than that, Adam Weishaupt, the founder of this new elite, approached Robison to join an inner circle known as Illuminism. It was the quiet flame that burned in the French intelligentsia such as Voltaire, Robespierre, Mirabeau, and the Duc D'Orleans.

The Illuminist plan was to unseat the present powers of hereditary aristocracy and replace them with an intellectual aristocracy, using a staged revolt of the masses to do this.

This, indeed, was exactly what the French Revolution appeared to be—key people catalyzing great numbers of people.

Robison warned the royal family of England that hidden powers were pulling strings—that the French Revolution was not a historical accident happening by whim, but that it was manipulated by geniuses who had their own agenda. There was one genius in particular behind Illuminism. Like Karl Marx, he was of Jewish descent, but had temporarily joined the Jesuit Order. Later he got into league with some powerful German merchants who were initiates in the occult. Adam Weishaupt was a professor of canon law at the University of Ingolstadt. He started the Order of the Illuminati on May 1, 1776. His plan was to use the Grand Orient Lodges of Europe as a filtering mechanism through which to screen out talent and build a hierarchy of inner circles. Like the Mafia of today, only the inner inner circle could be trusted with the true purpose of the Order.

The true purpose of the Illuminati, according to Professor Robison, was world hegemony: a world order ruled by an elite pretending to represent the common man, an elite who had penetrated every aspect of society from the arts to politics and law while shaping public opinion with more subtlety than the average citizen was able to detect. Weishaupt's plan involved a communistic order outlined a full 70 years before Marx came on the scene.

Weishaupt was exposed in 1785 when the Bavarian government stepped in and seized his papers. An unknown variable had caused exposure. The hidden hand was forced to come out of the shadows for a moment. The horseman, named Lanze, carrying various secret papers and plans to France, was struck and killed by lightning in Regensberg. The local police handed the papers over to the Bavarian government. When the Bavarian government questioned four professor colleagues of Weishaupt, they testified to the conspiracy. On historical record is the attempt of the Bavarian government to warn other European governments in an official document entitled *Original Writings of the Order and Sect of the Illuminati*. Four years after lightning struck the horseman, the French Revolution rocked Europe.

Rumor remained that the Illuminati then shifted locations to Italy, calling itself "the invisible 40." By the early 1800's, Weishaupt and his conspiratorial Illuminists were mentioned in the correspondence of George Washington, Jefferson, Madison, and John Quincy Adams. They did not want this plan infiltrating America any more than Robison wanted to see it in England. They had seen the ruthlessness of France's "Reign of Terror."

George Washington wrote in 1798: "It is not my intention to doubt that the doctrine of the Illuminati and the principles of Jacobinism had not spread in the United States. On the contrary, no one is more satisfied of this fact than I am."[1] That was 200 years ago, and indeed a connecting thread existed through the 1800's. It had to do with merchant bankers and occultists, as well as other invisible players.

200 YEARS LATER

Today, the power of a certain group of bankers is colossal according to Harvard and Princeton professor emeritus, Carroll Quigley, who confessed to being an insider and confidant of this elite group. Professor Quigley's *magnum opus, Tragedy and Hope: A History of Our Time*, rocked those who saw it when it came out in 1966. This 1300-page book named major insider power groups attempting to manipulate a world socialist order. Quigley ardently supported the plan, but said that it should no longer be under cover. His book was a triumphalist announcement of the inevitable, since the plan had virtually reached completion. He had been among the intellectual brain trust rubbing shoulders with the insiders. The problem was that he had said too much. The Macmillan first edition of 1966 suddenly disappeared almost overnight, even from public libraries. When Professor Quigley took his final academic post and taught at the Georgetown University School of Foreign Service, an acquaintance of mine in the sixties took every class under Doctor Quigley that he could enroll in and spoke of this Ivy League professor in almost messianic language.

When I got a copy of Quigley's book, *Tragedy and Hope*, printed in Taiwan (an exact copy of the original Macmillan book which my friend owned), I was amazed. Indeed, Professor Quigley had let too much out of the bag. That book and others opened a cryptic doorway. It enabled me to glimpse the reality of some of the elite insiders manipulating world events in order for their plan to take shape. The reality of what was happening was even more incredible than Robert Ludlum's *Matarese Circle*. Here finally was tangible evidence of insiders who were so well-versed at removing their own fingerprints that they slipped detection. Evidence had previously come in faint traces here and there; certain names kept cropping up. When author Ian Fleming, who for years had been a member of the British Secret Service, wrote about James Bond combating such secret conspiratorial groups as Smersh and Specter, one wonders whether he was indulging in more than just fiction and showing insider's knowledge thinly veiled. According to Quigley, yes, such hidden groups most certainly do exist, and they are beautifully camouflaged. The average person would not think twice as their stretch limousines with tinted windows glide down Park Avenue or London's Bond Street.

Harvard professor emeritus Quigley divulges the following about this "international network" in *Tragedy and Hope*:

> This network which we may identify as the Round Table Groups, has no aversion to cooperating with the Communists or any other group, and frequently does so. I know of the operations of this network because I have studied it for twenty years and was permitted for two years, in the early 1960's, to examine its papers and secret records. I have no aversion to it or to most of its aims and have, for much of my life, been close to it and to many of its instruments.[2]

In the next sentence, Quigley differs on only one point with the insider network: "It wishes to remain unknown." Other sources have led me to believe that Quigley went very deep, but that there are things even deeper.

Quigley summarizes the insider's grand plan: "Their aim is nothing less than to create a *world system* of financial control in private hands able to dominate the political system of each country and the economy of the world as a whole. The system was to be controlled in a feudalistic fashion by the *central banks of the world acting in concert*, by secret agreements arrived at in frequent private meetings and conferences."[3] This is almost a perfect description of the secret international meetings of the Bilderbergers: "secret agreements arrived at in frequent private meetings. . . ."

One fact that Quigley and others reveal is that the banking houses owned by the great family dynasties are also the banks behind the International Monetary Fund, as well as The World Bank. The same names keep cropping up. They are king makers and nation breakers. The goal is a global central bank—once national banks have been established and conditions are right.

So far, the central banking system projected for Europe in 1992 is a major milestone to this goal—and not a small part of this gradualist agenda is America's own central bank, the Federal Reserve Bank. National debt is highly in their favor. The two trillion dollars now owed to them by the United States, as they wear the outer attire of the Federal Reserve Bank, gives this inner circle of select banks yearly interest payments of over 100 billion dollars.

Elections and stock markets can switch directions overnight with a directive from the Federal Reserve. Alan Greenspan, the visible chairman of the Federal Reserve, could change the prime lending rate and cause a panic, a recession, indeed, a depression with a single word. The politician who does the bidding of the insiders gets in the door. It is always good policy to justify substantial loans from these banks. The rhetoric is irrelevant and has been for a very long time—just watch one president after another promise to balance the national debt, then watch it quietly climb off the graph. The debt will soon equal the sum total assets of the nation.

How do banks and money barons manipulate conditions?

According to Harvard economist John Kenneth Galbraith, Winston Churchill was shown an interesting object lesson by

New York banker and industrial magnate Bernard Baruch in 1929. Baruch, of the lineage of the money changers, was an advisor to President Wilson at the Treaty of Versailles, beside that other great advisor, "Colonel" Mandel House. Baruch also advised Roosevelt and was a member of his brain trust. During World War I, Baruch, when he was chairman of the War Industries Board, made hundreds of millions of dollars from lucrative contracts in the war and munitions industry. He was at the right place at the right time. According to Harvard economist Galbraith, Baruch walked Sir Winston Churchill out on the floor of the New York Stock Exchange the morning it fell.[4] Churchill was brought to witness the crash firsthand on October 24, 1929, because it was desired that he see the power of the banking system at work. This presumes plenty of lead time for Winston to take the ship from England to the United States, hang out for a while, maybe start the day with a good breakfast at the Waldorf, and make it there in time to see the floor open up. This is insider knowledge that would pale Simon Boesky's. We will see later why Baruch gave Churchill this object lesson.

The American market collapsed that day of 1929, and so did the world market not long after. Economic conditions for the next world war were set up, greatly aided by America's Great Depression. Billions of dollars shifted hands overnight. Some had gotten out in time—the big hitters—while scores of the wealthy were destroyed. Then, after the crash, when railroads and industries plummeted, the big hitters came back on the stock market floor and bought industries at whim for a dime on the dollar. One such "fortunate speculator" was Bernard Baruch who had boasted to Churchill that he had liquidated his stock holdings when the market was at the top and bought bonds and gold, while retaining a huge cash reserve. Now he could buy companies like pieces on a Monopoly board.

Millions of lives were wrecked, and America suddenly needed a "New Deal" in the form of social welfare. The Great Crash created another precedent for free America: gradual socialism, as the Fabians had been doing in England. Why would any banker or insider be the least bit attracted to socialism? Because the idea that socialism is a share-the-wealth program is strictly a confidence game to get the people to surrender their freedom to an all-powerful collective. It is a means to consolidate and control wealth. Once this is understood, it is no longer a paradox that the super-rich promote it. Here is another riddle: Once the central banks become "socialized" as in Britain, the ownership remains the same. Rothschild still controls the Bank of England, and the Bank of England is still a private bank. As a central bank, it is literally above the law.

While wars and revolutions have been useful to international bankers in gaining or increasing control over governments, the key to such control has always been control of money. You can control a government if you have it in your debt. A creditor can demand special privileges from the sovereign. Money-seeking governments have granted monopolies in state banking, along with natural resources, oil concessions, etc. But the monopoly that the international bankers most covet is control over a nation's money. The famed quote of Lord Rothschild to his friend Benjamin Disraeli, England's first Jewish prime minister, was, "As long as I control a nation's currency, I care not who makes its laws." Disraeli's novel *Coningsby*, a thinly veiled story that involved Rothschild, contained the following interesting quote: "The world is governed by very different personages from what is imagined by those who are not behind the scenes."[5] This is true.

International bankers actually own as private companies the central banks of the key European nations. The Bank of England, Bank of France, and Bank of Germany are not owned by their respective governments, as most people imagine, but are privately owned monopolies that were granted by the heads of state. That is precisely why the *London Financial Times* of September 26, 1921, revealed that, even at the time, "Half a dozen men at the top of the Big Five Banks could upset the whole fabric of government finance by refraining from renewing Treasury Bills."

But Professor Quigley revealed that these visible heads at the top of the Big Five Banks were only front men, the *agentur*

of the invisible international bankers. Again, it was impera-
tive that the shadow figures stay in the shadows and work
behind front men. Quigley directly addresses the issue of the
front men of the state banks of Europe:

> It must not be felt that these heads of the world's
> chief central banks were themselves substantive
> powers in world finance. They were not. Rather,
> they were the technicians and *agents* of the domi-
> nant investment bankers of their own countries,
> who had raised them up and were perfectly capable
> of throwing them down. The substantive financial
> powers of the world were in the hands of these
> investment bankers (also known as "international"
> or "merchant bankers") who remained largely be-
> hind the scenes in their own unincorporated private
> banks. These formed a system of international co-
> operation and national dominance which was more
> private, more powerful, and more secret than that
> of *their agents* in the central banks.[6]

Such a front man was Montagu Norman who was governor
of the Bank of England. He suddenly came to America the
year of the Great Crash, in February of 1929, to confer with
Andrew Mellon, the Secretary of the Treasury. *The Wall Street
Journal* on November 11, 1927, had already referred to Norman as "the currency dictator of Europe." Wrong. He was the
front man for Lord Rothschild, the true currency dictator of
Europe. Norman, a close friend of J.P. Morgan, had said of
himself, "I hold the hegemony of the world," according to
Dr. Quigley. John Hargrave who wrote the biography about
and entitled *Montagu Norman*, cited the dream of this titular
head of the Bank of England: "that the Hegemony of World
Finance should reign supreme over everyone, everywhere, as
one whole supernational control mechanism."[7] Norman was
parroting someone else's view behind the scenes.

The Fabian Society of Britain, another of Quigley's inner
circle round table groups who were present at Versailles, had
worked up the gradualist agenda for the spread of socialism.

Americans needed the backdoor approach. So after the crash, which in turn started the Great Depression, in came the Trojan horse of socialism in its first small increments as Roosevelt was cast in the light of the savior of the people with welfare and government programs. Not far behind were his liberal advisors, including Mr. Baruch who had also advised President Woodrow Wilson (having contributed generously to both Wilson's and Roosevelt's campaigns). Take note that within a decade of Churchill's object lesson on the floor, he became one of Britain's greatest prime ministers. His bid as prime minister had failed repeatedly, but with the right support, he was elected.

CREATING AMERICA'S CENTRAL BANK

How did America finally get a central bank like its European cousins? Let's look back again. There were numerous attempts in the 1800's to create a central bank in America—most of these attempts point back to the Rothschilds.

The Rothschilds had their invisible hands in many of the early major American banking houses. One banker was August Belmont, a superstar of Birmingham's *Our Crowd* (whose original family name was Schoenberg). He used to put ads in the New York paper advertising himself as Rothschild's agent. He became incredibly wealthy. In the South, Rothschild had the Erlangers.

It is interesting that both the original American banking houses that represented Rothschild—August Belmont and the Erlangers—funded the North and the South respectively during America's Civil War. Rothschild sent August Belmont to the United States during the Panic of 1837 and empowered him to buy government bonds. Right then the Civil War started. Whichever side won owed its respective banker for the victory. Could the goal be monopoly of capital?

It seems Abraham Lincoln saw the power play behind this masquerade as one bank was seemingly played against the other. The invisible hand underneath was never seen by the multitudes. Lincoln did see it, for he had resisted the pressure to create in America a central private bank that would print its money. He also spotted the "divide-and-conquer" movement where the North was pitted against the South with both sides financed by the same money elite.

Abraham Lincoln battled for the right of Congress and the Treasury to hold the awesome power of coining money. He knew that to surrender this power to private banks was ultimately to surrender the sovereignty of America. Adams and Jefferson had warned of this all along. Defying the hidden bankers, Lincoln issued the greenbacks. Interestingly, Lincoln was soon assassinated.

Forty years later there was another event: John Pierpont Morgan created the Panic of 1907 and was amply rewarded. He gained numerous holdings, as well as his bid to be the Rothschild's number-one American agent. J.P. Morgan's real feat and service to Rothschild in the Panic of 1907 was that he created a mood in America that was receptive to a central bank—to be known as the Federal Reserve Bank. Morgan's own bank, The Morgan Guaranty Trust, was allowed to be among the inner circle of primary owners of the Federal Reserve. It is interesting that Morgan had spent five months in Europe right before the 1907 Panic, shuttling between London and Paris. He was gaining an inside look at Europe's central banks.

The New York Times, October 26, 1907, noted in connection with J.P. Morgan's actions during the Panic of 1907, "In conversation with the New York Times correspondent, Lord Rothschild paid a high tribute to J.P. Morgan for his efforts in the present financial juncture in New York. 'He is worthy of his reputation as a great financier and a man of wonders. His latest action fills one with admiration and respect for him.' " This is the only time a Rothschild praised another banker outside his own family. A few decades later, *The New York Times* dropped another nugget. On March 28, 1932, during the Great Depression, *The New York Times* noted: "London: N.M. Victor Rothschild, twenty-one-year-old nephew of Baron Rothschild, is going to the United States soon to take a post with J.P. Morgan & Co., it was learned tonight."

Soon after J.P. Morgan had created the Panic of 1907, the American people were in the right mood to believe that a central bank would prevent such a panic from occurring again. When the moment was right, Senator Aldrich—who later married into the Rockefeller family when his daughter Abbey married John D. Rockefeller, Jr.—was in place to push through the Federal Reserve Act. That delicate moment was during a lame duck Senate, right before the Christmas break on December 22, 1913. Immediately before that, Aldrich, representing the Rockefellers, with Paul Warburg, who represented the Rothschilds as well as the Kuhn Loeb Bank of New York, had gone to Jeckyl Island, Georgia, in a sealed train, away from the press, to iron out how they would present the Federal Reserve bill to the House and Senate. Paul Warburg was the banking genius who understood the labyrinthine structure of the Federal Reserve Bank, and Aldrich was the public relations man in the Senate.

Warburg had some interesting connections. Paul Warburg had come to America ten years prior, in 1902, from the Warburg Bank of Germany. He married Nina Loeb, daughter of Kuhn Loeb founder Solomon Loeb, while his brother, Felix, married Frieda Schiff, the daughter of Jacob Schiff, who was head of Kuhn Loeb. Jacob Schiff was the ruling power of Kuhn Loeb. Both Paul and Felix were made full partners of Kuhn Loeb, and Paul was finally paid an annual salary of half a million dollars (then!) to enlighten the public on the need for a central bank. His father-in-law, who paid him this colossal salary to set up the Federal Reserve, was Jacob Schiff. Stephen Birmingham writes in his authoritative bestseller *Our Crowd: The Great Jewish Families of New York*, "In the eighteenth century the Schiffs and Rothschilds shared a double house" in Frankfurt. Jacob Schiff reportedly bought his partnership into Kuhn Loeb with Rothschild money—hence, the Kuhn Loeb connection with Rothschild.

Once Senator Aldrich had gotten the Federal Reserve Act through the Senate, Woodrow Wilson, under the nod from "Colonel" Mandel House, signed the Federal Reserve Act. Among the international financiers who contributed heavily to Woodrow Wilson's campaign were Jacob Schiff, Bernard Baruch, Henry Morgenthau, and *New York Times* publisher Adolph Ochs. Insider banker Bernard Baruch was later made absolute dictator over American business when President Wilson appointed him chairman of the War Industries Board, where he had control of all domestic contracts for Allied war materials. Hence his war industries profits of over two hundred million dollars.

Yale professor Charles Seymour, whose collection of secret papers of Colonel Edward Mandel House are at the prestigious Beinecke Rare Books Library at Yale, revealed in his book *The Intimate Papers of Colonel House*, that "Colonel" (who was never in the military) Edward Mandel House was the "unseen guardian angel" of the Federal Reserve Act. His father, Thomas House, reportedly a Rothschild agent during the era of the Civil War, made millions of dollars running supplies through the blockades. Then he retired to Texas and sent his son Edward to Europe to be educated. "Colonel" Edward Mandel House almost never left Wilson's side.

After Wilson signed the Federal Reserve Act, none other than Paul Warburg became the first chairman of the Federal Reserve Bank. Naturally he had to temporarily give up his partnership of Kuhn Loeb. Paul Warburg remained chairman of America's new central bank until it was revealed that his third brother, Max Warburg, who was still in Germany, headed the Central Bank of Germany! It just seemed too much of a coincidence. Paul's brother Max Warburg, by World War II, also headed up German Secret Intelligence, which has baffled many fellow Jews—as has the fact that some of Hitler's major funding came through the Warburgs, who controlled the Mendelsohn Bank of Amsterdam through which they sent loan money.

Once America had a central bank in place from which to borrow money, World War I suddenly arrived just in time for America to take some substantial war loans and get into the action. Versailles was the urban renewal after the "war to end all wars." The goal was the League of Nations: guaranteed peace through world unity—again, "world unity."

THE CHALLENGE OF SOVEREIGN STATES

While Europe was ready for the League of Nations,

America was not. So those insiders meeting at Versailles after World War I now had to regroup to get America ready for globalism. The coming Crash of '29 would help. Meanwhile several semisecret groups were formed. According to Professor Quigley, they were round table spawns. One in America was named the CFR, or Council on Foreign Relations, a boringly neutral name. But try to become a member or walk through the door! The founders included many of those who had been at the signing of the Treaty of Versailles after World War I, including Colonel Edward House and Walter Lippmann. Finances for the CFR came from: J.P. Morgan; John D. Rockefeller; Bernard Baruch; Paul Warburg; Otto Kahn; and Jacob Schiff. The CFR began on July 29, 1921, in New York City. Its building is on the west side of fashionable Park Avenue at 68th Street. Facing it is the Soviet Embassy to the United Nations on the opposite corner.

The flame for the League of Nations had to be kept alive at all costs, and the best and the brightest had to be tapped as members of these groups. One of these groups, the CFR, traditionally divulges almost nothing about its aims and purpose, but something did leak out once. The CFR's *Study No. 7*, published November 25, 1959, openly declared its true purpose: ". . . building a New International Order [which] must be responsive to world aspirations for peace, [and] for social and economic change. . . . an international order [code for world government] . . . including states labeling themselves as 'Socialist.' "

The roster of CFR members is thoroughly impressive—so are the power groups who have representatives in it.

International banking organizations that currently have men in the CFR include Kuhn, Loeb & Co; Lazard Freres (directly affiliated with Rothschild); Dillon Read; Lehman Bros.; Goldman, Sachs; Chase Manhattan Bank; Morgan Guaranty Bank; Brown Bros. Harriman; First National City Bank; Chemical Bank & Trust; and Manufacturers Hanover Trust Bank. The CFR is totally interlocked with the major foundations (Rockefeller, Ford, Carnegie) and the so-called think tanks (Rand, Hudson Institute, Brookings Institute).

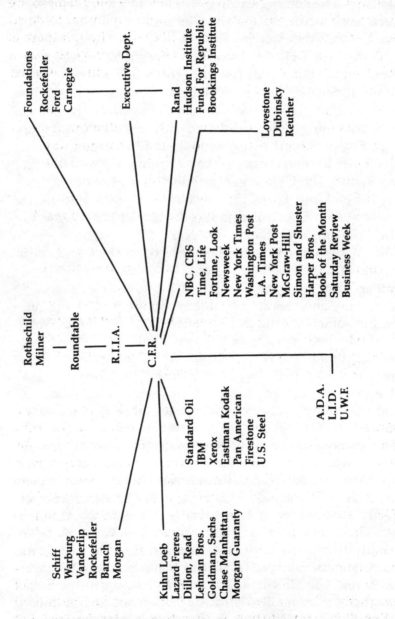

Figure 1. The CFR

According to Article II of the CFR bylaws, no minutes are to be taken and no member of the CFR is to divulge the content of any of its top-secret meetings. If a member should do so, he is to be expelled immediately. One former member to do so was Rear Admiral Chester Ward (USN ret.). Though there is an elite of high military in the CFR, Chester Ward was a patriot. They misjudged him. The former rear admiral warned the public about the CFR saying:

> The most powerful clique in these elitist groups have an objective in common—they want to bring about the surrender of the sovereignty and the national independence of the United States.
>
> A second clique of international members in the CFR . . . comprises the Wall Street International bankers and their key agents.
>
> Primarily, they want the world banking monopoly from whatever power ends up in the control of global government.
>
> They would probably prefer that this be an all-powerful United Nations organization; but they are also prepared to deal with, and for, a one-world government controlled by the Soviet Communists if U.S. sovereignty is ever surrendered to them.[8]

Less than 20 years after the CFR was founded, World War II had arrived. Once that war had ended, America was now ready to join "the League of Nations," now incarnating as the United Nations. America sat down in San Francisco with Alger Hiss and joined the United Nations, the successor to the League of Nations—Alger Hiss, a charter member of the CFR; Alger Hiss, whose sympathy with communism can no longer be denied. The CFR's chairman is David Rockefeller, and the United Nations' 18 acres of prime Manhattan land was donated by the Rockefeller family. The United Nations charter and constitution is a thin paraphrasing of the Soviet model which Alger Hiss borrowed from when he coauthored it. The U.N. constitution is therefore a Marxist socialist paradigm. According to Quigley, this is far from being an accident. World socialism, communism and bankers!

There was always the Communist question. Bankers kept cropping up in this area as well, which is odd—unless one understands the logic of Hegelian synthesis: the logic of propping up two counterforces who are to oppose one another until they merge. It is also a great way to run up national debt—weapons systems that take billions to create, that through a disarmament treaty are then trashed. This happened again and again. Did the bankers have goals for Russia? There are shrouded historical facts.

Jacob Schiff, head of Kuhn Loeb, had given Trotsky (alias Bronstein) 20 million dollars in gold bullion in 1917 and sent him to Moscow to trigger the Bolshevik Revolution with his 275 comrades (now bearing new Russianized names) from the lower East side of Manhattan. When this long roster of names entered the United States Congressional Record, many saw a pattern and it took the full weight of the Antidefamation League to silence them. *The New York Journal-American* of February 3, 1949, cites Jacob Schiff's grandson and says, "Today it is estimated by Jacob's grandson, John Schiff, that the old man sank about 20,000,000 dollars for the final triumph of Bolshevism in Russia." But there was a brief embarrassment. Trotsky (or Bronstein) and his 275 comrades on the S.S. *Christiana* were held in Halifax, Canada—their first port of call. World War I was going on, and Canada was suspicious. Trotsky spent five days in jail in Canada, but the powers-that-be moved the Canadian government. Soon Trotsky with the 20 million dollars in gold bullion and his 275 comrades were again back on their way to Russia. What happened?

The British, through Kuhn Loeb partner Sir William Wiseman, and the United States, through "Colonel" House, put the heat on Canada. Trotsky even got an American passport out of the deal. William Wiseman, who had also been sent by British intelligence to help bring the United States into the war, was amply rewarded for his services. After World War I ended, he stayed in America as a new partner in the Jacob Schiff and Paul Warburg-controlled Kuhn Loeb Bank.

While Schiff was sending Trotsky on his way, the German Warburgs gave Lenin five million dollars and sent him through Germany in a sealed train. The world was distracted by World War I. Lenin was installed, and by the end of the war the Communist takeover of Russia was well in effect. Loans to Russia continued. World War II solidified things even more. By then, Stalin had come to power.

After World War II came Yalta where Churchill and Roosevelt gave Stalin all sorts of concessions as they drank gallons of whiskey and ate pounds of caviar. Stalin was handed 11 nations including East Germany, Albania, Latvia, Lithuania, Hungary, Bulgaria, Estonia, Rumania, and other satellite landholdings. Soon enough Stalin got Poland and Czechoslovakia through unhindered invasion. It was Roosevelt who had held Patton back from finishing the war against Germany and marching right into Moscow. Had Patton been allowed to do what he had wanted to do and continue his march, which moved without obstruction, there would be no Russian occupation of East Germany and countless other satellite countries. After World War II, the Communist bloc was far more solidified. Nations and power groups were being shuffled like cards in a deck, with decisions as weighted as Olympic scoring.

Now another irony: Russia has apparently needed the capitalists. This is clear in the ten books by Antony Sutton, British scholar and member of Stanford University's Hoover Institute. Sutton wrote *Wall Street and the Bolshevik Revolution*, tracing all kinds of capital flowing from Wall Street into Russia. Sutton also wrote *National Suicide: Military Aid to the Soviet Union* (New York: Arlington House, 1974) about how one military secret after another has somehow leaked out of America and into Soviet hands—how we somehow keep giving them our secrets after spending hundreds of millions of dollars on research to get that edge which we lose almost instantly. Several news leaks stated that in one day the plans for the cruise missile went from a Pentagon desk top out the door. They were very top secret. Just an innocent mistake! Months later, Russia had its own version of the cruise missile—so too with Polaris submarines. Sutton cites volumes of "coincidences." But there were earlier precedents for leaking secrets. Oddly enough, it was Alger Hiss' friends Julius and Ethel Rosenburg who shared with the Stalin government the secrets from the Manhattan Project on how to build the atomic bomb. Close to the Rosenburgs was Communist sympathizer and genius of the Manhattan Project, Robert Oppenheimer.

To this day, superbillionaire Armand Hammer, owner of Occidental Petroleum among other things, can arrive in Moscow and get any dissident he wants freed, including the Jewish Nobel-prize-winning physicist Sakharov, builder of the Tokamak linear particle accelerator. Armand Hammer is of that very group whom the Russians "persecute," yet he gets special treatment. Why? Is there something we are missing? What about other supercapitalists visiting this bastion of communism?

What about the trip to Russia in October 1964 of David Rockefeller, the chairman of the CFR and the Chase Manhattan Bank? What an odd place for a money superbaron to go— a capitalist, no less. And what about the coincidence that happened after Rockefeller left Russia? A few days after Rockefeller ended his only vacation to Russia, the head of Russia, Nikita Khrushchev, was recalled from a vacation at a Black Sea resort to learn that he was no longer premier of the Supreme Soviet. He had been fired—Khruschev who pounded his shoe on the desk at the United Nations General Assembly, the killer from the Ukraine who said to the capitalists, "We will bury you." He was fired after David Rockefeller's visit— amazing. Also amazing was the low-key reporting of these "coincidences" by the press, until you examine the interlocking boards of directors of the CFR and the New York media: publishing, radio, and television. Then it is not so amazing, nor is it amazing when very powerful publishing houses push bestsellers and create hot topics. *Avant-garde* and *chic* is always in. Traditional values are always out. Some topics are strictly taboo—Christian bashing, unfortunately, is not one of the taboos.

The Rockefeller empire took off at the beginning of this century. Today it is colossal, though it is sometimes hard to see where their ownership ends and that of other bankers begins—and that includes the Rothschilds. Compared to the Rothschilds of Europe, who have been in the banking business for 200 years, the Rockefellers are merely country squires. But let us look at these country squires for a minute. Seeing the panorama of their holdings is like trying to photograph a mirage—things shift in and out of view. At another time, we will look at the Rothschilds.

In the 1970's a report was sent to Congress by two University of California professors revealing the extent of the Rockefeller empire. The findings were reported in January 1975 in the *Intelligence Digest* of the United Kingdom. Here are those findings—

At that time, 15 members of the Rockefeller family were directors of 40 corporations which had assets of 70 billion dollars. The boards on which the Rockefellers served had interlocking directorates with 91 major U.S. corporations controlling combined assets of 640 billion dollars. The Rockefellers have more than 200 trusts and foundations where tremendous deposits of wealth are placed.

The Rockefellers' first business is the oil empire of Exxon with its 300 subsidiaries and affiliates worldwide, and secondly, the banking empire—the Chase Manhattan, the Citi, and Chemical Banks. Closely related to these banks are three gigantic insurance companies—New York Life, Equitable Life, and Metropolitan Life—which have interlocking boards of directors. More than these main banks and insurance companies, the Rockefeller investments account for about 25 percent of the assets of the 50 largest commercial banks and 30 percent of all the assets of the 50 largest life insurance companies in the USA. Similar influence holds true for their holdings in major corporations, including Mobil Oil, Marathon Oil, IBM, Westinghouse, Boeing, Xerox, Avon, TWA, Eastern, United, National, Delta, Northwest Airlines, Penn Central, Safeway, General Foods, Allied Chemicals, Anaconda Copper, Shell, Gulf, Union, Continental Oil, American Motors, and so on.

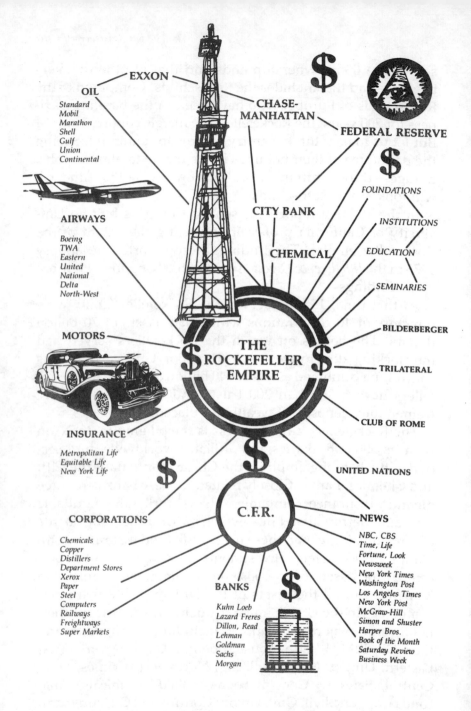

OIL

Standard
Mobil
Marathon
Shell
Gulf
Union
Continental

EXXON

CHASE-MANHATTAN

FEDERAL RESERVE

CITY BANK

CHEMICAL

FOUNDATIONS

INSTITUTIONS

EDUCATION

SEMINARIES

AIRWAYS

Boeing
TWA
Eastern
United
National
Delta
North-West

BILDERBERGER

THE
ROCKEFELLER
EMPIRE

TRILATERAL

MOTORS

CLUB OF ROME

INSURANCE

Metropolitan Life
Equitable Life
New York Life

UNITED NATIONS

C.F.R.

NEWS

CORPORATIONS

Chemicals
Copper
Distillers
Department Stores
Xerox
Paper
Steel
Computers
Railways
Freightways
Super Markets

NBC, CBS
Time, Life
Fortune, Look
Newsweek
New York Times
Washington Post
Los Angeles Times
New York Post
McGraw-Hill
Simon and Shuster
Harper Bros.
Book of the Month
Saturday Review
Business Week

BANKS

Kuhn Loeb
Lazard Freres
Dillon, Read
Lehman
Goldman
Sachs
Morgan

Figure 2. The Rockefeller Empire and CFR Connections

The main homestead of the Rockefellers has been the occasional meeting place for the secret meetings of the Bilderbergers. This homestead is the palatial mansions at Pocanto Hills in New York State. It is more than 4000 acres in size, with 70 miles of roads. In 1929 it had 75 buildings. No expense has been spared. Some rumor it makes Buckingham Palace seem like a barn. It has underground archives to store family records that cost almost five million dollars to build. Between them, the Rockefellers have about 100 residences internationally, with palaces, estates, and plantations from Ecuador to Rome, from Hawaii to Manhattan.

But again, compared to certain other banking dynasties, the Rockefellers are *nouveaux riches*, mere upstarts of this century. There exist powers within powers that they have only tapped. The grand directors—the illumined seers—are in other drawing rooms—older, larger, more palatial drawing rooms way out of public view.

THE MONEY CHANGERS
AND THE TEMPLE

After Christ had cast the money changers out of the temple, they went out into the greater marketplace of the world and in time captured it. They did this colossal feat through "money changing" in all its aspects. The greatest international banks on the face of the earth now belong to them.

The following are the international banking aristocracies of the earth, those temple money changers who have resurfaced as international bankers. They include the banking dynasties of Rothschild (in the five pivotal nations of Europe), Warburg (Germany and Holland), Sassoon (the Far East), Lazard Freres (France), Mendelsohn (Amsterdam), Israel Moses Seif (Italy), Kuhn Loeb (New York), Goldman Sachs (New York), and Lehman Brothers (New York). All but one of the above are among the select "primary owners"/class A stockholders of the Federal Reserve Bank of the United States that collects over a hundred billion dollars of interest a year from the United States government on America's national debt to them. (Note: The primary banks alone participate in the profits, not the hundreds of associate member banks protected by the Federal Reserve. The secrecy of the primary banks has been so great that from 1914 until now only certain insiders even knew who they were.)

There is a primary member of the Federal Reserve Bank who is not from among the lineage of the money changers. It is the Rockefellers of the Chase Manhattan and CitiBank of New York—though the Rockefeller's Chase Bank had merged with the Warburg's Manhattan Bank to become the Chase Manhattan Bank. Each of the above dynasties presides over multiple banks, and many of them have interlocking director-ates.

Most of these banks are private partnerships, family-run dynasties. As partnerships, they are free from auditing. Those that are central banks of nations are especially free of auditing. They loan to nations as well as major corporations and individuals.

Lincoln made the following interesting observation about conditions around him, an observation that equally applies today: "When we see a lot of framed timbers, different por-tions of which we know have been gotten out at different times and places and by different workmen, and when we see these timbers joined together and see that they exactly make the frame of a house or a mill, all the lengths and proportions of the different pieces exactly adapted to their respective pieces, and not a piece too many or too few, not omitting even scaffolding, or if a single piece be lacking, we can see the place in the frame exactly fitted and prepared to yet bring such a piece in; in such case, we find it impossible to not believe that they all understood one another from the beginning, and all worked upon a common plan or draft drawn up before the first lick was struck."

Fifty years after Lincoln's statement, America finally did get a central bank. The blueprint for that was the one used by the same architects who established the central banks of Europe. Now the building materials for the grand pyramid—hewn, polished and assembled—finally stood ready to form the grand structure of the supreme builder masons. This

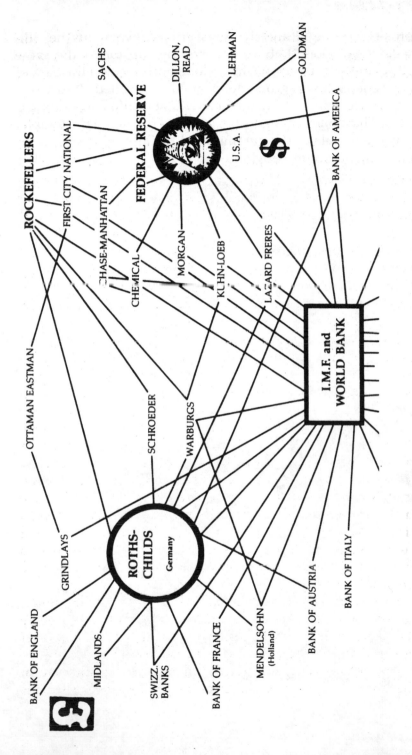

Figure 3. A Part of the International Banking Framework

project is to be ultimately overseen, as always, by the "all-seeing-eye" poised above the missing capstone—the same all-seeing-eye, mind you, as the one portrayed on the back of the Federal Reserve one-dollar-note and called "the Great Seal"—the pyramid and the floating eye printed on a banking note. The money changers have indeed reentered the temple. It is the temple of the pyramid and the all-seeing-eye, commercial and occult Babylon.

21

When the Last
Piece Fits into Place

The pieces of the New World Order seem to be fitting into place very quickly. Economic Babylon is unfolding. The political powers of unity are marching ahead. And a social corrupting process combined with a spiritual apostasy is moving at an unprecedented rate. But no one looking on can really set the timetable. I have always had the feeling that I would live to see this critical apocalyptic period of the world's history; but, of course, I could be wrong as so many others have been wrong through the centuries. It is merely a gut sense.

The biblical mandate is that we are not to set dates concerning the prophetic timetable. Hundreds of Christian amateurs and pseudoprophets have been discredited for doing exactly that—inventing their own schema to set dates on the prophetic calendar—when even Christ himself clearly announced in Scripture that no one knows the day or the hour of the Second Advent except God. Date-setters usually extrapolate the Second Advent from something that they have targeted nearby it on the prophetic calendar. It never works. It is to remain a mystery. The church is given signs to look for, yet it is still supposed to watch and expect while remaining active and diligent in life, not passive and monastic.

Most likely the New World Order must be set in place before the final world ruler can ascend the throne. I am speaking of the Antichrist. This presents another time variable. Who can guess the time period between the establishment of the interlocking world order and the appearance of the one who is to ascend the throne? It might even be decades, maybe longer. Likewise, the knowledge of God still must be abolished far more extensively before a sufficient apostasy can take effect that the inhabitants of the world will fully reject God and instead worship the dark god and his instrument. This is especially true if Satan worship becomes blatant, where there is no longer a camouflage. Yet clearly, a corrupting and apostatizing process is at work in our culture that none but the most self-deluded can ignore. It is happening before our eyes daily. Once-dependable pillars of tradition are collapsing—these collapsing pillars are important for the global puzzle. Let us look again at what has happened in our own lifetime to two key pillars of the old world order: gender and the family. God made the two with absolute purpose. They are part of the protective lymph system of society. When tampered with, there are dire results. This was true in the ancient world, as Edward Gibbon and other historians have shown with Rome, Greece, and the antediluvian world.

In the 1940's and 1950's, Norman Rockwell's depictions of the happy American family sitting in a country church or at the family dinner table summed up the soul of mainstream America. There was little Johnny smiling with innocent good cheer at his strong, stable, and loving father who was seated at the head of the table, while the mom humbly and affectionately served the dinner—each comfortable and secure in their own role. There was a feeling of stability, security, and love. These were happy people who loved one another and loved living in a free world. Not that all marriages then reflected this, but at least the consensus was that this was an ideal worth emulating. That was the model. People knew it took commitment, and they were willing to work toward it. What made it easier then was that they had the full sanction of society on their side.

But today, where are these people whom Norman Rockwell portrayed? Where have they gone? They have all but become extinct with the buffalo. They are a distinct minority—not at all popular, neither do they have the sanction of society on their side anymore.

Today's emerging consensus abhors and jeers at these "stereotypes" as they are now called. If this representative Norman Rockwell family could somehow be lifted out of the 1940's to appear on the Phil Donahue Show, these folk would be publicly ridiculed. Donahue would concoct his most passionate tone of moral outrage. He would then inform this wholesome, old-fashioned family that Dad should be a "house husband" as Mom goes out to drive a big rig while Johnny gets to experiment with open sex-role options like leotards, jelly slippers, and stick-on nails—that is, if little Johnny even exists. First he must survive that risky trek of gestation through his mother's liberated womb without her exercising her own "freedom" to have him cut up and removed to join that mountain of 27 million other aborted babies—Donahue would intone this with his hands outstretched, pleading to his audience the obviousness of what has become the conventional wisdom.

For talk-show icons such as Donahue, this issue is a "moral" crusade. If Donahue were to suddenly change his mind about such things, the shadow figures behind him who control the media would have him off the air immediately. A new talk-show sensation would suddenly be "discovered." At the annual dinner of the American Press Association in 1914, John Swinton, editor of the *New York News*, later the *Times*, summed up the reality behind the media even in those early years: "There is no such thing as an independent press in America. . . . Not a man among you dares to utter his honest opinion. . . . We are the tools and the vassals of the rich behind the scenes. We are marionettes. These men pull the strings and we dance. Our time, our talents, our lives and our capacities are all the property of these men—we are intellectual prostitutes." This took courage, and I am sure Swinton headed for early retirement. Can you see Dan Rather, CFR member, sacrificing a two-and-a-half-million-dollar annual salary to give this type of confession? Think of what the media has done since Swinton's era of 1914. It has worked miracles on changing America, especially with sex roles and the family.

In the late seventies, it was with great pride that Phil Donahue introduced to his television audience a family model he could get excited about, applauding their "courage." Husband and wife had gone to John Hopkins Medical Center and had extensive surgery to reverse their genders. They were true transsexuals. The dad was now the wife, and she was now the husband—right down to prosthetic penis and breasts. No, there was no feeling in "the act" anymore (neither emotional nor physical—just nerve-less pseudoorgans flopping back and forth). The one who was once the father was now experimenting with strong feelings for men. Donahue glowed with admiration. Literally, the castration of the man had been made complete, with the wife now wearing the pants. James Thurber's metaphor had become literal. The young daughter was still learning to "understand" her new parents, "bravely" hiding her deep bewilderment. To the liberated, obviously this was better than Norman Rockwell's American family of the fifties with the dad, pipe in mouth at the head of the table with all that hierarchy and affection. Almost anything but the old family model is permitted. If science in a few short years has provided discoveries which have destroyed much of the earth's critical ozone layer with flurocarbons, which are now changing the earth's climate, that is insignificant compared to destroying the family. The fallout from that will be staggering.

Among other things, it took men like Hollywood producer and playwright Norman Lear, head of *People for the American Way* (which should be named "people who want to destroy America") to further bury the traditional family. Lear's TV superhit, "All In the Family," starring the inflexible "male chauvinist pig" Archie Bunker, showed that the traditional family model was archaic in a modern world, and indeed laughable. Dad bullied a passive mom. The strong dad could only be a buffoon and a bad guy who should have his authority taken away from him—yes, even by the state, if it took that. And Bunker's catholicism made him prejudiced and out-of-step. There was old world Archie Bunker to whom you could apply the most-feared labels of all: He was "sexist" and "racist." Of course, Lear is not from the Catholic tradition. He is free of all prejudices, right? Except when it comes to men of the type who founded America—those Christians who loved God and country. Norman Lear made millions while he grinned all the way to the bank. He also set the caricature in the public mind. The traditional hierarchical family was obsolete. Roles had to change, and certain religious views were old paradigms that helped create today's problems.

Meanwhile, ACLU legal precedents have been keeping a close pace with the media Frankenstein. Reality is catching up with film. A recent ACLU legal victory enabled the courts to take a ten-year-old boy from his evangelical mom (described in court as "fanatic and bigoted") to be placed into a more suitable household. The boy was awarded by the courts to his divorced homosexual father dying of AIDS and living with a gay lover—obviously a better environment for a growing boy than a Christian home.

Norman Rockwell's little Johnny has come a long way! America in the 1980's has him living with his divorced homosexual dad whose live-in lover is a man. In Rockwell's era, Johnny was reading about "Dick and Jane." Now there are magazines lying about like Dick and Frank, and chances are good that Johnny is learning all about sodomy. There are videos and open doors. Johnny can come home from fourth grade with his chums, while the dad and his gay lover are off somewhere arm-in-arm, and play their videotapes—not old Walt Disney films, but movies like *Heavy Bondage* with men wearing leather masks sodomizing, "fisting," and torturing each other.

All this because the ACLU really cares about Johnny! They are deeply caring people when it comes to the American way—that is why they are spending millions of dollars on extremely clever legal arguments that are sealing the coffin on old America. Their very efforts prove that they have an agenda: to destroy the old America for the new.

Meanwhile, if Johnny has any survival sense at all, at this point he will join that sad legion of street runaways and end up in Los Angeles on Hollywood Boulevard. At least he may have a better chance of avoiding molestation and AIDS, or his mother might risk arrest and run away with him. This is America right now—the same America where little Johnny can go to public school and in fourth grade buy crack—cocaine that's so strong that grown-up professionals once addicted to it can't kick it apart from months in Phoenix House. (After cocaine's years of trashing society, the experts are willing to admit that maybe it's more of a problem than they thought.) Little Johnny's peers can score it in ten minutes within a hundred yards of the elementary school.

Let it sink in. This is not fantasy. There is no turning back apart from a revolution or a miracle. Most Americans will predictably sit with their heads in the sand (it's easier that way) until they are hit, but by then it will be too late. These changes have all crept through the gate while the nation was asleep. People will adapt to anything you dish out to them if you don't hurry the process.

How are the youth of these non-families developing?

If you time-grafted today's youth culture next to the era of the fifties, no one would believe it. Who would have ever thought that God, goodness, and doing right would be despised by the majority of today's youth? But it is. Try talking about these things on the University of California at Berkeley campus, which often sets the pace by five or ten years ahead of most other campuses. The reaction will be incredulous hostility or mockery the minute you mention that one name that can only bring a caricature to their minds. They think of Jim and Tammy and the telechurch, or the empty church down the street full of old people. They are sealed off. End of discussion.

But if you talk about lesbian rights, they will cheer you on. To be lesbian is in. Several candidates for the 1989 University of California at Berkeley student government ran on the lesbian platform—ditto for gays, ditto for Marxists, ditto for anarchists. These platforms were underground 30 years ago, but not any longer. These changes of belief are reflected in other ways—even in superficial ways, such as appearance.

In the fifties a social outcast was depicted as some fellow with long hair, perhaps in eye shadow, with maybe one big earring, wearing outlandish or foppish attire. He might even shave his head in odd places or color it green or have a tiny pigtail. It was the sissy look. Imagine a student in the fifties appearing in class at Oklahoma State looking like that! For girls in the fifties with pretty long hair, a stylish dress, and a feminine demeanor, a freak to them was exactly what is now "in"—namely, a woman with a crew cut or flattop and a hard look in the eyes, wearing boots, jeans, and anything else to look masculine. Femininity is defiantly trashed—so are men; so is the family. This pseudomale butch and her colleague-in-arms would be an object of derision, shock, and disgust 30 years ago—reactions that are healthy, by the way. Now they are "in." Too bad. It is an ugly and hideous turn of events—that the androgynous role-reversal is what is in. It seems impossible that this has all happened so fast. To me, these are indicators of other things on the way.

All these happenings comprise what the Bible predicts when it describes the "great rebellion" and "the great falling away." It's as tangible as sea lions choking and dying from the poisons in the ocean, except this is spiritual pollution—and it must happen for other pieces of the puzzle to fit into place.

An interesting detail is in the Bible. Paul described "the last generation" to Timothy. It is a description that seems to be getting closer and more fitting every day. It is the psychological profile of those in "The Great Rebellion." Paul says:

> But mark this: There will be terrible times in the last days. People will be lovers of themselves, lovers of money, boastful, proud, abusive, disobedient to their parents, ungrateful, unholy, without love, unforgiving, slanderous, without self-control, brutal, not lovers of the good, treacherous, rash, conceited, lovers of pleasure rather than lovers of God (2 Timothy 3:1-4).

This is an apt description of the popular youth culture of today. We see it in all the teen movies, from *Less Than Zero* and *The River's Edge*, to *Fast Times at Ridgemont High*. But there are higher octane rebellions. Picture Billy Idol or Mottley Crue and their audiences. Picture modern satanists, and you're all the way there. Yes, another "modern" development to come in our lifetimes is satanism. It is getting so serious that police departments have special departments and agents assigned to this growing phenomenon—people who have been ritually murdered and dismembered, and kids who have been kidnapped—never to be seen again. Then exsatanists try to confess the horrendous things that go on. Human sacrifice in the 1980's—that's modern progress for you. It certainly shows how effective "education" has been—that god of the culteratti. It also is a perfect profile of the last generation.

The old world order must really be expunged before the New World Order can come into place. This is the transformation threshold, the critical mass, the full paradigm shift heralded today. At some point it will probably be lightning-fast once certain things are aligned.

The New Order

The New World Order will be different from anything the world has ever seen. It will be an impressive monolith of colossal power. There will be things about it that will surprise all of us—things we did not foresee. But some elements come into clearer focus every day. I have had what I think are glimpses of forces behind this emerging reality—spiritual forces. I believe but cannot prove that these glimpses were given to me by God. One of them was soon after I returned from India after being there several years. I was a young Christian recuperating in my parents' London house in Kensington. Dad, a diplomat, had retired in London for ten years. I was still battling serious intestinal problems from living in the wilds of South India. A dream is a dream, but what I experienced was something else entirely—massive color: panoramic, superscreen, bigger than life. It was not at all foggy, but I was present in the experience with all of my faculties. I knew it was not just another dream but something, perhaps instructional, to prepare me for a future reality.

I am a very difficult person to scare. I used to go to horror films alone even when I was seven. But in the darkness of

5 A.M. after the panoramic experience was over, I was in a cold sweat, breathing heavily. I was certain that it was not just another dream—I had spent years gear-shifting to different levels of altered consciousness. This was unique. Now that I was a Christian, it felt as though the Holy Spirit impressed this direct connection with a certain reality right into my soul.

In the early to midseventies, I recounted this experience to a number of close college friends who are among my best friends (Charles Jarvis, former deputy director of Legal Services Corporation; Dr. Preston Campbell, the Vanderbilt University Faculty of Medicine; Dr. Bob Brown, the Faculty of Medicine of the University of Virginia; Dr. Tony Morton, a U.S. Naval Flight Surgeon; Dr. Rick Ciccotelli, Ph.D. from Princeton University and former philosophy assistant professor at Notre Dame). I emphasize the importance of the date because, among other things, in 1981 AIDS hit national headlines.

The Main Vision: It is the Place De Canon in downtown Brussels, the city of my father's final diplomatic post. It is the large medieval cobblestone square surrounded by impressive regal buildings. A terrible laughter fills the air and spiritual airwaves—omnipresent. As I round the corner I see a huge canvas canopy covering a throne.

A huge swollen leg maybe 20 feet long rests on a ramp. A grotesque gigantic being that is the source of the laughter is mounted on the throne. I almost do a demonic mind meld with its thoughts. I cannot begin to describe the hideous cascade of direct feeling. I realize that this image represents the reality behind the triune Antichrist. One head is astoundingly intelligent, maybe an IQ of half a million, and another head swings around flopping on the chest—it is insane beyond belief. The third head is entirely sinister, pure evil. It wants to destroy. It is the source of many embodiments. I recognize India's Siva, who I once meditated on, as being an outward type of this creature.

The being knows I am watching and that I have some understanding of its real mission—to unify and possess the human race, to penetrate every soul. Satan himself has entered this creature. A bent and mythologized history of the cosmos emerges with every hideous screaming laugh. It is trying to unmake God. It is trying to keep out the knowledge that the holy God in fury will consign this creature to the lake of fire. It wants to destroy the apple of God's eye.

I notice that sticking in the leg there are hundreds of hypodermic needles. Dazed, unaware people in some kind of trance approach the leg. This is the moment they are to lose their souls forever. They play with the hypodermics, forcing polluted blood to go in and out. A slurping sound is emitted. Then they plunge the needles into their arms, joining blood with the creature. I can see their consciousness changing the minute the blood has entered them—there is no turning back. The dazed lack of awareness of the brainwashed subjects is terrible beyond belief. They seem unreachable as they walk to eternal destruction.

After that, I sit up in bed and look out into the black early morning of London through the window of my bedroom. This mood haunts me the whole day. No, it's not just another dream—almost ten years later AIDS appeared in headlines. But blood can have other contaminants, from heroin to cocaine, and who knows what else awaits down the road? Just a dream? I'm not so sure. I feel it was a glimpse at a spiritual reality operating behind the scenes.

Some of the great writers have tried to see into the future to glimpse this invading global reality. Aldous Huxley saw the manipulated masses in his *Brave New World* as being reduced to trivial hedonists, living for the moment, enthralled with designer drugs, with no purpose for living beyond the next shallow thrill. These drugged subjects were putty in the hands of the state. They had no will, no character—they could not fight the system even if they wanted to. But they were not the gray masses living on the edge of absolute poverty that Orwell envisioned in his tyrannical world order. Huxley's world was one of numbed thrill-seekers.

George Orwell, that famed British author and former member of the British secret intelligence, speculated about things probably from what he knew then as an intelligence insider. His *1984* is a classic, with graphic insights that have been almost prophetic. From the forties, when Orwell wrote *1984,* he envisioned a collective semiglobal system. People were slaves without free will. They were the brainwashed masses who had no concept of history, since all books were destroyed. And what passed the censors had been rewritten to fit the confines of permitted thought. History was skewed with new interpretations yearly. One thinks of the father of American progressive education, John Dewey, and his idea to influence youth in state schools through textbooks—schools, mind you, with no prayer and no God. Like Lennon's "Imagine," it would be a world without heaven and hell, with only exalted man to govern his own affairs.

The populace of *1984* were surrounded by subliminal messages and the centralized eyes and ears of the state. Double-think slogans were everywhere—slogans that went against the natural gut sense of the conscience and common sense, just like so many of the high-sounding social agendas of today. Orwell's "antisex league" brilliantly foresaw the anti-sexism leagues of today—that liberal collective who have invaded college campuses with their nonsexist and antifamily agenda; this new consensus of today comprised of gays, lesbians, and "minorities."

In Orwell's *1984* there was not a moment to think in privacy. "The individual is only a cell." Reality is in "the collective Mind, the Mind of the Party, collective and immortal." One's own child could be an informer to the ever-present central control. Orwell's two-way telescreen foresaw the host of technological breakthroughs of today that could one day be used to invade privacy. The science of psychology had become a power, not to heal wounded psyches—its alleged purpose in the past—but to invade and take over wanton parts of the individualist mind that had engaged in "thoughtcrime." No private thought could escape the all-seeing-eye of Big Brother. The science of behavior could even turn to the most elaborate forms of torture, in Room 101, to flush out anything it wanted and remake the mind in any fashion it so chose. Room 101 was deep in the massive gray structure known as "the Ministry of Love," where thoughtcriminals were "cured." "Power is tearing human minds apart and putting them back together by your own choosing." The hero was being made an "unper-son" and told that as a heretic, "We will lift you clean out of history. You will be annihilated in the past and in the future. But first we will make you perfect. Your mind will be perfectly remade, and only then, destroyed." It's a vision of total dehu-manization—an apt portrayal of the system of Antichrist.

People were seduced and manipulated from every side. And when they got their supersystem, it turned on each one of them, to invade them, to possess them. They had surren-dered bit by bit to this emerging reality over the decades without the need for a single shot to be fired. It was the frog-in-the-heating-water analogy.

In Orwell's futuristic world of 1984, there were no families, and sex roles had been obliterated. This fact seemed very important to George Orwell. Intimacy and trust and attrac-tion between the sexes had all but vanished. Tenderness was gone. Innocence and vulnerability were gone. Love between men and women was abolished forever. The family was obso-lete. Men and women were neutered in drab uniforms. A member of the Party told a rally of the brainwashed that "unorthodox loyalties lead to thoughtcrime; that the family leads to unorthodox loyalties," encouraging "ownlife." There-fore "the introduction of 'artsem' [artificial insemination] combined with the neutralization of the orgasm will render impossible the family until it becomes impossible to concep-tualize." Even the memory of the family will be blotted out of history.

In the end, all human passion and genius is destroyed in Orwell's world. The free-thinking individual has become anathema. The state has become God. Of course, George Orwell was a secularist, so it is natural that he would omit the metaphysical and spiritual dimension. If we added the spiri-tual reality of supernatural evil, we would be closer to the mark—that is where the abyss of horror deepens far more than the dull grays of Orwell's future world. Orwell's evil would have dimension and color and free reign once the spiritual reality was added, combined with the enormous stakes of the eternal worth of each soul. That is exactly the biblical prediction. Much worse than Orwell's Big Brother is the embodied Antichrist. And much worse than the collective mind of the Party is the spiritual reality of a demonic mind meld—unified mass possession by which spiritual beings of evil possess human minds like empty clearinghouses. It is a hideous mass haunting where humans do unimaginable things to one another, taking Orwell's dehumanization a step farther. Evil intent is amplified.

But there is another difference between Orwell's future world and biblical reality. The vision in Room 101 for the human race is: "Picture a boot stamping on a human face forever." The biblical picture does not permit this. The prophetic picture is simple and final—God intervenes. End of story. The God of history absolutely forbids the final triumph of evil, and what he does to the powers of evil and their system is horrifying beyond imagining, should you happen to be on the wrong side. Wrath explodes from the all-powerful God who is great enough to create the galaxies with a single word. His power is terrifying. He demolishes those who hated and destroyed good, those who terminally rejected God and wrenched others' souls apart, and those who chased God's elect to the ends of the earth, persecuting and destroying the church. It is not for nothing that since the ancient church, the Second Coming of Christ has been called the "blessed hope," and so it is for God's people, for the pure-hearted and the innocent. But for the enemies of God, it is something else entirely.

The one whom the dark rulers and their anti-God subjects thought they could erase from history and expunge from the universe suddenly cracks the sky apart. His light floods the souls of those who thought they could mythologize him out of existence. The faulty cement of the New World Order comes unglued, and this brief global experiment ends. The global banking fraternity watches helplessly as Babylon falls in a single day. The economic spell ends as the cleverest plans are laid waste. The old apostle on the Isle of Patmos describes this moment when commerical and occult Babylon falls. John observes, in the Book of Revelation:

Fallen! Fallen is Babylon the Great! She has become a home for demons and a haunt for every evil spirit, a haunt for every unclean and detestable bird. For all the nations have drunk the maddening wine of her adulteries. The kings of the earth committed adultery with her, and the merchants of the earth grew rich from her excessive luxuries (Revelation 18:2,3).

" 'Woe! Woe, O great city, O Babylon, city of power! *In one hour your doom has come!'*
"The merchants of the earth will weep and mourn over her because no one buys their cargoes any more—cargoes of gold, silver, precious stones, and pearls . . . and the bodies and souls of men" (Revelation 18:10-13).

Babylon is destroyed in a single hour! That would be impossible, but for the recently emerging reality of globally interlinked computers. John saw this 2000 years ago, a thousand years before the Dark Ages. Think about it—a system that could only be possible with twentieth-century technology, and John describes how the world economy collapses in a single hour. Already we see the New York, London, and Tokyo stock exchanges affecting each other in a matter of hours. But a unified system with something suddenly going radically wrong—such as a massive interlocking debt system finally collapsing—makes a lot of sense. It really could happen in a single hour.

John Lennon, in perhaps his most famous and influential song, "Imagine," pictures a world with no heaven or hell. Then the key refrain soon follows: *"And the World Will Be as One."* Lennon's song sums up the one-world dream.

He also sings of those who have this dream: "You may think I'm a dreamer, but I'm not the only one." Lennon, of course, would include those countless contemporary idealists on his wavelength. But he may have been referring to others as well, a much more esoteric group who helped him in his ascent from Liverpool to becoming the greatest rock legend of all time. He had every instrument needed to broadcast his message, from his own prodigious talents to the media at his feet. His lyrics were a messianic message for a world ("I'm more famous than Jesus Christ," he once said). And doubtless Lennon entered, upon occasion, even larger drawing rooms than the ones in Buckingham Palace, and met those who might not just be imagining, but actually pulling the levers for the world to be as one.

Yes, we can imagine the Lennon/Illuminist dream for a season, but it cannot endure because its foundation stone is the falsehood of human imagination and cunning grafted to a deeper satanic plan. It's the promise of perfection and harmony—but with God clearly left out of the picture. As such it is a Frankenstein monster, as empty and dead as a body without a soul. It is the final experiment that is doomed to fail. This pretended paradise will become hell on earth. The Book of Revelation pictures the earth as a tortured planet: its oceans poisoned from pollution, its weather and seasons in upheaval, its atmosphere heating up to agonizing temperatures, boils and skin cancer breaking out, and a world government gone haywire. God, in passive wrath, will allow the momentum of human folly to show its inevitable fruits. But man's hatred of God and man's embracing of a demonic system headed by Satan himself will ultimately bring God's active wrath. These are the vials of judgment in the Book of Revelation, and they will bring terror to many.

In the end, the world will require something drastic, something far beyond the ability of any man or machine to solve. The apostle Peter reveals what will happen to this despoiled and tortured planet:

> But the day of the Lord will come as a thief in the night; in which the heavens shall pass away with a great noise, and the elements shall melt with fervent heat, the earth also and the works that are therein shall be burned up.
> ... Nevertheless we, according to his promise, look for new heavens and a new earth, wherein dwelleth righteousness (2 Peter 3:10,13 KJV).

The dazzling empire that came in like a rainbow will be no more. The New World Order will be blotted out, replaced by the New Creation. Only God can remake the universe—not with the glue of human or diabolical cunning, but with a single word uttered from highest heaven!

NOTES

Introduction—The New World Order
1. *The Utah Independent*, Sep. 1977.

Chapter 1—Contact
1. Kubler-Ross, *Death: The Final Stage of Growth* (Englewood Cliffs: Prentice-Hall, 1975), pp. 164-66.
2. Jon Klomo, "Channeling," in *The New Age Journal*, Dec. 1987, p. 37.
3. Ibid., p. 38.
4. Ibid., p. 38.
5. Ibid., p. 34.
6. Whitley Strieber, *Communion* (New York: Avon Books, 1988), p. 16.
7. Ibid., p. 100.
8. Ibid., p. 123.
9. Ibid., p. 21.
10. Ibid., p. 245.

Chapter 3—Opening the Third Eye
1. Tal Brooke, *Avatar of Night* (New Delhi: Vikas Publishing, 1982), pp. 9-13.

Chapter 5—Higher Guidance
1. J.D. Salinger, *Nine Stories* (Boston: Little, Brown, and Co., 1951), pp. 287-88.

Chapter 6—Voices from Out of the Rainbow
1. John Randolph Price, *Planetary Commission Update*, Aug. 1986, p. 4.
2. Ken Wilber, *The Atman Project* (Wheaton: Theosophical Publishing House, 1980), p. ix.

3. Peter Russell, *The Global Brain* (Los Angeles: Tarcher Publications, 1983), pp. 210-11.
4. Robert Muller, *New Genesis* (Garden City: Doubleday & Co., 1984), p. 100.
5. Russell, *The Global Brain*, p. 231.
6. Note: The list of New Western Hybrids was put together with the aid of Robert Burrows.
7. Alice Bailey, "Externalizing the Mysteries," Part I, *The Beacon*, Nov./Dec. 1975, p. 171.

Chapter 7—Wheels of Influence: The Therapist's Office
1. William Kirk Kilpatrick, *The Emperor's New Clothes* (Westchester: Crossway Books, 1985), p. 27.
2. Ibid., p. 28.
3. Ibid., p. 28.
4. Ibid., p. 36.

Chapter 8—Wheels of Influence: The Marketplace
1. Peter Waldman, "Motivate or Alienate? Firms Hire Gurus to Change Their 'Cultures,' " *The Wall Street Journal*, Section 2, July 24, 1987.
2. Ibid., p. 78.
3. John Bode, "The Forum: Repackaged est?," *The Chicago Tribune*, Feb. 27, 1985, Section 5.

Chapter 9—Wheels of Influence: The Schoolroom
1. Marilyn Ferguson, *The Aquarian Conspiracy*, p. 283.
2. Felix Frankfurter, "The Supreme Court and the Public," *Forum* magazine, June 1930, pp. 232-33.
3. Francis Adeney, "Educators Look East," *SCP Journal*, Vol. 5, No. 1 (Winter 1981), p. 29.
4. The Society for Accelerated Learning, "New Dimensions in Education—Confluent Learning," San Francisco, Apr. 25, 1980.
5. Connecticut Citizens for Constitutional Education, Jan. 22, 1980.
6. Jack Canfield and Paula Klimek, "Education in the New Age," *The New Age Journal*, Feb. 1978, p. 27.
7. Ibid., p. 27.

8. Ibid., p. 28.
9. Ibid., p. 28.
10. Ibid., p. 30.
11. Ibid., p. 36.
12. Ibid., p. 36.
13. Ibid., p. 39.
14. Ibid., p. 39.

Chapter 10—Dress Rehearsal for a New Age Christ
1. Thomas Sugrue, *There Is a River* (New York: Holt, Rinehart, & Winston, 1942), p. 361.
2. Robert Skutch, "The incredible story behind . . . *Course in Miracles*," *New Realities* magazine, July/Aug. 1984, p. 17.
3. Ibid., pp. 18-19.
4. Ibid., p. 19.
5. Robert Burrows, *SCP Journal*, Vol. 7, No. 1, 1987.
6. Skutch, *New Realities*, p. 21.
7. Ibid., p. 23.
8. Skutch, *New Realities*, p. 19.
9. Skutch, part II, p. 11.
10. Ibid., p. 12.
11. *A Course in Miracles*, p. 165.
12. Ibid., p. 150.

Chapter 12—Erasing God from the Universe
1. William Barrett, *Irrational Man* (Garden City: Doubleday, 1958), p. 217.

Chapter 13—Letting Mr. Gumby Control the Universe
1. Henry Thoreau, *Walden* (New York: New American Library, Signet Classic, 1960), p. 67.
2. Walter Pater, *The Renaissance* (New York: Mentor Books, 1977), pp. 157-58.
3. Ibid., p. 158.
4. Alan Bloom, *The Closing of the American Mind* (New York: Simon and Schuster, 1987), p. 141.
5. Diogenes Allen, *Philosophy for Understanding Theology* (Atlanta: John Knox Press, 1985), p. 265.

6. Gunther Stent, *The Coming of the Golden Age: A View of the End of Progress* (Garden City: Natural History Press, 1969).

Chapter 14—Bridges to the New Consciousness

1. James Webb, *The Occult Underground* (La Salle: Open Court Publishing, 1974), p. 86.
2. Ibid., p. 101.
3. Ibid., p. 101.
4. M.K. Neff, *Personal Memoirs of Helena P. Blavatsky*, p. 244.
5. Ibid., p. 291.
6. Madame Helena P. Blavatsky, *The Key to Theosophy* (Chicago: Theosophical Publishing House, 1930), p. 111.
7. Madame Helena P. Blavatsky, *Collected Writings*, Vol. 8, p. 277.
8. Madame Helena P. Blavatsky, *The Secret Doctrine* (Los Angeles: Theosophy Co., 1925), Vol. 3, p. 386.
9. Ibid., Vol. 2, p. 132.
10. Ibid., Vol. 3, p. 246.
11. Ibid., Vol. 3, p. 376.
12. Blavatsky, *The Secret Doctrine*, Vol. 4, p. 52.
13. H.T. Edge, *Theosophy and Christianity*, p. 52.
14. Ibid., p. 37.
15. Ibid., pp. 85-90.
16. Ibid., p. 168.

Chapter 15—Going Beyond Good and Evil

1. Malcolm Muggeridge, *Eternity* magazine, Apr. 1972.
2. John Whitehead, *The Stealing of America* (Westchester: Crossway Books, 1983), p. 53.
3. John W. Whitehead, *The Stealing of America*, pp. 43-44.
4. Walker Percy, *Lost in the Cosmos: The Last Self-help Book* (New York: Simon & Schuster, 1983), p. 44.
5. Ibid., p. 44.
6. H.J. Blackham, *Humanism* (London: Penguin, 1968), pp. 13, 19.
7. Henry Miller, *The Tropic of Cancer* (New York: Grove Press, 1961), p. 232.

8. Soren Kierkegaard, *Fear and Trembling* (Princeton: Princeton University Press, 1941), p. 30.

Chapter 17—Building the New World Temple
1. Virginia Hine, *The Networking Newsletter*, Fall 1983, p. 10.
2. Ibid., p. 12.
3. Marilyn Ferguson, "Marilyn Ferguson: Changes for a New Age," *Yoga Journal*, July/Aug. 1981, p. 6.
4. Ibid., p. 6.
5. Ibid., p. 8.
6. Ibid., p. 8.
7. Ibid., p. 8.
8. Ibid., p. 10.
9. Kubler-Ross, *Death*, p. 3.
10. Dean Halverson, "Transformation Celebration," *SCP Magazine*, Jan. 1984, p. 4.
11. Ibid., p. 4.
12. Ibid., p. 4.
13. Ibid., p. 100.
14. Robert Muller, *New Genesis* (Garden City: Doubleday & Co., 1984), p. 19.
15. Mark Satin, *New Age Politics* (New York: Dell Books Inc., 1978), pp. 20-23.
16. Ibid., pp. 24-25.
17. Ibid., pp. 25-27.
18. Ibid., pp. 30-32.
19. Ibid., p. 90.
20. Ibid., p. 94.
21. Ibid., p. 96.
22. Ibid., p. 99.
23. I had a private after-class conversation with him in October 1985.
24. Planetary Initiative for the World We Choose, *Organizing Manual*, Project Description/Attachment III-a.
25. David Spangler, *Reflections on the Christ* (Scotland: Findhorn Community Press, 1978), pp. 40, 44.
26. *SCP Newsletter*, Aug./Sep. 1982, p. 5.
27. Bruce Larson, *The Whole Christian* (Waco: Word Books, 1978), pp. 16, 176.

Chapter 19—The Great Lie

1. Austin Farrer, *Love Almighty and Ills Unlimited* (New York: Doubleday and Co., 1961), p. 126.
2. Alexander Hislop, *The Two Babylons* (Neptune, NJ: Loizeaux Publ., 1916), pp. 20, 78, 96.

Chapter 20—The Hidden Aristocracy

1. *The Writings of George Washington*, published by the U.S. Government Printing Office, 1941, Vol. 20, p. 518.
2. Carroll Quigley, *Tragedy and Hope* (New York: The Macmillan Company, 1966), p. 950.
3. Ibid., p. 324.
4. John Kenneth Galbraith, *The Great Crash, 1929* (New York: Time Inc., 1954), p. 102.
5. Benjamin Disraeli, *Coningsby*, p. 233.
6. Quigley, *Tragedy and Hope*, pp. 326-27.
7. John Hargrave, *Montagu Norman* (New York: Greystone Press, 1942).
8. Rear Admiral Chester Ward, *Review of the News*, Apr. 9, 1980, pp. 37-38.

OTHER GOOD
HARVEST HOUSE READING

AMERICA: THE SORCERER'S NEW APPRENTICE
by *Dave Hunt* and *T.A. McMahon*

Many respected experts predict that America is at the threshold of a glorious New Age. Other equally notable observers warn that Eastern mysticism, at the heart of the New Age movement, will eventually corrupt Western civilization.

The question is, *Who is right*? Is there really a threat to the American way of life as we know it? Will we be able to distinguish between the true hope of the Gospel and the false hope of the New Age?

Dave Hunt and T.A. McMahon, bestselling authors of *The Seduction of Christianity*, break down the most brilliant arguments of the most-respected New Age leaders. This bold new book is an up-to-date Christian apologetic, presenting overwhelming evidence for the superiority of the Christian faith.

THE SEDUCTION OF CHRISTIANITY
Spiritual Discernment in the Last Days
by *Dave Hunt* and *T.A. McMahon*

Since its release in August 1985, *The Seduction of Christianity* has become one of the most talked about books in Christian circles. Examining dangerous and extrabiblical practices that are influencing millions, the book emphasizes that Christians need to become aware of fake doctrine so they won't fall prey to the seduction of Christianity.

THE CULT EXPLOSION
by *Dave Hunt*

This book exposes the real danger and the strategies employed by cults of our time. Must reading for anyone who wants to understand the subtle ways cults prey upon the fears and needs of so many people.

SATAN'S UNDERGROUND
by *Lauren Stratford*

Lauren Stratford was abused and tortured as a child, and as a young adult found herself caught in a painful web of pornography, satanism, and ritualistic abuse. Her story is a difficult one to hear. Lauren openly shares her dramatic story from personal devastation to complete liberation so that others may find healing and freedom through the love of Jesus. It is a true testimony of the power of God to take the most tragic circumstances and turn them into blessings. Foreword by Johanna Michaelsen and Hal Lindsey. Highly recommended by Mike Warnke.

THE BEAUTIFUL SIDE OF EVIL
by *Johanna Michaelsen*

Hal Lindsey's sister-in-law shares her extraordinary story about her involvement in the occult and how she learned to distinguish between the beautiful side of evil and the true way of the Lord.

A PROPHETICAL WALK THROUGH THE HOLY LAND
by *Hal Lindsey*

An authoritative guide to the mysteries and beauty of the Holy Land as seen by world-renowned Bible prophecy expert Hal Lindsey. Illustrated with beautiful photography, this book portrays the fascinating places where God's promises have been fulfilled down through the ages and where the most momentous events of all time will soon take place.

ASTROLOGY: Do the Heavens Rule Our Destiny?
by *John Ankerberg*

Forty million Americans today believe in some form of astrology. Its influence is felt throughout government, industry, the sciences, education, the church, and the home.

Well-known occult authorities John Ankerberg and John Weldon examine astrology's major issues and answer most commonly asked questions:

- What exactly *is* astrology?
- Do the heavens really influence life on earth?
- What are the dangers of astrology?
- How much does astrology actually influence Washington?
- What does the Bible say about astrology?

Astrology thoroughly researches astrology's claims, assesses its occult aspects, and emphasizes the personal consequences of its use.

Dear Reader:

We would appreciate hearing from you regarding this Harvest House nonfiction book. It will enable us to continue to give you the best in Christian publishing.

1. What must influenced you to purchase *When the World Will Be As One*?
   - ☐ Author
   - ☐ Subject matter
   - ☐ Backcover copy
   - ☐ Recommendations
   - ☐ Cover/Title
   - ☐ _____

2. Where did you purchase this book?
   - ☐ Christian bookstore
   - ☐ General bookstore
   - ☐ Department store
   - ☐ Grocery store
   - ☐ Other

3. Your overall rating of this book:
   ☐ Excellent ☐ Very good ☐ Good ☐ Fair ☐ Poor

4. How likely would you be to purchase other books by this author?
   - ☐ Very likely
   - ☐ Somewhat likely
   - ☐ Not very likely
   - ☐ Not at all

5. What types of books most interest you?
   (check all that apply)
   - ☐ Women's Books
   - ☐ Marriage Books
   - ☐ Current Issues
   - ☐ Self Help/Psychology
   - ☐ Bible Studies
   - ☐ Fiction
   - ☐ Biographies
   - ☐ Children's Books
   - ☐ Youth Books
   - ☐ Other _____

6. Please check the box next to your age group.
   - ☐ Under 18
   - ☐ 18-24
   - ☐ 25-34
   - ☐ 35-44
   - ☐ 45-54
   - ☐ 55 and over

Mail to: Editorial Director
Harvest House Publishers, Inc.
1075 Arrowsmith
Eugene, OR 97402

Name _____

Address _____

City _____ State _____ Zip _____

Thank you for helping us to help you in future publications!

DATE DUE